REACHII
BLACK
MALES
THROUGH
SPIRITUALITY

ERRATA

On Page 96 after the word "relationship.", it should read - "**In her book, _Afrocentric Theory and Applications, Volume II_, Nsenga Warfield-Coppock on pages 39 and 44 provides us with examples of program goals, curriculum and needed resources. While she lists them as success indicators, for the purpose of this program I see them as goals. They are as follows:**"

On Page 105 after the word "others.", it should read - "**Referencing Perkins (1986) Warfield-Coppock says,** additional criteria . . ."

On Page 108 after the words "being ordered to do so.", it should read - "**Malidoma Some', _The Healing Wisdom of Africa_**"

REACHING BLACK MALES THROUGH SPIRITUALITY

BABA KOLEOSO KARADE
a.k.a Nashid Fakhrid-Deen

SHEKHEM PUBLISHING, LLP

Shekhem Publishing, LLP
P.O. Box 593
Union, KY 41091
Website: www.shekhempublishing.com

Library of Congress Control Number: 2004108438

ISBN: 0-9745070-1-6

Edited by T. A. El Amin & Tessaat Nefer Shekhem Ur Khufu
Cover Design by John M. McAtee

My beloved Brother, should you find yourself with a copy of this book as the result of a gift from your mate, girlfriend, lover, or etc., please do not get upset. She has only been the vehicle that spirit used to get the book in your hands. If it were not for her love for you, spirit could not have used her. It is my prayer that you read between the lines, find true self love, spiritual liberation, and stand in the world as a light for others to follow.

With the Name of God, Most Gracious, Most Merciful and in the Presence of Our Ancestors, Both Seen and Unseen.

Dedication

This work is humbly dedicated to the Most Honorable Elijah Muhammad, a man who with courage, faith, dedication and love stood at the edge of the universe and reached across time and helped me and millions reclaim our lost manhood.

Acknowledgements

To my father N.T. Thompson for his confidence, who with an 8th grade education became one of the first black men in the history of Chrysler Motors to become a supervisor. Dada, I was watching.

To Minister Louis Farrakhan, who has such love for the work of his spiritual father, The Honorable Elijah Muhammad that he went down in hell to resurrect the Nation of Islam and help save me from my own faithlessness.

To Imam Warith D. Muhammad, who with vision instructed us to study and see other aspects of the religion. Thank you for liberating me from my myopic vision.

To Minister Donald Shabazz : who showed me first hand what it meant to be a Muhammd Man. Each time I wanted to punk out, he made me reach deeper for the courage to follow Messenger Muhammad. Minister Donald, I could never thank you enough.

To Na'im Akbar, who continues to demonstrate how our Ancestors so freely use us to speak their truth. Naim may you forever remain a clear channel for their message. Most of all thank you for ensuring I was not crazy!

To Baba Ifa Karade, thank you so very much for opening that portal in 1998 and allowing me to walk through, thank you for your wise counsel and guidance. Thank you for your courage to follow our ancestral without compromise.

To the FOI of former Temple #61 Grand Rapids, Michigan, it was from soldiering with you that I learned to love, respect and rely on my brothers.

Special Acknowledgements

To Rashidah, thank you for being beside me all of these years and teaching me such valuable lessons. Your devotion and dedication to our family is without equal.

To Osunnike, thank you for bringing the love of Oshun into my life and teaching me to breath again, for in your being I have experienced the mercy of God.

To my children, it goes without question that you are my wealth, thank you for giving me the honor of being your father.

To my granddaughters, Ameera, Nasia, Khari, Waliyah and Janece, may I learn the lessons that you beautiful flowers have come to teach. May you grow and go forth into the world as the embodiment of the sacred feminine.

To the Karade-Anke spiritual family, 'I am because we are'. May we all stand on the shoulders of our Ancestors and seek to return the people to tradition.

To the brotherhood in Tennessee, Pittsburgh, Ohio and Michigan may you keep the Spirit Fires of the Sweat Lodge burning with the love of our Ancestors.

To all of the spiritual sons who have watched me closely insuring that I walked my talk thank you.

To my God daughter Omiesun, thank you for your devotion and assistance in doing the editorial corrections. Your Joy is infectious!

To the publishers at Shekhem Publishing, LLP, thank you for believing in this book and your courage to walk the waters.

Finally to T.A. El-Amin, my beloved brother we have walked many roads together and watched each other as we have evolved. Words cannot express the gratitude to God for your being in my life. You have been an example for me as well as a stabilizing force. You have been a light house when I was loss in this quest for spiritual realization. Most of all you have been a friend. Thank you for reading, editing and the Preface for this work. T.A. the world awaits your book (smile).

CONTENTS

FORWARD

When attempting to introduce readers to a subject as broad as this, one is humbled by the request to try and write an introduction that gives due credence to the author, the Exalted Ancestors that came through him and The Creator from which it flowed, while keeping himself out of the way. My hope is that these words will assist the reader in opening-up to the information contained within, and actively involve themselves in this great call to *reach the Black Male through Spirituality and rites-of-passage*, so he can become a contributing member in properly-raising the next generation of Afrikan men here in America.

Baba Koleoso Karade, aka Nashid Fakhrid-Deen, JD, has undertaken the task of presenting us with a manual, a guide if you will, that can be used by groups across the Diaspora to assist their young men in recognizing, and understanding, what kind of beings they truly are. He uses the vehicles of history, culture, spirituality, health, and tradition to enlighten us on this crucial subject.

Having edited several of the previous works by Baba, I had a feel for the types of communications he receives, as well as a vast knowledge of his research and experiential experiences as it pertains to spirituality, religious traditions, cultural differences, and similarities of peoples around the world. All of his writings are designed to bring us closer to the knowledge of who, and what, we are as spiritual beings having a human experience sent directly from The Creator to do various works in each lifetime.

We are given Koleoso's mission in the Preface. Here, he sets the tone for the body of this work, as it relates to guiding us, as men, along the path to self-correction, to our spiritual selves, to our initiation into manhood, using time-tested proven systems from around the world. The questions he poses to us, upfront, make us think about what we are about to read and prepare us to think deeply, then act upon our findings so we can become the men The Creator intends for us to be.

The book is constructed as a training manual, which includes various undertakings by the initiate, the student, designed to get us on the road to "becoming".

He begins with The Call. Here, cosmology is explored and explained, giving us deep insights into this ancient science of the 'knowledge of self'. Most Afrikans, born in America, have never been exposed to this term, much less the meaning of it. He takes us back to the origins of the "Man, Know Thyself" dictum and shows where it is our divine right and inheritance to know these ancient truths and how they affect us today. He references the works of Ra Un Nefer Amen, Iyanla Vanzant, Sun Bear, Nzinga Warfield-Coppock, R.A. Schwaller De-Lubitz, and other scholars, shamans, priests, and deep-thinkers to give us a broad base of information that covers most areas of life that concern us as men.

Next, we are given the reasons and rationale for establishing and going through rites-of-passage so we can become more akin to our true selves. His sources cited are well documented and thorough in detailing what is missing in the growth and development of Afrikan men in America. All of this detail is done to help us know the depth, the sincerity and correctness of the ideas presented later on in the work. He works his way through the writings of John S. Mbiti, Frances Cress Welsing, and Na'im Akbar, Amos Wilson, Nzinga Warfield-Coppock, and the Willie Lynch piece, and references Paul Hill, Jr.—founder of the Rites-of-passage Institute in Cleveland, OH. The need is clearly established in this section, and the prescription is being written for our healing.

From this point, we are given a look at the Nation of Islam and its rites-of-passage program as an example that achieved much success, using a religious format, in bringing Afrikan men to manhood, having them take on the role of family head, forcing them to respect themselves, their women and children, and the laws of their captors, in order to rebuild the family unit destroyed during our sojourn in this wilderness. We are given a brief look at numerology and its impact on things on this planet historically, and also the use of this science in building character in men throughout the ages. Koleoso's use of history, as a teacher, is phenomenal in that the lessons are short, yet deep, while still being clear and to-the-point.

Spiritual cultivation, or the essence of rites-of-passage initiation, is dealt with from the perspective of practicing spiritual leaders and guides: Ra Un Nefer Amen, Koleoso's teacher, Baba Ifa Karade, and Malidoma Some'—a shaman from the Dagara people of Burkina Faso. This short section lays the foundation for the spiritual undertaking in the initiation process. All of these references and sources are essential to establishing a firm foundation for the methodology of the program being prepared.

For those of you well versed in the Kamitian (Ancient Egyptian) spiritual systems, the section on "Ready to Recover the Phallus is very informative and instructive. He takes us into the story of Auset's (Isis') ordeal in trying to reconstruct Ausar's (Osiris') body, after Set's (Satan's) misdeed of having him "cut" into 14 pieces. His treatment of this very deep subject matter is supported by other writers when they talk about our being dismantled and our women struggling to find all the parts necessary to restore us to our traditional manhood. His connecting of the phallus and fish discusses sexual potency as it relates to spiritual power, subjects many of us would never research. How he connects the sex act with spiritual growth is profound and an object lesson.

References to the Chinese Health and Healing Systems, Egyptian Yoga, religion and war, then living in the light carefully guides the reader to understand the true roles of religion in bringing us back to our natural path, our natural way of living in the world.

The actual program is structured to comprise nine (9) months of activities, beginning around the spring equinox, March 21st and running through the winter solstice, until December 31st, the next-to-last day of Kwanzaa, the only Afrikan cultural holiday in this country. Baba lets us know that this is not a one-time fix, but an ongoing effort that becomes a permanent part of the community process. This allows for the building of a generational ideology that transcends our lifetimes and leaves a firm foundation for future Afrikan peoples to continue developing men in our communities. The goals cited in this section deals with building character, self-knowledge, responsible behaviors, self-esteem. It hopes to build positive images for male development, build positive male/female, adult, and parent relationships. There are three phases of the program. The first includes sex education, social values, business and personal finance, law and justice, religion and science, and art and health. The second contains inter-community relationships, and pertinent issues dealt with in the first phase—going into more detail in each area. At the conclusion of the program, a large celebration is held to honor and welcome the new initiates home as men.

Critical to the whole program is the establishment of a Council of Elders, an essential component to intergenerational connections. There is an in-depth criteria for selecting the council, which includes their knowledge of community traditions and culture, their knowledge of the concept of Afrikan-centered thinking, the reading of major texts that deal with the histories of our people and the world, and a deep interest in instructing and guiding same-gender youth. Baba cites several sources to note the importance of sitting with and seeking council from our learned Elders, the histories of our peoples as it relates to their roles in building and maintaining a sense of community, and the pitfalls of not paying heed to those most-fit to give guidance to our community on its journey toward building men.

We are exposed to a deep exchange between Baba Koleoso and one of his Spiritual Masters, in the section: El-Hajj Ray Rites-of-passage, 7 Doors to Manhood. It discusses the well-known Know Thyself phrase and gives us criteria to follow to get in-touch with who we are as men. He deals with divination, balancing the male and female aspects of the individual, spiritual baths, addressing the man in the mirror, and the sweat lodge ceremony—usually associated with the Native peoples of North America. The exchanges are so profound that one can see himself inside these discussions and gain much benefit from studying and meditating on the ideas brought forth.

Having had the great privilege of being in numerous sweat lodges with Baba Koleoso, I can attest to the power they bring to one's walk in this life and the revelations one receives while sitting in the tremendous heat of these ceremonies. The healing qualities of these sessions are unheard of in our daily comings and goings and lend much to developing good character, courage, stamina, spiritual enlightenment, and purpose in the participant. Koleoso has blended the Afrikan steam hut, Native American sweat lodge, and South American sweat ceremonies with insights from his guides and massive research into how the ancients went about building men in their communities. These efforts have made them healing sessions designed to help us break out of the psychological shackles we have labored under the past twenty-five generations in America. The rites-of-passage program, with all its component parts, allows us to move beyond our state of impotence to becoming the warriors we were created to be in the beginning. This section also informs us of some of our spiritual heritage, our spiritual teachings of old, our names for the Divine, how we saw God, how we can get back to seeing the world through Afrikan eyes, and how to use the healing wisdom of our Ancestors to resurrect the Afrikan man.

There is a serious discussion on Cleansing and Purifying that gets to the heart of what ails us, based on what we put into our temples, called bodies, and the proper ways to take care of these vessels. Ayur Veda is one of the ancient healing modalities we are exposed to in this section of the book. We get a historical overview of who created this system and how it fell into the hands of those bringing it back to the forefront in medicine, today. For those of us with serious medical problems, a look into The Raj, an Ayur Vedic Healing Institute in Iowa shows where we can go to become well, while not harming the physical temple with drugs and bad food. From the various experts on this subject, Baba gives us the origins of this practice, its "cosmic roots", our cosmic nature and treatment of said nature. He talks about using sound in healing, getting in touch with our conscious selves and our ego selves, both from a scientific and spiritual perspective. He covers beliefs and values we hold dear and makes us look deep into their origins and the related practices we follow to help us identify who and what we are. The piece on Phallic Purification Rituals was instructive, in that, most men I have encountered have never mentioned such, and few have written anything on the subject. Citing several powerful works, Baba Koleoso shares the historical view of the phallic symbol, the spiritual connection to the growth and development of man, what overindulgence does to men, how to reclaim the healing energy we lose when we give-up our semen, and prescriptions for renewing ourselves after losing our fluids in the sex act.

Finally, the "Living in Alignment with Absolute Truth" section of this work deals with the search for the self, as contained in a piece produced by the Siddha Yoga Foundation. It takes us on a wonderful journey with the student and master having an in-depth exchange, with the master trying to show the student that he is God, having a human experience, along with the billions of the other expressions of God on this planet. It really brings to life the message of us being created in the ' image and likeness' of the Divine. We are shown how there are many paths to follow in our trek towards God realization. The key being to select the path that best fits who and what type expression you are and which walk fits the individual best. The book ends with a critical discussion on the spiritual significance of male/female relationships. Quoting from such diverse writers as Rumi, the Sufi poet of old, On the Breath of the Gods by Tomioka, Africentric Guide to a Spiritual Union by Ra Un Nefer Amen and looking at the current statistics that deal with said relationships, Baba, once again, shows his tremendous grasp of the issues we face while trying to move from being males to boys and then to Afrikan men walking the way of the ancients—who were closer to God in their thoughts and actions—and rebuilding our families into the communities we used to live in before these schisms.

This synopsis of such a great work is done without thought of personal gain or to toot my own horn. It is done to help ease the way for the initiate, on the path to becoming a spiritual Afrikan, using a rites-of-passage program as the nexus.

May the Creator, The Exalted Ancestors, and The Deities guide you as you journey on the road to reclaiming your spiritual Afrikan self. Maat Hetep!

Professor T. A. El Amin

PREFACE

With the Name of God, Most Gracious, Most Merciful and in the Presence of Our Ancestors, Both Seen and Unseen.

This Book is not THE WAY, but a way, in my estimation to reach, not only Black Males but all Males. If you, the reader, find anything in this book to be of benefit, then Praises are due to God, the Divinities and the Ancestors. Should you find it offensive and of no use, then, the fault is mine. It means that I was too caught up in the calling of my ego to impress and have my ideas accepted by you. For that, I ask your forgiveness and patience with me.

We all are on a wonderful journey we call life. We all have come back this way for a grand purpose. This life we live is a gift, a gift from the Creator, and it is my prayer that we all appreciate this gift.

So many of our lives are filled with pain and suffering until we fail to realize the richness of life. We fail to see the wonder of walking this blessed earth. I say to you, when was the last time you looked up in the heavens and gave thanks for the stars and wondered what was behind the creation of them. When was the last time you walked in the grass with your shoes off and truly felt the energy of the earth moving through you?

My Dear Brothers, we have been so caught- up in what this world has said about us that we've accepted our station in this life. We walk about carrying tremendous burdens that we do not know how to release. One of the greatest burdens we carry is that of trying to figure out, and understand, manhood, Black Manhood. How can you understand Black Manhood, in a society that was built on the destruction of said, manhood? How can you look in the mirror and find satisfaction in that which you see, when the world has told you that you were less than a man, and fit for nothing? How is this possible? There are so many of us out here, struggling to find our place in a society that never really meant for us to have a seat at the table of humanity.

Yes, you may be a great athlete making millions, yet you know deep inside, there is a hole, which you long to fill. You may be a successful businessman, corporate executive, academician, a great rap star or gangbanger, yet you know there is a hole that must be filled. The hole I speak of is the question of your own manhood in a society that denied your ancestral men the right to be men. No matter how you try to hide it, or run from it, that legacy is passed on to you. Think of all that you have had to give up in your climb towards success? Think of the compromises you have had to make, knowing all too well that you were not being the man that you wanted to be. We say, this is the time when you must stop, look deep within, and see if you are truly the man that you seek to be. We say, step outside of all of your labels, riches and fame and ask yourself, who am I, really?

My, Dear Brothers, there was a time when manhood was understood and praised. There was a time when we were taught of manhood and we looked forward to taking our place of responsibility in the family. Yet, today, our manhood has been reduced to "sexing women and kicking ass, be it on the court, or in the streets." We have allowed ourselves to be hypnotized by the illusions of this world. We are, nothing more than, poor imitations of our former slave masters, imitations on every level.

The very men we should look to for guidance, our spiritual men, are so caught up in their own God complex, until they are of little or no help. We spiritual men are no more than religious pimps and spiritual oppressors. So, where does a brother turn? The first thing a seeker of truth must do is to be truthful to himself. Admit to self that you are not fulfilled as a man, that you really do not know what manhood is. Then, pray to God the Creator for guidance, next get up, and seek the answers.

Our Ancestors knew, full well, what a man was and how to bring men into manhood. It was rites-of-passage, a time when the elder men would come, collect the younger men, and initiate them into the mysteries of manhood. Tell me, who has come to get you? What elder men have come to get you and teach you of the mysteries of manhood? No one has come to get you, because we all have been so beaten down to the point that we have lost the meaning and desire of taking young men to manhood. We are too busy imitating the European image of manhood, thus we want nothing to do with the ways of our ancestors.

We say to you, look back! Take a good look back and you will see the image of men of the first order. They were strong men, who were able to endure the pain of captivity, slavery, lynching, segregation and still find self-dignity. Look back, beyond that period, and you will see the image of men who gave the sciences to the world, men, who where the first civilizers of humanity, men, who valued family, honored their women and loved their children.

Where are those men, today? Yes, there are a few, and those few are the exception, not the rule. It is time for these men to, once again, become the rule and not the exception. It is time for us, the elders, to go and retrieve our young men and teach them the secrets of manhood. No woman should be without a man in her life, no child without a father figure. Our greatest enemy should be ignorance, not the brother who is walking beside you. My Beloved Brother, I need you. I need your strength, your vision, your natural intelligence and spiritual understanding, that we might go forth together, in this world, and seek to make a change, that we might leave this world a better place than we found it.

In many respects, this book is dedicated to those men who endured all of the hardships of capture in central and west Africa, who were marched to the slave dungeons and held there for up to a year. It is dedicated to those men who endured the journey across the Atlantic and survived the hardships of slavery, Jim crow and untold harm and fear in America that I might be here. It goes without question that this is dedicated to the mothers of us all, those mothers who stopped and gave birth to us in the hulls of slave ships, in the cotton fields, the tobacco fields, in the sugar cane fields, in rice fields. It is to those mothers who kept our skies from falling, those mothers who rocked the cradle and taught us softness from hands hardened by work, from sun up to sun down. It is a tribute to those mothers who taught us love, love of God, family and community, in a time when we could not have community, nor family, and were introduced to another God. This dedication is to those men and women whose shoulders I stand on and seek to see what they could not see. It is to those men and women of toady, who withstood the dogs, the hoses and insults that I might walk into a school and receive every degree offered. I give thanks for them and their sacrifices for me.

This book it dedicated to the modern day mother who raised a man-child, by herself, in this promised land. It is dedicated to the untold fathers who stayed, who endured the pains of marriage, job disappointments and poverty, to ensure that their sons would know fathers, that their daughters would know the love of daddy and their wives would know the protection of husbands. We talk, all the time, about the fathers who left, the men who would not assume their responsibility, but nothing is said of the fathers who stayed. Nothing is said of the father who worked, two and three jobs, to make ends meet, so his family could survive. Nothing is said of the father who gets up each morning and goes to a job on which he is still reduced to a 'boy', yet, he does it in silence and dignity because he has accepted his responsibility of FATHERHOOD. Nothing is said of the father who endures his wife's disappointments in him because she, in her ignorance, is comparing him to a European standard of manhood, in which, he was never an equal player. It is to those modern-day men of courage that I dedicate this work. To the fathers who stayed, put up with everything and endured, I give thanks for you. To the fathers who gave up and ran, I say to you God is Most Merciful and ALL forgiving, your family still needs you – GO HOME !!!! Find them, and let them know that you LOVE them.

It is time for the men to gather and prepare our sons for manhood!

Peace and Love
Nashid "Koleoso"

INTRODUCTION

With the Name of God, Most Gracious, Most Merciful and in the Presence of Our Ancestors, Both Seen and Unseen.

The symbol on the cover is the "EYE of HERU"

About the symbol:

Ra Un Nefer Amen, Chief Priest and King of the Ausar/ Auset Society, informs us that the story of Ausar, Auset, Set, and Heru, is to our Egyptian Ancestors, what the Old Testament is to the Jews, and the Bible is to Christians. However, he makes it clear that to gain benefit from this story, one must keep in mind that the characters, i.e., deities, are personifications of faculties residing in the spirit of God and man. Ra Un Nefer Amen points out that Ausar is that faculty that embodies, or represents, the divine intelligence, divine wisdom and spiritual power of God and man. Heru embodies the faculties of divine law, justice and your personal will. However, man's will also suffers from the defect of spiritual blindness, thus, allowing evil to run rampant. Set (Satan) represents the partially developed will, combined with syllogistic intellect. This aspect of our self is dominated by the animal spirit. This is the principle of evil in man. Auset represents man's persona, when fully devoted to God. Without going into the entire story, I would like to draw from the aspect of it that deals with the symbol: "Eye of Heru." Ra Un Nefer Amen writes, in his book 'METU NETER Vol. 2, pages 150 –151 that "Heru gathered his army and went to confront Set. They first met at Edfu, where Set's army slew many of the followers of Heru." Ra Un Nefer Amen's commentary on this is:

> As we will see, ultimately, Set will be defeated through truth, but one must be prepared to stand up to him at all cost, and by all means necessary. Without this, you cannot get him to abide by the truth. Heru was defeated because he followed his own head (the intellect). Heru is our sense of freedom and independence.[1]

The story goes on to say:

> But, Heru and his followers, although greatly outnumbered, resumed the war. His greatest weapon was his faith in the council of Tehuti, whose words were God's words (the Metu Neter). They attacked Set again and drove him to the eastern frontier. He sought refuge, at Zaru, where Heru caught up with him, and the last battle of the war ensued.[2]

Ra Un Nefer Amen's commentary:

> His victory came from humbling himself to the intuitive guidance of the wisdom faculty, which is received through perfection in meditation, or oracles, or counsel from a sage. Intelligence has always defeated might and steel. As we will

see, ultimately, Set will be defeated through truth, but one must be prepared to stand up to him at all cost, and confront him with all means possible. Without this, you cannot get him to abide by the truth.[3]

The story goes on to say that "In this pitched battle that went on for many days, Set gouged out Heru's eye, which would have cost Heru the war had not Tehuti healed it. With his insight regained, Heru managed to castrate Set." Of this on page 151, Metu Neter Vol. 2, Ra Un Nefer Amen says:

> The eye of Heru symbolizes the visual thinking of the right side of the brain which governs understanding and spirituality. It is also the symbol of the omniscience and omnipresence of God, as shown in earlier chapters, thus it was attacked by Set. The healing of the eye by Tehuti is an allusion to the role that wisdom plays in our lives. Likewise, Heru attacked Set in the seat of his uncontrolled aggressiveness.[4]

By Set cutting out the eye of Heru, we see that Set attacked Heru's understanding and spirituality. We, as a people, have been separated from our spirituality! This separation from OUR spirituality is what keeps us alienated from our true selves. Remember, Heru's victory came from him humbling himself to the intuitive guidance from the wisdom faculty (Tehuti). This guidance comes through meditation, oracles, or counsel from the sage. Once, we humble ourselves to OUR spiritual ways and submit to the guidance of the sage, we will gain the victory. Thus, the eye of Heru (front cover) is a reminder that we have been attacked in our spirituality and that we can no longer follow our heads (intellect). It is submission to OUR spiritual ways, via God, Deities and the Ancestors, that will ensure our victory!!

*With the Name of God, Most Gracious, Most Merciful and in
the Presence of Our Ancestors, Both Seen and Unseen.*

Reaching Black Males Through Spirituality

The Ancestor, Ra Bena' Saa Tur, who comes through Nashid, spoke on
this subject of Reaching Black Males Through Spirituality, on March
20,1996,

"So you come to us to speak to you of reaching black
males through spirituality. Well, what is it you want to know?
It is, as we have said to you time and time again, the fact that
you are caught up in this world of illusion. The fact that this
world has you thinking you are something separate from your
spirit is what has you thinking that you have to reconnect to
spirituality to capture the black male. We say to you, you are
not separate from your spirit, your spirit is who and what you
are. We say to you, all that is necessary is for you to point them
back home. Point them back home to Africa and how their
Ancestors knew that they, and God, were one and the same.
That spirit was nothing foreign to them. That everything they
did was based on a high spiritual principle.

Dear One, you want to know the role of spirituality in
reaching the black male. We say to you, the role of spirituality
in reaching the black male is to acquaint them with who they,
truly, are. They are spirit, housed in a physical body. We say
to you, you are to tell them that they are created in the image
and likeness of God. That God is neither spirit nor material,
that God stands above and in creation and rules it. We say that
you are to point them to us and we will do the rest.

INTRODUCTION

So, you want to know the role of spirituality in reaching the black male. We say to you, the further you take the black male from spirituality, the harder it is to reach him, for you are taking him away from his nature. His nature is spirit, his essence is spirit, he is the spirit of God that took on form. He is that aspect of God that chose to manifest as the individual we see and hear each day. However, it is because he allowed his consciousness to become grounded in matter that he thinks he is something different, and today, you have to come and ask us the role of spirituality in reaching black males.

We say to you, look back in time, take a good, long, look back in time and see that spirituality was the essence of everything your Ancestors did. When we took you through a rite-of-passage, it was via the vehicle of spirituality. When you came from the womb of your mother, it was via the spirit. In fact, as a newborn child, you were viewed as a NETER, a God that had come back to the earth to perform a specific job. They looked to you for messages from the other side. They knew you were closer to God, because you had just come from the face of God. We say to you, you want to know the role of spirituality in reaching the black male. It is a vital role, an important role. For it, spirituality, acquaints him with who and what he is. We say to you, that is all he wants to know, 'who am I and where do I fit in the grand scheme of things'. Dear One, is that not what all of you want to know? Do you still search for meaning in your life, in spite of all your riches, power and status? You are still searching for meaning and your place in this creation. That is why so many of you are going to psychics, healers and seers, trying to get a vision of your essence.

Do you think it is any different for the young Afrikan male, an entity who knows, deep within his being, that he has a special role to perform in the transition of the universe? An entity who knows that he is to take over the throne of his father, who was killed by his evil uncle? These are the young men who will get the job done. They will succeed, where you have failed. They are strong, fearless, and powerful, yet, they need direction. However, they do not need to know how to make money, for many of them have, will make, more in one day than you will in a year. They do not need to know how to be obedient to the laws that govern this land, for they see them broken, each day, by the lawmakers. They do not need to be taught religious laws, for they see some preachers, etc. transgressing the laws and becoming nothing more than pimps. We say to you, they need to be taken to a higher level.

We say to you, their souls are crying for a great vision. They are longing to be taken to the edge of the universe and allowed to look into infinity and see their divinity. However, you cannot take them there, for in order to do so, you must be willing to embrace your culture, your heritage and your history. You must be willing to take the knowledge of today, go back, and mix it with the knowledge of yesterday, to give them a vision of the future.

We say to you, one such way is the way of the sweat lodge. We say to you, take them into the lodge. Take them into the womb of their mother and allow the heat to purify them. Take them into the sweat lodge and call the Ancestors to come and initiate them into mysteries that they cannot talk about, but experience. We say to you, take them into the sweat lodge and allow them to get a look at the death that they play with each day. For, as you know, initiation involves dying and

being reborn. All they are looking for is a symbolic death.
They want to die as little boys. They want to come alive as
men. Yet, there are no elders to show them the way.

We say to you, Dear One, you must take them by the hand
and show them the way. Allow the Ancestors to join them in
the sweat lodge and they, the Ancestors, will initiate them.
The Ancestors will cause death to look them in the face and
they will be, forever, transformed. You doubt what we are
saying? How many of those you have taken on this sacred
journey have been transformed? All, all, we say! Their lives
have been affected in a way that is even a mystery to them.
We say to you, Dear One, take them into the womb of the
sweat lodge and we, the ancestors, will do the rest. We say
to you, for those whom we touch in a special way, you're to
take them to the Sun Dance and allow them to experience the
pain of hanging from the Tree of Life by the chest. The pain of
pulling away. They will learn that power is not about a gun, in
hand. It is about manifesting God in your life. They will learn
that power is not about the woman beneath you in bed, but
the woman that is hiding in the recesses of your mind, who is
seeking to express herself, so that she might take you further
into the reaches of inner- space.

We say to you, introduce them once more to ritual.
Make everything you do a ritual. Show them the rhythm in
mathematics, that they are rhythm in motion, that they are
mathematicians manifest! Yes, we say to you, take them
back home. When you do this, they will liberate you from the
middle-class slavery in which you live."

Peace & Love
Ra Bena' Saa Tur

I

THE CALL

We are taught that man is created in the image and likeness of God, thus, the essential nature of man is God. While he may not have the same quantity of power as THE GOD, who created the heavens and earth, he has the same qualities. This understanding was taught, thousands of years ago, and was the guiding principle in the development of black men and women. Also, a blueprint (Cosmology) was known that would guide man to the realization of his God self. Speaking of Cosmology, Ra Un Nefer Amen writes:

> Cosmology, the study of Cosmogony has two fundamental goals. First, it provides an ordered and unified (synthetical) view of who and what is God, Man, and the forces that administrate and sustain the world. No understanding of a subject can take place without an ordered and unified presentation of its whole and parts. Second, cosmology (like all blueprints and maps) provides a framework that guides thinking and action through the vast array of seemingly un-related life situations to the successful identification and attainment of the goal of living. It achieves this, by showing how all the events in a person's life are integrally related to his/her destiny.[5]

Thus, it was via the vehicle of Cosmology that man was able to understand who and what he is in relationship to God and creation. It was Cosmology that allowed man to look at himself, not as separate from God, but as a manifestation of God, functioning in creation. Cosmology allowed man to understand how he came into being and how he was to function in this world. Ra Un Nefer Amen goes on to say:

> It is very important to understand, that contrary to popular opinion, cosmology does not attempt to explain how physical things, on the atomic and molecular levels, come into being. It concentrates on the coming into being of the metaphysical factors that will function as the vehicles through which the physical things will come into existence, as well as the means of regulating their structural and functional components, hence external behavior.[6]

Therefore, we see that cosmology is the embodiment of the biblical phrase, "In the beginning was the word, and the word was with God, and the word was God and the word took on form." It is cosmology that will allow us to understand how the word was with God and was God, pointing us to the spiritual and spirituality. On page 65 in Metu Neter Vol. 2 , Ra Un Nefer Amen goes on to say"

> Keeping in mind that the ultimate goal of Cosmology (the study of cosmogony) is the understanding of Self, the Ra conceptualization of the highest aspect of God's manifestation did not integrate with the fact, that at this level, one finds a separation of Being from one's faculties of creation, which are all combined in the symbol of Ra. In other words, while the faculties of creativity can be totally at rest, the Self is forever conscious.[7]

Now, what is this Self? How is it forever conscious and how can its understanding and access benefit Black Males, or anyone, for that matter? We all are familiar with the phrase, "KNOW THY SELF", but, is this the self that we think we know? Is it the personality that I call self, the ego I call self? It is our understanding that this is speaking of something, much more expansive and greater, it is speaking of God, the ultimate Self, of which we are all a part. While this is easy to speak of, it is the journey towards the experience of the Self that is the challenge. For the ancients, consciousness, or the Self, or God, were all synonymous, one and the same. In the <u>Siddha Yoga Mediation Teachings</u>, Ram states:

> The experience of the Self is not cold, or dry, or intellectual. The self is warm and euphoric; it exists within, as an inner smile. Our experience of "fun," "amusement," "humor," and "enjoyment" all arise from the Self. The Self is supreme contentment, supreme fulfillment. It is embodied in laughter, and its sensation is love. This Self is our own true and eternal nature. It is who we truly are, who we always have been, and who we always will be. Because of our mental conditioning, because of our ego, we do not see this Truth.[8]

In short, the Self is the divine consciousness within us. Thus, in the phrase "KNOW THY SELF," the ancients were directing us to know our DIVINE consciousness, the God in us who is the SELF. We are God. Ram goes on to say:

> The Self is Consciousness, and Consciousness is our Awareness. Our own Awareness of Being is not different from divine Consciousness itself. There is not more than one Self. There is only one inner-Self. You and I share the same inner Self. For this reason, when we truly know our own Self, we truly know each other. The same universal Self is shared by everybody, simultaneously. Everyone has the same inner Awareness, the same "I".[9]

Now, we can see why the bible says, "to know self, you know all men", we are the same Self. If I know the Self, then, I know the Self that is manifesting as you and others. So, what is all the fighting and warring about? In essence, when truly understood, we are only fighting and warring with SELF. On one level, we are fighting and warring because we do not understand, nor know, God. We have allowed politics to guide our spirituality and religiosity. To understand what I am saying, look at the words of Swami Rama in his book, Spirituality Transformation Within and Without, page 129:

> All religions of the world believe in the incarnation of God as messiah, prophet, or savior. Such a concept of God, or godly manifestations, restricts our worldview, and even forces us to divide humanity, in the name of God. Identifying God as a personal being, also, prevents us from experiencing God in every human being. As a result, we do not respect our own brothers and sisters, if they do not worship "our God." What ignorance to consider God to be, merely, our God, and not the God of all! Unfortunately, that has been the case with many of the followers of God. The destiny of mankind lies in experiencing the God beyond "my God," "your God," or their God.[10]

Where would we be, as a people, nation, and world, if this egotistical energy was channeled into the discovery of self, maybe the superior races we see on Star Wars, or once again, builders of great civilizations like those of the past? Before going any further, let's look at the concept of we, being the same Self, from a different perspective. Dr. Keith Wallace writes in his book, The Physiology of Consciousness, page 4:

> The recent achievements in mind-body research have paralleled breakthroughs in modern physics. In physics, matter and energy are viewed as expressions of four fundamental fields: gravity, electromagnetism, and the strong and weak nuclear forces. In the last few years, quantum physics has reached such a profound level of understanding that it has been able to locate one unified field of all the laws of nature at the basis of these four fields. While the complete mathematical description of this field is still developing, it is

clear, that the unified field of nature law is the source of all material diversity. It transcends all existence; it is a field of pure information from which all the different forces and laws of nature sequentially emerge in the first microseconds of the creation of the universe, and from which this process is continually taking place at every moment. Most striking, modern physics' description of the unified field of natural law, as a self-sufficient, self-interacting, field of infinite intelligence and dynamism, is remarkably similar to descriptions of the unified basis of creation given by the world's most ancient traditions of knowledge.[11]

Thus, it seems that even science is bearing witness to the unity of our being, that we are the same, coming from the same place. However, as was stated, it is our mental conditionings that keep us from this understanding. Our mental conditionings, in part, are a result of the society, culture and environments in which we live. Our western culture has done, and continues to do, a lot to keep most of us from the path of true Self-realization. Everyday, we are controlled by our conditioned responses. If the brain is like a computer, transmitting and receiving messages, it can only put out in reference to the manner it has been programmed, or conditioned. If we have been programmed, or conditioned, by our culture, that the individual is more important than the group, then, our conditioned response is for the benefit of the individual and not the group, i.e., the individual is greater, and more important, than the we. Yet, the Africans say, "I am, because we are. We are, therefore, I am" and the Native Americans say, "We are all Part of the great Web." This all points to the fact that we have a common origin, bond, and interest which we all share. If we have been programmed, or conditioned, that God is outside of us, beyond ourselves, then, we will not look for God in us. We will not see ourselves as having a common origin. Therefore, we never get to the Self, the higher Self.

REACHING BLACK MALES THROUGH SPIRITUALITY

Today, there is a reawakening taking place among black males, and central to this is the understanding of spirituality. The Million Man March was an example of the divine spiritual unity of black men. Spirituality should not be confused with religiosity. Working from a western orientation, religiosity denotes the degree to which one relates to their particular religious doctrine (Christianity, Islam, Judaism, etc.). Spirituality denotes the transcendence above the religious dogma and the celebration of the oneness of all. However, it is our lack of comprehending spirituality and our dogmatic adherence to Western notions of religion that continue to separate us as black men and human beings. At this point, it is necessary for us to raise the question, "What does spirituality really mean? What are the demands of spirituality?" The root word of "spirituality" is spirit, the spirit is free, boundless, and unconditioned. Iyanla Vanzant gives us a definition of spirituality. She says:

> Spirituality means faith in self, as a divine and noble expression of the Creator, and faith in spirit as your guide in life. Spirituality means viewing life through a spirit's eye - the third eye, which is not limited by ego, perception, or intelligence. Spirituality means seeing the truth, value, and beauty in all life forces and dedicating one's self to the expansion of those lives. Spirituality is a journey inward, which connects you to the pulse of the universe as it is expressed through your being.[12]

Therefore, we see that spirituality requires one to journey within, and, for most of us, this is a serious undertaking. We have been so externalized and alienated from self, until our definition of self comes mainly from the media. Were one to take the journey within, they would learn the truth of the biblical saying, "To know self is to know all men." For, all men/women are the essence of God and it is cosmology that will teach us this. Spirituality demands that you take this journey within, that you cannot learn of self and your divine essence, primarily, from outside of self. Spirituality requires a different mindset and worldview. In fact, it requires that one give up their present way of looking at the world. Vanzant goes on to say:

> Spirituality is the recognition of your connection to the essence of the Creator, as the source of your power. Spirituality simply means that you recognize and accept your individual connection to the Creator and use that 'spiritual connection' as your guiding force.[13]

To understand spirituality, is to understand how to conquer fear, hate, anger, depression and loneliness. To understand your individual connection to the essence of the Creator was, and is, the goal of all spiritual systems. It is these systems that liberate the individual from the conditionings that keep them from realizing the God within. These systems serve as the foundation of the African and Indigenous Educational System.

Today, we search for ways to reach black males, in reference to their education, career, social and moral duties. Our African and Native American Ancestors had the answer in their cultural educational systems. We must understand, before colonialism, and the arrival of the white man, Africans and Native Americans were a people who lived profoundly on this earth. They were a people who lived in reciprocal, respectful, relationship within the environments of which they saw themselves as an intimate part, and whose sacred nature they knew, understood, and respected. The everyday activities of the lives they lived were more akin to ritual, or sacrament. These daily activities were paced by the rhythms of nature and linked to and in harmony with the greater movements of the cosmos. As such, each present moment was a blending of the sacred and profane, past and future, and time and timelessness.

These were a people who inherited an uninterrupted transmission of the knowledge of a way of being, a way of life, that stretched back to their distant ancestors. They knew and understood the anatomy of the land in which they lived, they learned what it taught, shared its visions, and felt the pulse stream of life flowing through the veins of the universe that they felt flowing through their bodies. It was on this pulse stream of universal life that they founded their educational and religious systems.

For too long, because of our western indoctrination, we have looked at their beliefs as merely 'superstitious', 'primitive' or 'backward'. Yet, today, we are realizing that their lives and beliefs were dynamic and vivid ways of experiencing and understanding the universe. These ways of experiencing the universe were far truer, and far beyond anything our modern scientific belief systems, or our pale intellectual analytical interpretations of religion, have been able to give or teach us. As we, in the west, function in our material arrogance, we suffer from cultural amnesia. We cannot feel our bodies and their connection to the universe. As a result, our present educational systems lack the understanding of the universal rhythms of the past, which can assist in reaching black males, or any male for that matter.

One role of African education was the bridging of the gap between the adult generation and the youth. This education was not just there to be acquired, it was to be lived! It addressed every aspect of the individuals' lives, and gave them their assigned roles within the social order of that community. More importantly, it allowed the individual to comprehend his/her relationship to God and the cosmos. The children gained education by participating in the social, political, and religious institutions that ensured effective communication between generations.

THE CALL

But who will provide our youth with access to these Ancient systems, today? The African Shaman, Malidoma Patrice Some' says:

> When an elder fails to perform his work with respect to the spiritual, the future of this elder is threatened, not the present. Where ritual is absent, the young ones are restless or violent, there are no real elders, and the grown-ups are bewildered. The future is dim.[14]

The question becomes, 'what is the work of an elder with respect to the spiritual?' It was the elders, who initiated the youth and showed them their place in the community. It was the elders, who provided spiritual guidance in all areas of life. Our Ancestors understood that it took the moon 28 years to return to the same point it was at the time of your birth. Therefore, the first 28 years of the life of an individual is spent under the influence of the moon. The moon, indiscriminately, imitates the light of the sun. Our Ancient Elders knew that their youth would, indiscriminately, imitate all that they saw. Therefore, the elders were strong role models of the God in man, thus, allowing the youth to imitate them. Today, it does not take much to see how our youth are indiscriminately imitating the violence and low behavior that is placed before them by the media, and so-called role models. Again Malidoma says:

> The fading and disappearance of ritual in modern culture is, from the viewpoint of Dagara, expressed in several ways: the weakening of links with the spirit world, and general alienation of people from themselves and others. In a context like this, there are no elders to help anyone remember, through initiation, his, or her, important place in the community. Those who seek to remember have an attraction towards violence. They live their lives constantly upset or angry, and those responsible for them are at a loss as to what to do.[15]

Our young people are angry. They are looking for their important place in the community and they are looking for us to initiate them, looking for the Elders of today to test them. This is but one reason that gangs are so attractive to our young people. Bloch and Niederhoffer (1958) suggested that the study of the commonalities in gangs will aid in understanding the developmental phase of our young people and what they are looking for. They suggest that gangs offer:

1. The power and authority desired in the gang's attempt to gain status and a voice in their community.
2. The gang offers ego, support, and courage
3. A sense of manhood not provided to the person as an individual
4. Formal and public recognition for social maturity
5. Decoration/adornment is common
6. Training of novices by older members for new roles and incorprAtion into an older group.
7. Show of sexual virility
8. Symbolic death and rebirth into a new personality/phase

Nsenga Warfield- Coppock and Bertram Atiba-Coppock point out in their book, Afrocentric Theory and Applications, Volume II: Advances in the Adolescent Rites of Passage:

A reason, then, that accounts for the increase in gang activity is that these social units take the place of families and communities that are dysfunctional, or negligent, in raising the young people. " The child who is not raised by its mother will be raised by the world"....... The gang also offers what every person wants and needs—friendship, a sense of belonging, discipline/boundaries, nurturing/bonding, security, support, a means to financial income, and the ritual of passage.[16] (Warfield-Coppock, 199b; Prothrow-Stith, 1991; Perkins, 1987)

Also, it is the breakdown in intergenerational communication that is contributing to the development of conflicting values in our society and the emergence of rebellious youth. At some point, we, the Elders, must face the truth. Our communities are dysfunctional, and our major institutions have failed our young people. The responsibility of our young people does not rest with the city, state, or national government – that responsibility belongs to the African American community. We, as elders, must prepare the vehicles of initiation for our youth in the tradition of our Ancestors. It is no longer, whether or not, we need rites-of-passage programs, the behavior of our youth is demanding it!

To better illustrate this notion of how our young people are demanding rituals and rites of passage ceremonies, consider the words of Sun Bear. In his book, <u>Black Dawn Bright Day</u> he writes:

> Right now, you're seeing a lot of major Earth changes happening. You're also seeing very erratic behavior in human beings as a result. In the past decade there's been a very large number of suicides. In some cities across the United States, there are special squads that try to stop suicides. And more and more young people are committing suicide. What does it say about society when the young - those with most of their life ahead of them - kill themselves? And what can we do? Consider what happened recently on a reservation in Wyoming. Many young people were killing themselves. This suicide epidemic didn't stop until medicine people brought the sweat lodge and pipe ceremony to the young people.[17]

It has been argued by many that the behavior of our young black males is suicidal. Many of them, knowingly, place themselves in situations where they know there is a great possibility of their being killed. In fact, today, many young black males do not see themselves living past the age of twenty-one. It is our contention that a lot of this violence would stop if we were to bring back our Ancient rituals. Rituals that caused a total transformation in the life of the young men and women, rituals that are in harmony with the rhythm of life. Rituals that expand the consciousness, while, at the same time, demanding the endurance of pain prolonged silence and collective work. Rituals that bring the adolescent face to face with his/her inner-most fears then liberates them from the hold of childhood; rituals that reinforce the intergenerational communication, a communication that is vital to the survival of us as a people.

We must reach back, and bring forth the systems of initiation that will ensure that our youth pass through the different phases of life, with an understanding of where they belong and what is expected of them. We must understand that central to these systems of initiation were the African Secret Societies. It was the Secret Societies that were formally charged with the responsibility of overseeing the initiation ceremonies of boys and girls. Felix Boateng writes:

> In Western cultures, social scientists agree that the transition from youth to adult with its sexual ripening, is accompanied with prolonged conflicts, marked by varying degrees of frustration, guilt, and at times a total break in intergenerational communication. In traditional societies, secret societies, or initiation ceremonies, helped the African youth to avoid this break in communication and all the attendant negative reactions, the most important and most widespread role of the secret society, separate education of the adolescent boy and the adolescent girl and the final admission of each into an adult society.[18]

As one studies the initiation ceremonies of the Africans and Native Americans, they will see that the essence of these ceremonies was spiritual. Each aspect of the ceremony had rich symbolic meaning, which the initiate was to learn and understand. To understand the spiritual significance of dying as a little boy or girl, and coming alive as a man or woman, the learning of ritual dances, magic, sacred myths, secret languages and religion, was of importance to the young initiate, if they were to successfully complete their initiation and gain their place in the larger society.

As an aside, much of this is seen today in the initiation process to our Black Greek lettered organization. Unfortunately, these organizations have deteriorated to no more than quasi, college educated, gangs, with boys trying to initiate boys by taking out their adolescent frustrations on the new initiates. As a result, many young initiates into these organizations have been seriously hurt, or even killed, all of which speaks to the need for the ELDERS of these organizations to oversee the initiation process, as did our ancestors. You do not see young boys in Africa circumcising the new initiates, you see elders doing this, for elders know what they are doing. It was the Dagara ELDERS that guided Malidoma Some through his 40 day initiation, should it be any different today?

These initiation systems must, once again, employ the rich symbolism of our Ancestors, for it is with the use of symbols that one is able to express the spiritual nature of a thing. Among other things, it was the use of the symbol that allowed the Ancestors to awaken the spiritual faculties in man. As R. A. Schwaller DeLubicz writes:

> The ordinary consideration of the Egyptian symbol reduces it to a primary, arbitrary, utilitarian and singular meaning, whereas in reality it is a synthesis which requires great erudition for its analysis and a special culture for the esoteric knowledge that it implies.[19]

Here, DeLubicz is telling us that the symbols used by our Ancestors cannot be viewed in the ordinary, logical, reductionist sense. They require deep and extensive learning to understand and a special culture for esoteric knowledge to flourish. The Ancients understood that, the more a student studied the symbols, the greater insight they would gain into themselves. In this sense, the symbols of Ancient Egypt could be said to hold great psychotherapeutic value.

One example is the Great Pyramid. Following is my observation of this great symbol which is, as yet, still to be verified by our scholars. However, this is my understanding of the symbolism involved in the Great Pyramid and how it relates to reaching black males through spirituality.

The Great Pyramid sits on 13 acres of land. It stands approximately 485' high and is approximately 775 feet square at the base. You can take 1/2 the perimeter of the base, divide that by the height, and you get 3.14 which is Pi. In geometry, we are taught that Pi is a function and not a number. This leads one to wonder, what does the pyramid represent a function of? Louis Farrakhan once said, "He who gives you the diameter of your knowledge circumscribes the circumference of your activities." Thus, he, who gives you the length, breath and width of your knowledge, can limit the sphere of your activities.

All of our knowledge, thus far, has come from the one who has oppressed us. As a result, we still do not see ourselves as free and liberated. At any rate, how do you figure the circumference of a circle. C= Pi x D. If I give you the diameter of your knowledge and multiply it by this Pi, or function, then, I can limit your activities. It is my thinking that Pi represents the function of man, and that the symbolism of the pyramid is, it stands as a sign, representing the function of man on this earth plane. Why do I say this? First of all, the pyramid sits on a square of 13 acres. The square represents the four elements. Man is, basically, composed of those four elements: fire, air, earth and water. The triangle represents God, or, in the Christian faith, the Father, Son and Holy Ghost, or the Godhead. Thus, man is to stand in this material world and reflect the light of God. The 13 acres: in numerology, 13 represents death, transition and transformation. That means, man must continually die to his ego-self, as he seeks to transform himself into a God!

One such system of transformation is the Native American Sweat Lodge Ceremony. The Native American Sweat Lodge Ceremony is a sacred purification rite, in which, all the powers of the universe are utilized - fire, air, earth and water. It brings the participants in contact with themselves, the Ancestral spirits and Divine and Universal energies. It transforms the participants and allows them to see what is important, i.e., attuning self to universal harmony.

Essentially, the sweat lodge is a dome shaped structure, covered with skins and tarps to keep out light. Rocks are heated on an open fire, until red hot, and brought into the lodge. Herbs and water are put on the rocks to produce an intense heat, which purifies the participant, not only physically, but mentally and spiritually. Every aspect of the sweat lodge ceremony is sacred, from the initial purification of the ground all the way down to the every last round in the lodge. At every step, spirit is consulted and honored. Please understand, the sweat lodge is something that is not to be taken lightly. It is a holy, sacred rite, and should at all times be treated as such. If one is interested in learning more, I suggest they read, "The Sacred Pipe: Black Elk's Account of The Seven Rites of the Oglala Sioux" or "Native American Spirituality." I strongly suggest that we treat ourselves to this most sacred and wonderful experience.

At this point, I would like to digress for a moment and speak of my perceptions, regarding the spiritual path. It is our prayer that the Divine Creative Principle, which stands behind creation and is yet creation, will guide our hand as we endeavor to write this work. As we all seek to understand our purpose for existence, and strive to live in harmony with this purpose, we seek clear vision and direction. It is not our intention to claim perfect sight, only to offer another perspective to the collective vision of humanity.

In this age of information (in-form-ation) technology, one must be vigilant not to become a slave in this new era, for true knowledge remains in the hands of a select few, and just enough is given to the masses to maintain a sophisticated system of control. There is a need to keep subjects less powerful than the rulers. The average person does not believe, for one moment, that the same God, they worship, is not beyond them, but is them! That true wealth is not one's material possessions, but is in one's family and friends. What if women understood that the greatest role for a woman is as mother, that the hand that rocks the cradle rocks the nation, that to educate a woman is to educate a nation? What type of communities would we have? What if men really understood that we are to protect, maintain, and provide for our families? Then, all women and children would have male influence in their lives? Yet, we spend the majority of our time trying to have a free voice in a deaf world.

As we sit in front of our computers, 'surfing' the net, gathering all of this 'in-form-ation', do we give any thought to what we are being 'formed' into by this so called information? As we seek to actualize our purpose for existence via a spiritual path, is any thought given to the underlying assumption of that path? Are the custodians of these various paths and traditions spiritually liberated, or have they fallen victim to the crass ' individualism', which is the hallmark of the western mind? While many may claim to be 'Keepers' of the traditions, in reality, we are nothing more than adolescent imitations of the oppressive ruling elite. Instead of keepers of the traditions, we have become 'dictators' of the way. We are so starved for recognition and power that we have turned spiritual ideologies into dogmas, which stunt and destroy the human spirit.

THE CALL

The need to control and dictate the direction of one's life is at such a high today, until we are not free to experience freedom and liberation. There is a need for healing, healing of the human spirit. However, when one seeks to heal their spirit, they are confronted with the same things that made them sick in the first place. They are confronted with the toxic, inflated, egos of individuals who have been enticed by the western mentality of self-importance. The very practices that were given by 'Spirit', for the healing of our souls, are now being claimed as exclusive property, or are being exploited by cultural oppressors.

The human fabric is so fragile that spirituality is being used to manage and control people, as opposed to being the tool of ultimate liberation. Instead of facilitating the expansion of consciousness, many individuals, hiding behind the mask of spirituality, are giving us limited thinking so we can be managed. It is all about control and management, control of the human psychic and enslavement of the spirit. While we all are looking for a healing, if you do not have an idea of what you are looking for you can be given anything and told this is what you were looking for! Because we have no idea what to look for we are being exploited and taken full advantage of. Could it be that the inability to assimilate into the larger society is causing a rise in spiritual elitism, turning many well-meaning priests, priestesses, shamans, and medicine people into cheap imitations of their European oppressors?

People are hurting and they are looking for a place to heal, a place to find comfort. Yet, many are finding the same system of oppression, clothed in a thin spiritual veneer of illusion and rhetoric. There is a spiritual elitism that mirrors the elitism associated with the 'Blue Bloods'! Many come to the different spiritual practices seeking to find themselves, but too often they find nothing more than the same system of oppression they left. Many come with wonderful spiritual gifts, needing only to be supported and shown how to develop their gifts, but they are stripped of who they are and made into the image of their new spiritual oppressors, their new masters! As one examines this process, it is similar to the slavery process. Our ancestors came to this country, a spiritually whole people, but were stripped of their God, culture and rituals. They were made to walk around the tree of forgetfulness, just as many are made to make the same journey when they come to the various spiritual traditions. People may come to the spiritual path from Christianity, Islam, Hinduism, etc., yet they are stripped of the very things that got them to the door of our spiritual houses in the first place. If we take a deep look into the various religious traditions, we find a thread of unity underlying these belief systems.

It is our contention that it is the responsibility of the spiritually enlightened to find this unity, welcome all from the various traditions, heal them, and send them on their way. The hospital takes in all manner of illness. It is staffed with specialists of many different specialties. Such is the call to us of the spiritual path. Our people are coming from all directions and belief systems and we must be able to accommodate them. However, we will not be able to do this as long as we are myopic, self-centered, boasting in the illusion of our own spiritual purity!

There is a need to understand that this is a process of continual evolution, always moving towards the Godhead. We all are the collective results of our accumulated experiences. One is who they are; we all are a manifestation of the collective results of our accumulated experiences. We all are a manifestation of the unlimited aspects of the Creator, yet many seek to limit us. It is our responsibility to be able to show the spirit of God, moving through all traditions and show the unity, not the disunity! Barbara Marciniak writes in her book, Family of Light that "(Y)our history is filled with fights in all countries, in all corners of the world, over whose God is God, whose beliefs are correct, who are the infidels and who are the righteous ones."[20]

THE CALL

This scenario is being played out with extreme intensity in many, so-called, spiritual traditions and communities. Everyone is claiming to have the deepest knowledge, the correct way and the so-called real deal! Yet, how many are able to sit with someone and be shown the beauty of the spiritual path in his, or her, present belief system? How many can see the rich spiritual insight in the words of Jesus, then see the same richness in Islam, Hinduism, Kemetian, Yoruba and Native American spirituality. This is the call, to be able to show that the spirit of the Creator is moving through it all, that it is all of God and is God. The reader must understand that this is not an attempt to justify the adaptations or modifications of the various spiritual traditions, it is only an attempt to heal and point to the unity of creation. It is said that many Native American people could not conceive of ownership of the earth, yet today ownership of spiritual traditions is being claimed and in many cases, vigorously, defended. The identification and preservation of one's spiritual traditions is honorable, however, to claim exclusivity is to limit God's expression.

Our writing of this work is but an attempt to show that God is unlimited and is not owned by anyone. While the sweat lodge ceremony is a spiritual tradition given in this country to Native American people, by no means is it their exclusive property. Research shows the same ceremony to be found in Africa. In fact in their article "Using the Sweat Lodge Ceremony as Group Therapy for Navajo Youth" which appeared in the Journal for Specialists in Group Work, vol.24, no.1, March 1999, Stephen A.Colmant and Rod J. Merta writes:

> Sweat baths, sweat houses, and sweat lodges have been used in many different cultures and by many Native American tribes. Vogel(1970) cited references of sweat baths as old Celtic and Teutonic practices; he noted its importance in tribes of Africa, Melanesia, New Guinea, and Polynesia, and even how it was practiced by the Aztecs. New World anthropologists, such as Speck among the Nas-

kapi, Tanner among the Cree, and Luckert among the Navajo (as cited in Quinn& Smith, 1992), have reported the use of the sweat lodge in hunting rituals of purification. Quinn and Smith contend that it was in North America that the sweat bath procedures reached their highest development.[21]

Native Americans have been stripped of their culture and for a while (until 1979) their spiritual practices were made illegal. One can clearly understand and support the defensiveness and caution in reference to the preservation of sacred traditions. However, to claim exclusive ownership is antithetical to their spiritual teachings. Yes, all spiritual traditions should be honored and protected from cultural bandits and oppressors but somehow, these same spiritual traditions can be vehicles of universal healing.

It is our contention that the 'sweat lodge ceremony' is one such vehicle that can be used in the healing of humanity and can be, and was, adapted to accommodate any culture. Thus, we give thanks to those custodians of the traditions and their willingness to share, guide and pass on this knowledge. We give praise to the Divinities as they continue to guide us all towards spiritual reclamation. We thank our Ancestors for their sacrifices and their continued intervention in my life, keeping me on the path. We say to those whom spirit has called, and given a new vision, please ensure that your intentions are pure and not motivated by egotism. In fact, my wife, a Yoruba priestess, Osun-nike Anke, said to me that Ego means, "Easing God Out." Let us all make sure that such is not the case as we work to heal humanity and ourselves.

For several years, with the assistance of the Ancestors, I have been in the process of incorporating into my sweat ceremonies many African elements. Those of us who are of both Native American and African ancestry are being called to stand in the world as a reflection of the unity that exists between these cultures. There is a need to understand that many of our Ancestors found acceptance among the Native Americans. Once among them, our ancestors found that central to the Native Americans was a love and concern for the children. Such is the same among our African Foreparents. Critical to Native Americans is the respect and honoring of women and female energy. The great African Scholar, Cheik Anta Diop, pointed this out to us about our African ancestors in his book, <u>The Cultural Unity of Black Africa</u>. As one looks closer at Native American spirituality, they will see the same elements running through African spirituality. For many, Native American spirituality will become a bridge for them to make the journey back home to Mother Africa. When we talk about the journey back home, we mean that we will pick up our culture and live it! It is one thing to go to Africa - to wear the clothes, however, it is another thing to LIVE Africa. How many are ready for true African spirituality? We say that Native American spirituality is one bridge that will safely take us back home. Better yet, spirituality is the bridge.

REACHING BLACK MALES THROUGH SPIRITUALITY

II

RITES-OF-PASSAGE IMPERATIVE
Whose Bitches are We?

It has often been said that we are the only people on the planet who refer to their women as 'BITCHES'. It is saddening to hear us men use such terms in reference to our women. However, it is equally saddening and dangerous to hear our young women accept such labels and even refer to themselves as such with pride i.e., *Bitches with Attitudes*. While it may be argued, by so-called generation X, that this is their way of relating to each other, it stills speaks to the acceptance of self as less than human. This negative acceptance of self is not the fault of generation X, it is our fault, as Elders (42+ years of age), for not properly instructing them and pointing out their important place in the community.

Our youth are in pain and confusion, when it comes to the understanding of self and their place in the community. It is time for us to stop our maddening race towards European assimilation. Now is the time that we should give serious thought to healing our community. We must take time to sit with our youth and hear their stories, while, at the same time opening up our lives to them that they might profit from our mistakes and benefit from our successes. It is time to let them know they are loved and that their Elders are here to guide them towards greater success.

As one investigates the cultural ways of our ancestors, you quickly see the importance placed on children and their rearing. The children are one of the most important aspects of their communities, for they were, simultaneously, the future and the ancestors returned!!! John Mbiti says:

> In African societies, the birth of a child is a process which begins long before the child's arrival in this world and continues long thereafter. It is not just a single event, which can be recorded on a particular date. Nature brings the child into the world, but society creates the child into a social being, a corporate person. For it is the community which must protect the child, feed it, bring it up, educate it and in many other ways incorporate it into the wider community. Children are buds of society, and every birth is the arrival of "spring" when life shoots out and the community thrives. The birth of a child is, therefore, the concern not only of the parents, but of many relatives including the living and the departed. Kinship plays an important role here, so that a child cannot be exclusively "my child" but only "our child".[22]

Thus, the child is the responsibility of the community. Yes, it is very true that it takes a village to raise a child! However, today, we look at our youth as aliens, to be feared and criticized. We are so caught in our preoccupation of seeking to imitate the European status elite that we are destroying our future – our children! We rationalize our behavior with statements such as, "We are working so hard to give our children better than we had." So, we give them better things, but fail in giving them direction in life, direction into manhood and womanhood. In our quest for the impressive job, promotion, large home, expensive cars and luxury vacations, our youth stand as a testimony of what we truly have gained – a nightmare! The behavior of our youth lets us know clearly the words of James Weldon Johnson, "Lest our feet stray from the places, Our God, where we met Thee, Lest, our hearts drunk with the wine of the world, we forget Thee."

Drunk with the wine of the world, material consumption, we have forgotten God and God's pattern of how we should assist our youth in their growth toward adulthood. How can we go to our different houses of worship and pray to God for help with our youth, while, at the same time, we are in these places (houses of worship) making dates, having affairs, stealing in the name of God, etc.? Could it be that we ALL do not know our important place in the community? We are all manifestations of a loving and merciful Creator, yet our behavior demonstrates that we have forgotten God. The God-inspired 'Day of Atonement', The Million Man March, Million Woman March and the Million Youth March all serve as spiritual signs that we are seeking to heal ourselves. That we are seeking to atone, reconcile, not only with each other, but with God, the Deities, Orisha, and Ancestors. We seek to reconcile with our cultural ignorance and atone for our timidity in accepting and living our divine heritage.

Now, to the question of, whose bitches are we? First, I would like to apologize for the use of this word, however, it is necessary to get the point across. One of the quickest ways to get into a fight with a black male is to refer to him as a bitch, punk or whore. The code is: you cannot let someone punk-you-out, you must stand up and prove yourself. Unfortunately, many young men have lost, and will continue to lose, their lives because of this. Today, one of the signs of being a man in prison is your ability to make another man submit to your will, i.e. you make him your Bitch. You look to see if he has any bitch in him (overt effeminate ways), then, you work to bring these out. You force him to dress like a woman. He acts like a woman, goes to the toilet like a woman, etc. In essence, you make him submit to your Will, i.e., he becomes your Bitch.

Well, then, whose bitches are we, when we speak another man's language, carry another man's name, seek to live another man's culture and lifestyle, and worship another man's God? Just as that man who has been punked-out, turned into a bitch denies reality when he goes to the toilet, we do the same. Here you have a man with male genitalia in hand, yet, he uses the toilet like a woman. I know this example is simplistic, yet I seek to make a point. In spite of the fact of his obvious male stature, his mentality has been turned into a woman. Likewise, in spite of the research of our scholars, men and women who have given us back our history and culture, we still choose to submit to the ways of another man. Even though history clearly shows us this is not our religion, our culture, our lifestyle and God, just like the man who has been punked-out, we still seek to assimilate. So, my beloved brother, the next time you call a sister a bitch, ask yourself, whose bitch am I? The answer should be clear.

Let us look at this a little closer. Dr. Frances Cress Welsing writes in her book, The Isis Papers: The keys to the Colors:

> During the past 400 years, Black men in the U.S. have been forced into passive and cooperative submission to white men. The major strategy has been the installation of an overwhelming fear. Specific tactics range from actual physical castration and lynching, to other overt and more subtle forms of abuse, violence and cruelty. We should not be ashamed to recognize these tactics used to oppress Black men. It is the truth. It is reality. Ultimately, this is the meaning of black oppression.[23]

Please note, she uses the word, "FORCED" into submission. Is this not what takes place, in one form, when you make a man a bitch in prison, you FORCE him into submission to your will? Likewise, we were forced into submission to the culture, life style, education, religion, etc., of another man. Dr. Welsing goes on to write, "Additionally, white males fully understand that males who are forced to identify as females will be programmed simultaneously into submission to the males they call *The Man*, as opposed to aggressing against those same men."[24]

Thus, today, we see our men imitating the, so-called, man. Our young rappers call themselves gangsters, smoke cigars and seek to oppress their own in a vain attempt to deny the reality that they have been punked-out, by the so-called, man. The majority of our young men do not aggressively seek knowledge of self. They do not aggressively seek to understand our history, culture and heritage. Yet, they aggressively oppress and kill each other, to the delight of another man, i.e. the, so-called, man! Again, I ask, whose bitches are we? Dr. Welsing adds:

> White men in the world area have at least a vague, perhaps unconscious, understanding that after 20 generations (400 years), male passivity has evolved into male effeminization, bisexuality and homosexuality. These patterns of behavior are, simply, expressions of male self-submission to other males in the area of people activity called "sex." Males also can submit to males in any of the other eight areas of people activity – economics, education, entertainment, labor, law, politics, religion and war. Oppression is forced submission and cooperation in any of these areas of people activity.[25]

I ask the reader to look at Dr. Welsing's eight areas of people activity and tell me who do we submit to in these areas? In fact, we see the world is being forced to submit in these areas and whoever does not do so is labeled an enemy. In reality, the world is being made a bitch of , and by, the same man who made us his bitch! Look, world-wide, at how other people are abandoning their culture, their history, and their lifestyles. We see, with this cultural abandonment comes the destruction of that people. In all eight areas (economics, education, entertainment, labor, law, politics, religion and war), we submit to the way of another man. What do we know of the ways of our ancestors, in these eight areas? Knowledge of self is very important, in these eight areas if one hopes to gain any foothold in the world economy and self-liberation. Amos Wilson gives us an example in his book, Blueprint for Black Power : A Moral, Political and Economic Imperative for the Twenty- first century: in speaking of Joel Kotkins and his book Tribes, Wilson writes, "Furthermore, he predicts that 'it is likely that [globally dispersed ethnic groups] and their worldwide business and cultural networks will increasingly shape the economic destiny of mankind."

He argues that, although global tribes, such as British (and Western European Whites) and the Japanese, possess a different history, they all share the following three critical characteristics:

1. A strong ethnic identity and sense of mutual dependence that helps the group to adjust to changes in the global economic and political order without losing its essential unity.
2. A global network based on mutual trust that allows the tribe to function collectively beyond the confines of national or regional borders.
3. A passion for technical and other knowledge from all possible sources, combined with an essential open-mindedness that fosters rapid cultural and scientific development, critical for success in the late twentieth century world economy.[26]

Here, he states that those who run the world have a strong ethnic identity, mutual trust, and an open-minded trust for knowledge. What is our ethnic identity? We do not know if we are black, African American, Afro-American or what! Mutual trust? Let's be real! Open-minded trust for knowledge - we do not trust anyone who comes with knowledge, independent of that which our oppressors have authorized for us! Yet, history demonstrates that, in pre-colonial Africa and during the time of the great Kemetic dynasties, we had a strong ethnic identity, mutual trust and trust for knowledge that left the world irreplaceable architectural wonders, as well as civil and social systems that laid the foundation for today's world! However, today, we still choose to follow the ways of another man, whose bitches are we? According to Dr. Welsing:

> The death of adult Black males in the homes, schools and neighborhoods leaves black male children no alternative models. Blindly, they seek out one another as models, and in their blindness end up in trouble – in juvenile homes or prisons. But fate and the dynamics of racism, again, play a vicious trick because the young males only become more alienated from their manhood and more feminized in such settings. They are given orders by men to whom they must submit; they wait passively to be fed three meals a day by men; and finally, they have sexual intercourse with men. It is no wonder that they are unable to play the role of black men when they leave. One, ex-prisoner, patient told me, 'It is easier to endure the life on the inside than to try to put up with the pressures of being a man, a husband and a father in the street.' The intent of racist programming had been achieved; give up trying to be a black man. Why not be a woman. [27]

In a like analogy, the pressure of being a culturally conscious black man, husband and father, is too much for us, so, we become content at being the bitch of western culture. Dr. Na'im Akbar writes in his book, Visions for Black Men:

> Our major problem is that we've started imitating them (Euro-Americans) too much. Do you realize that the reasons our young people are in so much trouble right now is that this is the first generation of African people in the history of African-Americans who do not know that they were on a plantation? [28]

In his book, Dr. Akbar gives us a blueprint for the reclamation of our lost manhood. Central to this blueprint is the knowledge of self and the courage to define ourselves in light of our ancestral heritage. We, elders (42+ years of age), must once again pull our youth to us and educate them. However, this will require that we elders can no longer run around as cultural homosexuals, in love with another man's way of life. Again, it is as James Weldon Johnson said, "May we forever stand, True to our God, True to our native land."

We must look to our God for deliverance and direction. Look to our native land before Arab and European invasion, for the vital keys to our cultural liberation. One such key that was so vital to our definition of manhood were rites-of-passage. Nzenga Warfield-Coppock, in her book, Afrocentric Theory and Applications, Volume I: Adolescent Rites of Passage, defines rite of passage as "an activity or celebration marking the successful transition from one life stage to another."[29] John S. Mbiti speaks of how rites of passage move the child from the passive to an active role in the community. Thus, it is rites-of-passage that point out to the child his or her place in the community. It is rites of passage that define manhood and lay out social role expectations. Mbiti writes:

> The initiation of the young is one of the key moments in the rhythm of individual life, which is also the rhythm of the corporate group of which the individual is a part. What happens to the single youth happens corporately to the parents, the relatives, the neighbors and the living-dead.[30]

Thus, we see that initiation and rites of passage are all tied to the well being of the community. It is initiation and rites of passage that ensure the proper continuation of the community. They ensure that each initiate knows his or her role, and place, in the community. They are EXPECTED to assume the responsibilities that accompany initiation and rites of passage. Most young men and women are forbidden to marry until they have been initiated. The young men are EXPECTED and taught to become responsible protectors, maintainers, and providers. The initiated young men are expected to have their own homes and care for THEIR wife and children. Yet, today in our society, many of our tough O.G.'s (original gangsters) are living at home, hiding behind mama's skirts. They go out in the street and imitate the white man when they inflict oppression and punishment on each other, yet return home to mama to be babied and nursed. They go out and make babies, then bring the children and the girl home for mama to raise. Yet, they are tough and will kill you. No, we say what Elijah Muhammad said some 60 years ago, we are BLIND, DEAF, Dumb and haters of self. As Amos Wilson writes in his book, <u>Black-on –Black Violence</u>:

> The essence of the Black-on-Black criminal is self-hatred, or self alienation. These can only be learned. Self-hatred can only occur as the result of the self having been made to appear to be hateful, ugly, degrading, rejected, associated with pain, non-existent or devoid of meaning, and inherently inferior.[31]

We were stripped of our names, our culture, our history, our way of life, and FORCED into submission to another man's way of life, i.e. made into his bitch. Of this stripping of history Amos Wilson writes:

> When you steal a people's history, you can justify ruling over them and thus justify domination. More importantly, history may be used to influence personality, culture, roles, and to motivate us to commit suicide, to provoke us to commit menticide and may be used to create or rationalize fratricide, genocide and self-destruction.[32]

It is the stealing of our history that, in part, keeps us in the conditions we are experiencing at this time. As one studies the history of African and indigenous people, you learn that rites-of-passage and initiation play a vital role in the socialization of the people. Wilson writes:

> Having been removed against their will from their continent, the Africans have been denied access to their own self-generated time and rhythms: rhythms, the means by which time reveals itself to consciousness, rhythms that were the very evolutionary infrastructures of their minds, bodies, consciousness, social relations, social organizations, destinies and identities.[33]

Rites-of-Passage and initiation are examples of these rhythms. We can tell time by these rhythms of transition from birth, to puberty, marriage, elder-ship, and death. It is important we see how serious, and vital, rites-of-passage and initiations are. They are more than the cultural adaptations of our thinkers. They are the keys to the healing of our communities and youth. They provide the means for our cultural reclamation and liberation. At this point, the mother/ son relationship deserves some additional reflection, for in this relationship are many keys for our return to manhood in the years to come. In his book, Iron John, Robert Bly writes, "The possessiveness that mothers typically exercise on son—not to mention the possessiveness that fathers typically exercise on daughters can never be underestimated."[34]

One finds that African American mothers in most cases, are very possessive, and rightly so given our brutal history in this country as enslaved people. African men were beaten, castrated, and lynched, as part of the cultural fabric of this country, much of which still occurs today. In fact, Willie Lynch, in a speech, on the banks of the James River in 1712, supposedly, gave to a group of slaveholders the plan to make us slaves, forever. In the part of that speech dealing with, 'The breaking process of the African woman', he states, "Test her, in every way, because she is the most important factor for good economics. When in complete submission, she will train her offspring in the early years to submit to labor when they become of age."

Thus, he clearly saw the importance of the African woman in the making of slaves. We say, the hand that rocks the cradle, rocks the nation. Willie Lynch took this into consideration in his slave-making process. In speaking of the roles and relationships between African women and men, he points out how important it is to reverse the roles. He states:

> We have to reverse the relationships. In her natural uncivilized state she would have a strong dependency on the uncivilized nigger male, and she would have a limited protective tendency towards her independent male offspring and would raise the female offspring to be dependent like her. Nature had provided for this type of balance. We reverse nature by burning and pulling one civilized nigger apart and bull whipping the other to the point of death – all in her presence. By her being left alone, unprotected, with the male image destroyed, the ordeal caused her to move from her psychological dependent state to a frozen dependent state. In this frozen psychological state of independence she will raise her male and female offspring in reverse roles. For fear of the young male's life she will psychologically train him to be mentally weak and dependant but physically strong.[35]

It is clear, the same process is still in effect, today, for many African American mothers, for fear for their son's life, via streets, police or other wise, are very protective. Many of our young men are physically strong, yet very weak mentally. This can be seen in the number of tremendous athletes we produce. They are very strong, but lack mental strength, as seen in their academic performance while in college. Content to perform well on the court or field, they do not get involved in the liberation of their people and humanity. If any of these athletes do give to a charitable cause you can rest assured it is under the direction and approval of their new slave masters, the coaches, agents and owners. Also, many mothers, whose sons are not great athletes, raise them to be smart, get a GOOD JOB and not upset the apple cart! So we are good workers, very dependable, and will not upset the scale of balance at work. We are content to come into corporate American and deny our cultural heritage, in order to get into the front office, or, a vice presidency. In many cases, we become wonderful, black, white men, content to uphold European cultural corporate values as we run from Africa! It is something to listen to black executives and their wives speak of their trips to Europe, or speak of their trip to Africa as tourists, as oppose to taking a true, emotional, trip home. Yes, we have been trained well and we take pride in our ability to reflect this dominant culture. Willie Lynch goes on to say:

> Because she has become psychologically independent, she will train her female offspring to be psychologically independent. What have you got? You've got the nigger woman out front and the nigger man behind and scared. This is a perfect situation for sound sleep and economics. Before the breaking process, we had to be alertly on guard at all times. Now we sleep soundly, for, out of frozen fear, his woman stands guard for us. He cannot get past her early infant slave-molding process. He is a good tool, now ready to be tied to the horse at a tender age.[36]

Such is clearly the case today, as we find our women are out front and we, men, are hiding behind mama's dress. Good economics, one would say so, because all of the money we make we give it back to our former slave masters. She stands guard for our former slave master as she constantly holds up the standard of European manhood as the model to judge us by. It is something to hear an African American woman tell her man that he is not a man, or hear young African American females say that "they don't need a man, they can get everything by themselves." By what standard does she judge manhood? Better yet, what standard do we men use to judge ourselves?

If we are to be judged, let us be judged by our ancestral standard. To do so would require studying the ways of our ancestors. It would require serious introspection on the part of African American men and women. It would require our admission that, as Na'im Akabr says, "we are crazy." Once we admit our psychological confusion, we can get the necessary help. Yet, Harriet Tubman said, "I freed hundreds of slaves, I could have freed hundreds more if they had known they were slaves." The majority of us do not realize that we are still slaves in every sense of the word! Lynch says:

> Continually, through the breaking of the uncivilized savage niggers, by throwing the nigger female savage into frozen psychological state of independency, by killing of the protective male image, and by creating a submissive, dependent, mind of the nigger male savage, we have created an orbiting cycle that turns on its own axis forever, unless a phenomenon occurs and re-shifts the positions of the male and female savages.[37]

It is my contention that rites-of-passage is the phenomenon that can cause this re-shift. It is through rites-of-passage that young men are taught to be men. They are taught their place in the community and are expected to function there, yet given full support of the community. Mr. Paul Hill Jr., founder of the Rites of Passage Institute based in Cleveland, Ohio says on his website article at http://www.ritesofpassage.org/passage1.htm:

> Rites of Passage as a developmental and transformational process is culturally-specific, not universal. It is based on the multi-cultural premise that a group must recognize and affirm itself before it is able to share and appreciate the differences of others. Rites of Passage as a process also recognizes that entry into adult life involves the realization of social obligations and the assumption of responsibility for meeting them. What initiation does is to set a time on the journey for bringing the individuals into formal and explicit relation with their kindred. It also confronts them with some of their basic social ties, reaffirms them and thus makes patent to them their status

against the days when they will have to adopt them in earnest. Rites of Passage as a developmental and transformational process will not only provide self-development and cultural awareness, but will foster a sense of belonging; adolescents and adults will become part of community life- not person alone, lacking support, sanction, and purpose.[38]

We must applaud the courage and persistence of our cultural scholars in their research and application of our history in their lives and ours. They are to be honored for their efforts. Yet, there stands, in our community, a vehicle of rite-of-passage that has a 60 plus year history of taking young men and women to adulthood. It is cultural specific and has been on the forefront of allowing us to recognized and affirm ourselves. I speak of the Nation of Islam, while there are many more organizations that can be reviewed, the Nation of Islam has been chosen because of the writer's involvement with this organization and the manner that it brought him to the quest to reclaim his lost manhood.

III

THE NATION OF ISLAM
A Vehicle of Rites-of-Passage

Before we seek to examine the Nation of Islam as a vehicle of rites-of-passage, I would like to look at the nature of rites-of-passage from a different perspective. There are a number of excellent books available that speak to the process and procedures of rites-of-passage. My concern here is the spiritual philosophy underlining rites-of-passage. There is a need for us to seek to look at the underlying spiritual philosophy of the majority of our belief systems. For, it is in the underlying spiritual philosophy that we might tap into the underlying unity that exists in all of creation. For, we see that all of creation is the manifestation of one divine creative principle, which has manifested itself in the multitude of forms that we see, yet there is still a unity underlying it all. I strongly believe that we should seek the unity of our belief systems, instead of remaining fragmented and in competition for followers. There is a great unity that runs through all of creation and it is the comprehension and functioning in harmony with this unity that gives rise to great people and civilizations.

In all traditional rites-of-passage and initiation ceremonies, the sacred knowledge and stories are passed on to the initiates. These stories and myths explain creation, how their people came to be, the roles of men and women, etc. These stories are central to the initiation process and the well-being of the people, they are the why of the people. In keeping with the spirit of these creation stories and myths, I would like to examine the story of Ausar and the Student Enrollment Lesson Number 1 of the Nation of Islam as a lead into the discussion of the Nation of Islam as a vehicle of rites-of-passage. In speaking of the Egyptian story in which Set (devil) cuts the body of Ausar (God within us) into 14 pieces and Auset found the pieces and put Ausar back together, Ra Un Nefer Amen writes in Metu Neter, Vol. 2:

> She then hid the body in a secret place and hastened to Buto, in the city of Khemmis to give birth to her son Heru. Her triumph was short lived. While she was in Buto, Set came hunting the boar at full moon in the marshy swamps of the Delta and, by accident, found the chest. Recognizing it, he opened it and took the body of Ausar and cut it into fourteen pieces and scattered them in various parts of the country.[39]

Ra Un Nefer Amen's commentary on this is:

> The breaking of the body of Ausar symbolizes the fragmentation of consciousness by the left side of the brain which leads to a segregated view of the world. The fourteen pieces also correspond to the 14 psychic centers (chakras) of spiritual body. The dispersion of the pieces of the body of Ausar is the origin of the religious doctrine of the Diaspora – the dispersion of the elect.[40]

In the story, we see that Set cut the body of Ausar up into 14 pieces and it was Auset and her sister, Nebt-Het who went in search of these pieces. Once found, they erected a tomb where they found each piece, which became a place of worship by the people of the area. My reason for addressing this story is to simply analogize the 14 pieces of Ausar to the 14 questions and answers of the Lost-Found Muslim Lesson

THE NATION OF ISLAM
A Vehicle of Rites-of-Passage

No. 1, given to Elijah Muhammad by Master W. D. Fard Muhammad. Now, if it is, as Ra Un Nefer Amen states, that Ausar represents the God in us, that Asuar is that divine, in-dwelling, intelligence and the Student Enrollment (Rules of Islam) of the Nation of Islam states that "The Original man is the Asiatic black man; the Maker, the Owner; the Cream of the planet earth- GOD OF THE UNIVERSE," then, we see that the original man, God of the universe, Ausar, has been dismembered by one who is ruled by a Sectarian mentality. This one has fragmented the consciousness of the black man in America and throughout the diaspora. The story states that the spreading of the 14 pieces of Ausar is in part the dispersion of the elect. We have been taught by the Most Honorable Eljah Muhammad and presently by Minister Louis Farrakhan, that we Blacks, in America, are the ELECT of God. Just as it was Auset and her sister Nebt-Het, who went in search and found the pieces of Ausar, it was master Fard Muhammad who came in search of us, the lost found members of the Nation of Islam, the elect of God. The first step towards putting the pieces of Ausar, God of the Universe, the original man back together is seen as the mastering of the 14 questions and answers of the Lost Found Muslim Lesson No. 1, of the Nation of Islam. For those of us who received our initiation and rites-of-passage via the Nation of Islam, these 14 questions and answers represent the beginning of putting Ausar, Original Man, God of the Universe back together again.

Let us look at the number 14 a little closer. According to Faith Javne and Dusty Bunker in their book, Numerology and the Divine Triangle:

> The ancient symbol for the letter corresponding to the number 14 is a scribe, an individual who copied manuscripts by hand. Books were rare and very costly; therefore the scribe was in a unique position to glean knowledge that was otherwise denied to all but the wealthy and favored. As a result the scribe was exposed to philoso-

phy, religion, science and the Arts – all kinds of ideas that created an educated mind.[41]

It was Master Fard Muhammad who came with the knowledge of our history, philosophy, religion and science, knowledge traditionally known only by the wealthy and favored of this western society. They knew more about us than we knew of ourselves, before the coming of Master Fard Muhammad. He taught Elijah Muhammad, who taught us, and today that legacy is carried on in Minister Louis Farrakhan. Thus, we see, in the number 14, the 14 pieces of Ausar, the 14 lessons, that it is the scribe who comes with knowledge to put us back together again. Now, you take the number 14 and break it down to 5, $1 + 4 = 5$. In numerology, the number 5 represents freedom. It was basically the learning of the 14 lessons that began to free us from the intellectual bondage of the western world. John Anthony West writes in his book, Serpent in the Sky that "In ancient Egypt, the symbol for a star was drawn with five points. The ideal of the realized man was to become a star, and to become one of the company of Ra."[42]

We see, in the flag of the Nation of Islam, a five-pointed star. Could it be that the first step, towards becoming a realized man, one of the company of Ra (God), was the learning and actualizing the 14 questions and answers of lesson number 1? Could this have been one of the steps towards putting the 14 pieces of Ausar back together again? For many of us who were initiated in the Nation of Islam, my answer would be yes.

It is through initiation and rites-of-passage that indigenous man comes to learn and understand his place in the tribe. It is through this same process that he is given a proper image of himself and his relation to his community, and ultimately, the cosmos. It must be kept in mind that there are countless variants of rites-of-passage and initiation ceremonies. They all correspond to the different social structures and

THE NATION OF ISLAM
A Vehicle of Rites-of-Passage

cultural horizons that give birth to them. However, they all have one thing in common, they accord primary importance to the techniques and ideology of initiation and rites-of-passage. The initiation of the Native American youth is different from the African youth, and there is also tremendous variation among tribes. Therefore, it would stand to reason, if an initiation procedure were to evolve in America among African Americans, it would take on the flavor of the society and culture that gave birth to it, i.e., it would be culturally specific. What are the techniques and ideology of initiation within the Nation of Islam?

According to Mircea Eliade in his book <u>Rites and Symbols of Initiation</u>:

> The term initiation, in the most general sense, denotes a body of rites and oral teachings whose purpose is to produce a decisive alteration in the religious and social status of the person to be initiated. In philosophical terms, initiation is equivalent to a basic change in existential condition; the novice emerges from his ordeal endowed with a totally different being from that which he possessed before his initiation; he has become another.[43]

If we are a disenfranchised people, suffering from an inferiority complex and self-hatred, brought on by our sojourn in this country, then, where could we look for an understanding of our place in this community, world and cosmos? We would need an initiation, a rite-of-passage. Where is this body of rites and oral teachings whose purpose was to produce a decisive alteration in the religious and social status of the person initiated? For many of us, this body of rites and oral teachings was found in the Nation of Islam, however, there are many more communities that offer the same. There are the Yoruba communities, Islamic communities, the Ausar/Auset Society, the Black Hebrew Israelites just to name a few. While they all deserve attention, for they are doing great work in taking our people through the doors of cultural

75

manhood and womanhood, for the purpose of this discourse, I would like to address the Nation of Islam.

As thousands emerged from the ordeal of the 'nation' endowed with a totally different being, we became another. In fact, for many of us, it was our initiation via the Nation of Islam that opened the doors to our search for meaning and self-realization in the cultural ways of our ancestors. The Nation of Islam made us men and women and sent us into the world. Few can argue the physical and psychological changes the teachings of the Most Honorable Elijah Muhammad had on us. We were, literally, transformed, before the eyes of our families, friends, community and the world. We were taught who we were and shown our important place in the cosmic order of the Creator. Eliade continues:

> Among the various categories of initiation, the puberty initiation is particularly important for an understanding of pre-modern man. These 'transition rites' are obligatory for all the youth of the tribe. To gain the right to be admitted among adults, the adolescent has to pass through a series of initiatory ordeals: it is by virtue of these rites, and of the revelations that they entail, that he will be recognized as a responsible member of the society.[44]

In a like manner, the Nation of Islam has initiatory ordeals which all men and women were required to undergo in order, to be recognized as responsible members of the community. Among them were 'processing into the nation', selling of the newspaper and other products. Thus, becoming a responsible member of the community was not limited only to the Nation of Islam, but these initiatory ordeals prepared us for membership in the American and World community. The men of the Nation of Islam were REQUIRED to sell the information organ, the Muhammad Speaks, known today as "The Final Call". Now, many have argued that we were reduced to 'paper boys.' This is a sound argument for those with little or no knowledge of the initiation process. Here were men, many of whom had very poor self-images, and lacked confidence, who were made to put on a suit and bow tie, then go out into the public and stand up! Please seek to understand the transformative effect - before I hated myself, had no confidence, no knowledge of self, then I was taught that I am the God of the universe and am made to go out and demonstrate this to the world. We will discuss additional initiatory ordeals of the Nation of Islam as we evolve this discourse.

Eliade goes on the say:

> Initiation introduces the candidate into the human community and into the world of spiritual and cultural values. He learns not only the behavior patterns, the techniques, and the institutions of adults, but also the sacred myths and traditions of the tribe, the names of the gods and the history of their works. Above all, he learns the mystical relations between the tribe and the Supernatural Beings as those relations were established at the beginning of Time.[45]

For all familiar with the teachings of the Most Honorable Elijah Muhammad, it is clear that these teachings contain all of the elements that Eliade speaks of. We were introduced to the name of our God and gods and the history of how all came to be. We were taught the relation between our tribe, the Lost Tribe of Shabazz, and God we were taught about time before time. For a better understanding of these elements, I direct the reader to the works of the Most Honorable Elijah Muhammad and the Honorable Louis Farrakhan. My point is to demonstrate that within the working definition of rites-of-passage and initiation, as outlined by Eliade, the Nation of Islam fits. For many of us, it was the Nation of Islam that taught us the behavior patterns, techniques and institutions of adults. Like most rite-of-passage ceremonies that are gender specific, the Nation of Islam was no different. There were

REACHING BLACK MALES THROUGH SPIRITUALITY

weekly, separate, classes held for the men, F.O.I. (Fruit of Islam) and women, M.G.T. (Muslim Girls Training). The teachings given in these classes were sacred and not to be shared, not even with your mate. The same is seen in the initiatory rites of the Kurnai and most African rites.

Eliade goes on to say:

> The central moment of every initiation is represented by the ceremony symbolizing the death of the novice and his return to the fellowship of the living. But he returns to life a new man, assuming another mode of being. Initiatory death signifies the end at once of childhood, of ignorance, and of the profane condition.[46]

One such initiatory ordeal of the Nation of Islam that symbolizes this death and resurrection process, is the receiving of the 'X'. In short, the candidate undergoes a series of ordeals known as *processing*. This is where one is not a full member of the community (Nation of Islam) but is performing as such. They write a series of letters seeking acceptance and an 'X'. The 'X' stands for the unknown, we were taught that since we did not know our original names we would be given an 'X' until God would come and give us our names. Once the candidate has received their 'X'; they are no longer known by their old last names. That last name is dropped and replaced with an 'X'. James R Thompson dies and is resurrected as James R X! In many Temples within the Nation of Islam, a celebration is held in honor of this initiatory process. The candidate has moved from the childhood state of processing to that of adult responsibilities within the Nation of Islam. There are very few who came into the Nation that were not transformed for the better. Even if one was not a member of the Nation of Islam, a casual contact with the teachings brought about a transformation. The Nation of Islam has a 60+ year history of taking boys and girls and turning them into men and women. In fact, it is my assertion that the Nation of Islam is the quintessence of rites-of-passage and initiation among Africans born in American.

IV

SPIRITUAL CULTIVATION
The Essence of Rites-of-Passage and Initiation

In his book, "An Afrocentric Guide to A Spiritual Union", Ra Un Nefer Amen states that "Rites of passage are nothing more than a set of initiations aimed at leading individuals through the various evolutionary stages of life. For these initiations to succeed they must be based on a full understanding of the spirit of man."[47]

In His book , "The Handbook of Yoruba Religious Concepts," Baba Ifa Karade states:

> The function of the initiation rituals are to make the Orisha essence stronger within the devotee. The more rituals that are done, the more this essence is solidified and actualized. The essence then impacts upon the being of the devotee who now becomes an active element of it within a family, community, nation, and world.[48]

The statements by both of these spiritual men point to the higher aspects of initiation, that initiations are to awaken the spirit of man. Once initiation awakens the spirit of man then man must follow a system to ensure the proper development in reference to the new inputs. It is of extreme importance, for those of us involved with rites-of-passage and initiation programs, to have a complete system in place to accommodate the spiritual awakening of the initiate. For it is the spirit that is awakened and it must be guided. Ra Un Nefer Amen goes on to say:

> The procedures for awakening the higher dormant faculties and altering one's lifestyle to harmonize with the new inputs from these faculties is what is known as initiation. It is a system, not merely professing belief in God, or seeking divine assistance while remaining in a lowly state of ignorance, egoism, and impotence, but of growing and changing into our divine essence. God saves Man by endowing her/him with three divine attributes. The true worship, the true honoring, the true love and praising of God is in the striving to awaken the divine qualities that are the essence of our being.[49]

Thus, if we are going to reach the black male via spirituality, then it is important that we see him in the light that our Ancestors saw him—that he was a manifestation of God. We must seek to make all black men and women for that matter, conscious of their divinity. We must, in the spirit of Sankofa, return to the traditional ways of our Ancestors when it comes to the development of men. This world of illusion is failing when it comes to the development of men. While time is spent on the development of better material things and the acquisition of these things, little or no time is spent on the development of the God within. Importance is placed on how much stuff you have. In fact, in the western world, manhood is based on the stuff you have! We are familiar with the phrase, "he who has the most toys at the time of death wins." This is the thinking of the western mind. We find our young men preoccupied with trying to get this stuff and spend no time on inner cultivation of divine qualities. Among indigenous people true manhood and womanhood is based on how well you manifest the divine qualities of God that are in you, how well you accept your place in the community as a man or woman.

SPIRITUAL CULTIVATION
The Essence of Rites-of-Passage and Initiation

Today, our young men are once again defining themselves on sexual exploits and adolescent acts of macho imitation of TV. Our young women are defining themselves by their ability to give birth to children, get a man or be independent of a man. I ask the reader to go back to the period of forced slavery. This was a time when a man's worth was determined by the children he could sire and his ability to do work. A woman's worth was determined by her ability to work and have children. It appears that we are in the same place, today. However, it is time in our history for the elders (42+ years of age) to step forward with a strong voice, and once again, articulate direction for our youth.

We must come out of our domestic nightmare of living the western dream. We must come out of our illusion of being a successful imitation of the western status elite. We must, once again, join the battle and assume responsibility for the direction of not just our own children, but all children. It will be returning to the ways of our ancestors, it will be our taking the best of the western world and combining it with the best of our Ancestors and giving to the world a spiritually liberated black man, one ready to change the face of the earth!

When we suggest returning to the ways of our Ancestors we are talking about returning to a tradition that goes back thousands of years, a tradition that has produced the great builders of the civilizations that people marvel at today. We are suggesting that returning to our way is to ensure that our young men become men who are ready and willing to accept the responsibility of making the world we live in a better place. It is initiation and rites-of-passage that will assist our young men in understanding their purpose and where they fit into the world community. Malidoma Patrice Some' points out in his book, The Healing Wisdom of Africa on page 277:

Initiation consists of rituals and ordeals that help young people remember their own purpose and have their unique genius recognized
by the community. From birth to puberty, the tribal person is the
responsibility of the village; hence the saying that it takes a whole
village to raise a child. This collective attention and care prepare the
child for the delivery of his or her gift, potential, or skills. Rebirth
or rites of passage then mark his/her passage into maturity. Maturity
here must be understood as the awakening into one's gift and the
investment of self to a good that is greater than self. The mature person therefore is, tribally speaking, the initiated responsible person
fully aware of the reasons that brought him/her into this place, committed to carrying out his/her mission with unconditional support of
the village. Initiation thus ritually echoes and completes the passage
into life that began at birth.[50]

It is clear that we need rituals and ordeals to help our young people
remember their place in this community. We must begin to develop
the ways and means for recognizing their unique genius and allow
that genius to grow and add to the wealth of our communities. Look at
the genius of our young people, they have created a culture (Hip Hop)
that has affected the WORLD. They have taken the ability to use language to a new height, the rappers have taken this language, turned it
inside out and given it back to the world in a fashion that effects youth
around the world. One wonders if our Ancestors could be sending us
messages through our young rappers?

Now, if according to George G.M. James in his monumental work
'Stolen Legacy', that RHETORIC was part of the curriculum of the
Egyptian Mystery System and one of the meanings of rhetoric is skill
in the effective use of speech; then, what is being said by our rappers
today?? That our Ancestors have returned and they need direction,
guidance and initiation! Think, for a moment, what we could achieve
if this genius was harnessed and directed for constructive purposes.
In fact, in some areas, efforts are underway now to put many of the

subjects taught in school in a rap mode. This is just one example of the genius that MUST be awakened in our young people and put to benefit for our communities and not the benefit of record companies who give nothing back to our communities! Thus, it is in returning to our cultural and spiritual traditions that holds many keys to the healing of our communities.

V

READY to RECOVER the PHALLUS

The Kemetic story of Ausar and Set is described by Ra Un Nefer Amen in his book, <u>Metu Neter Vol.2, pg. 149</u> :

> On hearing about Set's deed, Auset set out again in search of the members of Ausar's body, this time accompanied by her sister Nebt-Het, who until then was married to Set. At length she recovered all the parts except the phallus which was swallowed by the Lepidotus, Phagrus, and the Oxyrynchus Fish....[51]

Drawing from this description and applying it to our present situation, it seems that our women have been searching for the parts of our dismantled manhood. They have been dedicated and patient with us. As the story says, Auset and Nebt-Het found all the pieces of Ausar except for the phallus, they could not find it, it was swallowed by a fish. It is we, the men, who must reclaim our phallus, the very tool that represents our ability to recreate life. Our women cannot reclaim it for us, they never could, it is our responsibility to confront the fish and reclaim it! Now, what does the phallus and the fish represent?

87

The connection of the fish and the phallus has to do with sexual potency and is a key index of spiritual power. The sexual potency must be nurtured, and the sexual act moderated for greater spiritual growth.

This nexus between sexuality and spirituality is a key, a vital key, that has remained hidden from the majority of humanity. It is through the control and regulation of our sexual urges that assist us in our spiritual development. It is through spiritual development that we learn of our divine nature. Once an individual becomes conscious of their divinity, the gravitational pull of this world of illusion begins to lose its hold on them. For the most part, they are no longer a slave to passion, anger, greed, jealousy and a host of other things that add to the in-harmony in the world and the individual. Thus, the loss of the phallus represents our inability to transform sexual energy into spiritual energy and spiritual liberation. In his book, The Complete Book of Chinese Health and Healing, pg. 273, Daniel Reid writes:

> In the Taoist and Tantric view, sex is sacred, and women are revered as the source of all life on earth. Before the rise of Christianity in Europe, sex was held to be as sacred there as in the Orient, as evidenced by the word 'sacrum' the body's sexual center, which is derived from the same root as 'sacred. In terms of practice, sexual essence and energy comprise our most potent tools for progress on the spiritual path.[52]

What does this have to do with the fish? Could this fish represent the age of Pisces (the fish) and the proselytizing effects of Christianity and the major world religions? Could it be that the fish which swallowed the phallus, the ability to recreate ourselves and advance along the spiritual path, is the major world religions? We are taught that the sun moves in a circle known to the Kemetic priest as a great year. It takes the sun 25,920 earthly years to move in a complete circle, passing through a different sign of the zodiac every 2,160 years. It is this present 2,160 year cycle, which will soon end, known as Pisces (the Fish) that Christianity and the other proselytizing religions began to seek to conquer the world in the name of God. It was, and is, in the name of God that people were classified as less than human and enslaved. Also, during this Piscean age, the truth of God would be withheld. As Dr. Muata Ashby states in his book, Egyptian Yoga, on pg. 23:

> It is a well known fact to religious scholars that the original scriptures of the western Bible included teachings which closely follow the Egyptian Mysteries-Yoga system,and the Indian Philosophical Yoga Vedanta system. At the Nicean council of Bishops in 325 A.C.E., the doctrine of self-salvation was distorted to the degree that the masses of people were convinced that they needed a savior as a "go between" to reach God. As their minds were thus conditioned, they forgot that they, the individuals, were as we are today, responsible for their own fate. A new religion, Christianity, was thus created by the Nicean council under the direction of the Roman Empire and the emperor decreed the destruction of all other philosophies, religions, and doctrines. It was at this time that reference to reincarnation and the ability of each individual to become a Christ were either deleted or misrepresented.[53]

Now it becomes easy to see that much has been withheld from the masses, many liberating secrets have been withheld, secrets that can help us all move towards spiritual liberation and enlightenment. Foremost, among the secrets, was the connection between sex and spirituality, i.e., the fish swallowing the phallus.

It was in the name of major world religions that our people were classified as less than human and enslaved. At the recent Millennium World Peace Summit held at the UN, David Little of the Harvard Scholars' Group said:

It is a very complicated question how religion is involved with war. In my own studies, I've found that religion is typically drawn in as a legitimating factor. That is, these conflicts are over national control. And religion sometimes willingly lends itself, so we can't say it is always exploited [by politicians].

As history demonstrates, it was religion that was used as a legitimating element of the slave trade. In the name of religion our culture was stripped from us and we were made to walk around the tree of forgetfulness. In the name of religion, Native Americans were viewed as savages who did not deserve the land, or life! It is in the name of religion that the majority of us remain isolated from our traditional ways, of which rites-of-passage is a central part. It is in the name of religion that we seek to dominate and control others. We have become prisoners of the very belief systems that are supposed to liberate us.

Today we cannot, and will not, come out from behind the security of these dominant world religions, namely Christianity, the religion of the Piscean age – the fish. Yes, I contend that the fish swallowed our phallus. Our ability to recreate ourselves has been swallowed up by the church. We are afraid to think outside the box. All thoughts and actions must be sanctioned by these dominant religions.

Today more and more men filter into the major world religions, and they become involved with the proselytizing of these faiths, the conditions of our people and the world seem to continue to deteriorate. Our own spiritual well-being has not gotten better, it has gotten worse. We take mood altering prescribed drugs to make it through the day and seek to sex ourselves into bliss. It is something to see, on any given video, rappers using foul language to describe a situation, or our women, while wearing a diamond studded cross around their neck. Yet, this is nothing but a reflection of our hypocrisy as adult believers and followers of religion.

READY TO RECOVER THE PHALLUS

How many of us, in the name of religion, have numerous girl friends and lovers? How many of us in the name of religion have taken advantage of each other? How many of us, in the name of religion, have used foul language to describe a situation or someone? I say this to say that our phallus has been swallowed up by the fish and we must get it back. We must develop the courage to confront religion. While more and more people are coming to these faiths, their spiritual emptiness grows deeper. Our phallus, (ability to recreate ourselves) is locked up in these major proselytizing religions, while they leave no room for freedom of expression and the development of spirit. You are told what to do, how to do it, what to believe and not believe. As a result, we know very little of the great religions of Africa, or of the Native Americans. We have no idea how liberating these faiths are and how in harmony they are with the universal order of things. We have been made to think that these belief systems are primitive and uncivilized; when in reality, it was conviction and adherence to these faiths that helped us through the Middle Passage, slavery, the Trail of Tears and much more. Reflect on the words of Shakti Gawain in the book, Living in the Light on page 39:

> Two examples, relevant to most Americans, are Native American and African Cultures. Both of these groups were devastated by their contact with European/American culture. However, a deep curiosity, respect, and appreciation for Native Americans has begun to surface in our awareness in recent years. And African culture, forcibly brought to this continent, has probably done more than any other culture to keep intuitive power alive in our country through its strong and soulful connection to spirit.[54]

Think on this, if we go to church, or the mosque, and give thanks for being able to pay our bills, our new car, good job, or fine home and etc., what do you think assisted our people to make it through the horrors of being captured, held in slave dungeons, packed in ships, raped, robbed and tortured, made to labor for another and used as toys? What do you think assisted our people to walk, in the dead of winter, from the east coast of America to Oklahoma as a result of forced migration and the taking of our lands? What got us through? What did we place faith in? Our ancestors had belief systems and it will be our going into the belly of the fish (Christianity) and looking at its effects on our manhood that will assist in our reclaiming our phallus.

Yes, it is time to go into the belly of the fish and reclaim our phallus; however, in many respects, this journey within the belly of the beast has taken place years ago. By virtue of the civil rights movement, we were forced to look within Christianity and find faith to face the forces of oppression. It took courage and great faith to face the challenges the early civil rights workers endured. The question is, from where did they gain this courage and faith? It came from the church and faith in God. It was those old preachers and believers who faced the dogs and water hoses, endured attacks, and insults while all the time keeping the faith. While many viewed this as being passive, we must look at and face the fact that their actions took great courage and faith.

They stood in the face of all opposition and said, "In the name of God, I will not be moved!" The men, the preachers, led many of the demonstrations; this can be seen as reclaiming the phallus. We used Christianity, a religion that was forced upon us, as a vehicle of liberation. While it was in the name of Christianity that this fish swallowed our phallus, it was in many respects the same fish (Christianity), which we modified, that gave our phallus back to us.

At this point, I would like for the reader to reflect on the courage and faith of our Christian brothers of the civil rights movement, who stood in the face of death as they sought equality. The courage of the early Black Nationalists and separatists, who stood on the backs of the civil right workers, said, we will meet force with force. Think on the courage and faith of these people and you will see that we have regained the phallus, yet, we stand in danger of giving it back due to our fascination with the pomp and glitter of this world. It was the church that brought us through and it will be the church, mosque, Yoruba house, the shrines, the spiritual societies, and nationalist communities, working together, that will assure that the fish will never again swallow our phallus. We can no longer, as men, allow ourselves to be separated based on beliefs. In the 60's, we dichotomized and polarized ourselves. Today, we need to see the unity in the diversity.

VI

THE PROGRAM

The supervised developmental and educational process of assisting young people in achieving adult status is called a rite of passage. The rite of passage involves going from a passive childhood state to active/responsible membership in the community. These rites of passage programs must become a *permanent* part of the community process, for it is not enough to give the young people a one-time fix. They must be fully integrated into their community, and their progress must be followed and supported until adulthood. Once they have completed the program, they will be expected to "give back"—to become peer leaders. Therefore, to begin a program involves a long-term commitment on the part of all involved.

The following is a proposed eight (8) month, three-phase program that is to flow with the natural harmonic cycles of the earth. The program will run from March 21st to December 31st. The first phase will begin March 21st, or sometime thereabouts, to coincide with the spring equinox—a time of planting new seeds. The next phase will begin June 21st with the summer solstice, a time of maturity. The final phase will begin September 21st, with the fall equinox, which will take us into Kwanzaa and the harvesting of our "fresh fruits" (our new initiates).

The Rites of Passage Program will have, central to it, an educational purpose, and can be adapted to an after school or weekend schedule. It will mark the beginning of acquiring knowledge, which is otherwise not accessible to our young people except through trial and error. As John S. Mbiti points out in his book, <u>African Religions and Philosophy</u> that the Rites of Passage Program "is a period of awakening to many things, a period of dawn for the young. They learn to endure hardships, they learn to live with one another, they learn to obey, they learn the secrets and mysteries of the man-woman relationship."

A) **Some goals of the program are:**
   1) To improve cultural awareness and knowledge
   2) To develop more responsible behaviors
   3) Improve socializing with peers
   4) Improve self-esteem and self-concept
   5) Improve sense of maleness or femaleness
   6) Improve relationships with adults, parents, elders, and members of the opposite sex
   7) Improve school behavior
   8) Improve academic performance
   9) Create a responsibility to pursue post-secondary educational or vocational opportunities
   10) Develop responsible job attitudes and behaviors.

B) **A sample of the program curriculum will include:**
   1) African History and Culture
   2) African American History and Culture
   3) African Women in History
   4) AIDS Education
   5) Arts and Crafts

6) Conflict Resolution
7) Dance and Drumming
8) Entrepreneurship
9) Family History
10) Finances
11) Future Planning and Careers
12) Health and Nutrition
13) Housekeeping
14) Human Development
15) Manhood
16) Martial Arts
17) Nguzo Saba
18) Self Defense
19) Sex Education
20) Spirituality
21) Substance Abuse Education
22) Value Clarification
23) Value Systems
24) Womanhood

C) Resources needed:
1) Council of Elders
2) Adults
3) Mentors
4) Sponsors

D) Orientation/Training
1) Parent orientation
2) Introduction/orientation separation ritual (retreat). *The separation ritual is very important because it marks the beginning and signals the initial move away from childhood.*
3) Training of staff, leaders, mentors, sponsors

4) Retreats—March 21st, June 21st, September 21st
5) Public ceremony acknowledging completion—city-wide Kwanzaa celebration December 31st or sometime during the week-long holiday.

Eight (8) Month, Three (3) Phase Program

As stated earlier, we propose an eight (8) month, three (3) phase, program which is to flow with the natural harmonic cycles of the earth.

Phase I

March 21 – April 20
April 21 – May 20
May 21 – June 20

Phase II

June 21 – July 20
July21 – August 20
August 21 – September 20

Phase III

September 21 – October 20
October 21 – November 20
November 21 – December 20

The Oracle of Tehuti, an Egyptian divination system, as well as Metu Neter, Vol I—both by Ra Un Nefer Amen—were consulted to determine what should be concentrated on during each phase, and the energy governing each cycle. Please understand that energy is always changing; therefore, the oracle should be consulted at the onset of your program to determine the energy governing it at that particular time.

A) Phase 1 will run from **March 21 – June 20**.

Phase Focus – A view of the whole, knowledge of the law, optimism, sharing attitude, outgoing joyful expression, the healthy urge to experience pleasure.

Course work should reflect this focus, with emphasis on male/female relationships, business, harmonious partnerships, and health.

Example: Initiates should be taught how to look at the forest instead of the trees. That joy comes from within and not in external material things. Too many of us get caught up in buying things, thinking that will bring pleasure. Importance should be placed during this phase on education regarding drugs, drinking, and the abuse of sex. Knowledge of law should be imparted: divine, societal, and national.

Phase I

♦ ***Sex Education*** – should include, but not be limited to:
a) Marriage
b) Pregnancy
c) Prostitutes
d) Romance
e) Sexual Pleasure
f) Venereal Disease
g) Wife/Husband—Role of
h) Bedroom—His/Hers
i) Intoxicants

♦ *Social Values* – should include, but not be limited to:
a) Concept of Charity
b) Cooperation
c) Indolence (Laziness)
d) Diplomacy
e) Ambassadors
f) Morality
g) Optimism
h) Sharing
i) Social Events
j) Law Abiding
k) Materialistic
l) Deferring to Elders
m) Sympathetic
n) Careless
o) Narcissistic

♦ *Business/Personal Finance*
a) Business Planning
b) Insurance
c) Trade, Foreign
d) Traveling Agents
e) Wealth/Wealthy People
f) Speculation (Stock Markets)
g) Managers

♦ *Law/Justice*
a) Judges
b) Legal Matters
c) Intoxicants
d) Lawyers
e) Bankers

♦ ***Religion/Science***
   a) Faith
   b) Cosmogony
   c) Cemeteries
   d) Books
   e) Astrology
   f) Copper
   g) Education—Higher/Spiritual
   h) Rain
   i) Yoga
   j) Scientific Theory
   k) Synthesis
   l) Vegetation
   m) Priest/Priestess
   n) Holistic

♦ ***Art***
   a) Gems
   b) Decorations
   c) Corals—Pink
   d) Ornaments
   e) Entertainment

♦ ***Health***
   a) Liver/Gall Bladder System
   b) Kidney
   c) Dietary Habits
   d) Reproductive Organs
   e) Heart
   f) Pancreas

Spring begins on March 21ˢᵗ, a time when there is equal day and night. This is a time when daylight will dominate our lives. It is a time of new spark, power, and inspiration, time to make a new start; time to plant seeds.

B) Phase 2 will run from **June21 – September 20**.

Phase Focus – Learning what it means to do things because they have to be done and not because you are told to do them or you want praise. Learning to exercise initiative.

Course work should reflect this focus with emphasis on spiritual growth and development. Learning our essential nature, spirit. All areas of the curriculum should reflect this. At this point Elders, teachers, and sponsors should begin to look for signs of initiative in the initiates and be prepared to feed it.

Example: Initiative should be reflected in the student's willingness to answer and raise questions. Willingness to ensure classroom is in proper order. Teachers can disorganize the room on purpose to see who will exercise initiative to put it back in order.

Phase II

♦ *Exercising initiative towards:*
  a) Elders
  b) Those Younger
  c) Family
  d) Community
  e) Personal Relationships

Instructors are free to expand on the concept of initiative as they see fit.

C) Phase 3 will run from **September 21 – December 21**.

Phase Focus – Learning the dangers of arrogance, incorrect use of the will, what is the will, strong-headedness, dictatorialness, unreceptivity to guidance combined with incorrect intuitions, misjudgments, bad counsel, and lack of faith.

Example: This focus can be illustrated in the story of Ausar, Set, Heru, and Tehuti. Young men **must** be taught about the rising of the male sexual energy and how it should be directed—taught the nature of a warrior.

Phase III

Areas of coursework should reflect how arrogance, incorrect use of the will, dictatorialness, etc. have destroyed:
Kingdoms
Businesses
Families
Leaders
Foreign Trade

♦ *Sex Education* – should include, but not be limited to, how these negative traits can destroy:
  a) Families
    i. Husband/Wife Relationships
    ii. Parent/Child Relationships
    iii. Grandparent/Child Relationships
  b) Nature of Fatherhood

♦ *Social Values* – should include, but not be limited to, how these negative traits can destroy:
  a) Friendships

b) Ability to Lead Effectively
   i. Presidents
   ii. Political Power
   iii. Kings
   iv. Judges
c) What is Courage?
d) What is Self-reliance?
e) What is Circumspection?
f) What is Will?

♦ **Business/Personal Finance** – should include, but not be limited to, how these negative traits can destroy:
   a) Foreign Trade
   b) All Aspects of Business Success

♦ **Religion/Science**
   a) Druggists/Chemists – Herbs
   b) Fire – Spiritual Aspects
   c) Nature of Men – Ages 28–56
   d) Heart – Spiritual Aspects
   e) Gold – Alchemical Process
   f) Oracles – Importance of

♦ **Art**
   a) Poets – all students encouraged to bring forth this form of creativity

At the conclusion of this phase, final separation is to take place, and a large celebration is given in honor of the new initiates, welcoming them home as young men. It is encouraged that all aspects of the community be represented. Allow spirit to guide this aspect of the rite- of – passage for it is a wonderful and meaningful time in the life of the community, enjoy it!

THE PROGRAM

Role of the Council of Elders

An essential part of any community is its Elders. There is a saying, "When an old person dies, a library burns." Elders are the linking pins between generations. It is necessary for us to turn to our Elders for guidance and wisdom. In <u>Afrocentric Theory and Applications, Volume I</u> (Warfield-Coppock, 1990), a guide was provided to assist in selecting Elders, the following is taken from her book.[55] The criteria included age (50 to 55 years), evidence of maturity, community residence and affiliations, wisdom and spirituality, respect and knowledge of young people, and commitment to our youth and the African American community.

We should identify several Elders that fall within this criteria and ask them to identify others. It must always be borne in mind that not all older persons are suited to sit on the Council of Elders. Unfortunately, many of our Elders are as alienated to themselves as our young people. We should respect *all* Elders, yet, it must be borne in mind that their level of consciousness may not be suited for an African-centered rite of passage. Many may still see Africa as jungles and its people as wild savages. The baggage of self-hate and self-doubt can be carried by anyone, young or old, and can be used to oppress one's self and others.

Additional criteria to be used in selecting Elders should include:

1. Highly respected and knowledgeable about the community's traditions and culture
2. Working knowledge of Afrocentricity
3. Read major texts
4. Read and knowledgeable in the subject matter of Rites-of-Passage, including manhood and womanhood.
5. Skill and interest in instructing same gender youth

Elders should serve in roles that are comfortable for them. They can serve as:

1. Advisors on matters of program planning and /or implementation
2. Assessors of the young persons' progress
3. Advisors on matters of conflict within the program, or between adults
4. Oversight of the procedures and practices
5. Oversight of and participation in the final ceremony
6. Provide insight into the African traditions of the community and people in general.

Elders are given the authority to query the initiates at any time they choose concerning their involvement in the Rites-of-Passage Program, thus insuring essential intergenerational communication.

At this point, I would like to say more regarding the eldership. It seems, in this country, in this day and age, it is a crime to become old. It seems that we fear getting old, that staying young is the goal. In our society, once you become old, there is no use for you, you are carted away to a 'rest home' to wait for death. It is as though getting old makes us all face our mortality, that we will leave this life, that we will, as the Native Americans say, " Lay down this robe," robe being the body. We have lost all regard for the elders in our community, thinking that we know more than them, yet they can lay their eyes on you and can tell you your real nature! Those elder mothers command respect with their piercing glance, and the elder men seem to stand ten feet tall for a life time of experience that we can only sit and marvel at. In his book, The Healing Wisdom of Africa, Malidoma Some' addresses the issue of elders among his people, the Dagara. He says that "Old means someone who is dry, solid, lasting. Thus the old and the elders embody stability, dependability, and wisdom. In this capacity, they become a frame of reference, a resource, a research center."[56]

In this day and age, when everything is so disposable and we are concerned with instant gratification, there seems to be no stability in the lives of our young people. The parents are too busy with their careers and chasing the American dream, or there is just one parent working him/herself to the bone with very little time to provide stability for the child. Yet, we have elders in all of our communities who embody stability, dependability and wisdom. They know from experience. We only have a lot of information but elders have the experience, plus knowledge, which gives rise to wisdom. They have come over a road that we, no matter our education, social status, and wealth, all must travel. We have in our elders rich repositories of tribal knowledge and life experience. Our elders are essential resources for the survival of the our communities, anchoring it firmly to the living foundation of tradition.

Our communities are dying; our way of life is changing in a direction I am sure that most will agree is not for the best. Our young men are searching for the meaning of manhood in all the wrong places. They get it from T.V. and movies, all of which seem to add to the collective insecurity of us all. Yet, we have elder men walking around who have endured unthinkable hardships and humiliation in an effort to provide for their families. They know full, well, what it means to be a man, what it takes to become a man and why it is necessary for our survival. They still understand the tradition of rites-of-passage, while it may not be in the traditional terms as outlined in this book, they still understand. Recall, the old men still out under the trees on a hot afternoon playing checkers and looking at us young men running after the girls. They would call us over and say "it's about time for you to go out with us behind the barn, " or, when we would be giving our mothers hell, they would say, "you are smelling your piss now." All of which meant that they had been watching us and it is time for us to be taught secrets, that of which we had only heard. It was time for the old men to take us to their world. "The old and the elder are the most revered members of the village community and its greatest preservers and nurturers."

Recall how the elderly of our community nurtured us all, how they looked out for us and made sure that we did what we were supposed to do:

> The gender of the elder is important in maintaining the stability of a social community. Female elders, though they have the same qualities as male elders, are more often in demand because of their role as containers and reconcilers. In the village, everyone knows that a female elder is less likely to curse than a male elder. Moreover, it takes a female elder to undo a curse inflicted on someone by a male elder. No one can undo the curse of a female elder. If two people are involved in an argument and a female elder shows up, they will stop before being ordered to do so.

Think of the posture of those church mothers, powerful women who, with a look, can make you stop. There was a time, in our community, when we had such respect for our elders until, no matter what we were doing wrong, we would straighten up when an elder showed up, particularly, female! It is time that we return to our traditions and seek to save our elders and place them in the revered positions they deserve. Why? "If a culture rejects the sacred, it rejects elders. If it rejects elders, it rejects the welfare of its youth."

What are we talking about other than reaching black males? Yet, if nothing is no longer sacred to us, then, we reject our elders. It does not take much looking to see that we have rejected the sacred. Church has become a place to get a date and religion has become a tool of oppression. What is sacred to us? We find amusement as our comedians make fun of our civil rights struggle! Have you ever heard a Jewish comedian making fun of the holocaust? I think not. It is not only a reminder for them of their sacrifice and the horrors they and their ancestors endured, but a manifestation of their sacred connection to the divine. Yet, it is nothing to turn on T.V. and see a comedian making fun of the church, black Muslims, and the civil rights movement. Here, Jewish people are influential in every aspect of American life, while we are the great imitators and clowns of society. I ask you, what is sacred to us? Sex is no longer sacred; it has become the subject of videos, and our young people get a healthy dose of it each day! Nothing is sacred, therefore, it is nothing for our young people to be seen cursing out elders, their parents, teachers, and whomever they please! As a result, we reject our youth! We create a never-ending cycle of oppression. When will it end? When we have courage to pick up the ways of our ancestors, honor our elders and live our traditional ways, among which, rites-of-passage is central.

.

VII

EL-HAJJ RAY RITES OF PASSAGE
7 Doors To Manhood Initiation

It is apparent, no matter the age, that we men need a rites-of-passage. There is a need for us to formally acknowledge our transition to adulthood. Face it, you know your woman, or mother, is still calling you her 'baby' (smile) and in many cases we act like it. For the most part, we act like babies before the world, refusing to accept our responsibility as men.

The program was named after a young brother El-Hajj Ray, who, when I met him at the age of 15, was very conscious and aware. There had been many elders in our community working with this young man, assisting him in his journey towards manhood. By the age of 17, he had been kicked out of every high school in Lexington, Kentucky; however, we managed to get him to take the GED. El-Hajj scored in the top 10 % in the nation, scored a 28 on his Act and won a scholarship to the University of Kentucky to study mathematics. He was always a bright spot and wonderful spirit. However, despite all of our combined efforts for some reason he was attracted to the street life. We were working to get him into the military and away from the streets. Two weeks before he was to go into the military, he was murdered. How is the story of this young man you? How is the story of this young man *me*? The question is, how does this young man represent all of us? How are all of us his story? In a sense, this program represents the rules, rituals and ceremonies designed to help us all break the cycle. The program is divided into 3, parts, KNOW THYSELF, CLEANSE & PURIFY and LIVING IN ALIGNMENT WITH ABSOLUTE TRUTH and is designed so several men can come together and assist each other in the process, working together is the most beneficial because it creates needed bonding, sense of brotherhood, and community.

The El-Hajj Ray Rites of Passage: 7 Doors to Manhood, Journey to the Godhead is a 9 month program that has grown primarily out of my 32 year search for the meaning of manhood in the context of this western society. The 7 doors to Manhood endeavors to take one deeper into their own psyche in an effort to open the doors to their spiritual liberation.

Why call it '7 Doors to Manhood'? As many of you know, 7 is a very significant number and carries very special properties in most ancient traditions:

* Seven Sea and Seven heavens
* Prophet Muhammad's journey to the 7 heavens
* Seven days of the week which correspond to the seven major planets in our solar system.
* Seven notes on the musical scale.
* Buddha sought enlightenment for seven years.
* There are seven sacred directions in Native American spirituality.
* Chakras are seven wheels of energy located in our spine which when activated it is said lead to illumination.

The list goes on and on, however, in his numerous writings and teachings Ra Un Nefer Amen informs us that man has more than one body and that man's spirit is divided into seven divisions. They are as follows:

1. The first division is the   'BA'
2. The second division is the   'Khu'
3. The third division is the   'Shekhem'
4. The forth division is the   'Ab'
5. The firth division is the   'Sahu'
6. The sixth division is the   'Khaibit'
7. The seventh division is the   'Khab'

In order to appreciate the relevancy of these divisions of the spirit they must be seen as being to the spirit what the physical organ systems are to the physical body. Now when we speak of man having seven bodies it must bore in mind that we are speaking in terms of African metaphysics. As Ra Un Nefer Amen writes in page 58 of Metu Neter Vol.1:

It must be noted that in traditional African metaphysics there is no distinction made between the physical, and Man's higher bodies. I.e., the physical body is considered an integral part of the spirit,- its densest component. The failure to realize that Man has seven, not one body, and that all things have a spirit, is one of the major causes of people's stagnation, and errors – both in thought and action.[57]

Thus one way to eliminate errors and stagnation in our life is to understand the 7 divisions of the spirits and how they function in our lives. It is understanding these divisions and working with them that will lead to our spiritual liberation. To be liberated spiritually is the highest form of liberation. To know that I am God, to live that I am God, to submit my will to God can be nothing but supreme liberation as was discovered by our ancient sages and seers.

7 divisions of the spirit can be seen as the path that the consciousness of man takes in its journey back to being conscious of itself.
In this journey it passes through 7 'Doors' and for most of us, our
consciousness is yet to reach the higher levels, i.e., The Ba , Khu and
Shekhem, which contains the divine faculties that connect earthly man
to his divine self. By our not having consciousness active in these three
levels we cannot take advantage of divine guidance in our life. Most
of us have consciousness active in the four lower divisions of spirit,
the Ab, Sahu, Khaibit, Khab. This, when rightly understood, explains
why we spend so much time caught in personality conflicts, fulfilling
sensuous desires, and intellectual bull baiting sessions with little or no
follow through. Also, even for those of us walking the spiritual path,
this explains why we may intellectually know the path but are unable
to realize it, i.e., back sliding from what we know is right. We are still
functioning out of the lower levels of spirit. They say that Kundalini
(life force) is coiled three and one half times at the base of the spine,
thus we see it is centered in the Khab (physical body), Khaibit (animal
spirit), Sahu (intellect, imagination and emotions) and part of the Ab
(the aspect dealing with the will). These seven divisions of the spirits
are akin to the seven Chakras. The initiate is strongly encouraged to
read the works of Ra Un Nefer Amen and Muata Asby for a deeper understanding. From the outset it is important for the initiate to conduct
additional study, for self-realization is a personal subjective experience. While we may be able to talk about manhood, ultimately it is
you who have to swim in the waters of your own understanding of it.

A. KNOW THY SELF

1. Excavating the real man – divination & incarnation objective
2. Balancing act – man of steel and velvet

3. Warriors time out – recognizing & healing our wounds
4. Rites of Passage – pathway to manhood
5. Spiritual baths
6. Mirror of Truth – identifying your masculine archetypes
7. Turn up the heat – sweat lodge & fire walk

B. CLEANSE & PURIFY

1. What's eating you – the effects of food on your nature.
2. Who do you think you are? – your beliefs, values and thoughts
3. A man's best friend – phallic purification rituals.
4. Tell it like it is – the bitch syndrome
5. Spiritual baths
6. Free your mind, body and spirit – cleansing & clearing rituals
7. The other side of daylight – introduction to feminine mysteries

C. LIVING IN ALIGNMENT WITH ABSOLUTE TRUTH

1. Can't live with her/can't live without her – developing &
   maintaining healthy intimate relationships.
2. Walking the walk & talking the talk – next steps.

At this point, throughout the balance of the book, the reader
will notice several dialogs between a Master and Student. Both the
Master and Student are fictional but the interchange between the two
is real and instrumental. The dialog is designed to pace the reader in
the presence of their own Master and Student located within them. As
you read the dialogs, imagine yourself as the Master or the Student
and how you would reply, take note of your reply, and where it is
coming from within you. You will find yourself opening up to your
higher self.

A. KNOW THY SELF:

As preparation to begin the first 10 days the initiate is to review the following lesson and follow the instructions given by the Master:

With the Name of God, Most Gracious, Most Merciful and in the Presence of Our Ancestors, Both Seen and Unseen.

June 4, 2002

KNOW THY SELF

The time had come for the student to learn the lessons of manhood. He had grown over the past several years but there still remained the journey into manhood he had to make.

Student: Master, teach me of manhood?

Master: Why must I teach you of that which God has placed in your nature to know?

Student: Do you mean that manhood is something that I should know, naturally?

Master: Yes, does not everything in nature function in accord to the nature in which it was created?
Student: Yes, but why do I have a question regarding my nature as a man?

Master: The world you function in has questions regarding itself. In fact, the world you function in is not sure of itself, therefore, it passes that confusion on to you.

Student: Therefore, are you saying that I function in a world that does not know its nature?

Master: Yes, and what's more, in not knowing its nature, all within that world is unsure of its nature. Let me give you an example. You go to the circus and you see elephants dancing, you see bears dancing, you see dogs wearing skirts and see all of these things and man takes pride in his ability to make animals function in opposition to the nature in which they were created. As a result of this, man takes pride in functioning in opposition to his own nature. So, the world in which you live is searching for its nature and everyone in that world is searching and questioning their nature.

Student: So, I am away from my nature?

Master: Your question reveals the answer. Now, let us go to the meditation hall, for you must access the universal record of manhood that you might re-member who and what you are.

With that, the student made the journey back to the great hall of meditation. He knew that this would be a 30 day guided meditation, back into the cosmos, back into that time before time, back into that universal knowing of all knowing, back into space between the manifested and un-manifested reality. Before proceeding into the hall, the student took a ritual purification for it is customary before undertaking any spiritual journey of enlightenment that one purify the body, mind and spirit. The student immersed himself in the healing crystallized waters seven times and anointed himself with myrrh oils. With that he was ready to enter the hall. Upon entering, he was greeted by the revered master of the cosmic journey. As he stood before this master, he seemed to lose himself in the loving vibrations of this galactic traveler. After bowing before the master, the student took his position among the sacred gems and crystals, all of which carried ancient vibrations and were tuned to frequencies of other worlds. The student sat in full lotus position, tuned all attention within, and thus, the journey began. As the student began to access the different levels of consciousness, he could sense the presence of the master with him, his mind and the masters mind became one. Then, something wonderful happened, he lost all sense of self and he and the master were part of what seemed to be a larger Self. In this ultimate Self, he became all-knowing and could sense all he needed to know. In this state of all-knowing, it became clear to him that manhood was a journey, whose destination was the reuniting with the ultimate self. In fact, it became known to him that marriage to the so-called opposite sex was the preliminary step towards this re-unification with the ultimate self. After this unification experience, the student found himself in what appeared to be an enchanted forest, full of life, songs, sunlight and a warm gentle breeze. There, beneath one of the trees, he sat and began to receive the teachings of manhood from the master.

Master: When you journey into the world and you are going to a town that you are not familiar with, what do you do?

Student: Get a map of the town?

Master: Very good. Now, what does the map do for you?

Student: It shows you the town and how to get to the different places that you need to go. It helps and keeps you from guessing and getting lost.

Master: Most men do not ask for directions and will not use a map. As a result, they get lost and everyone riding with them gets lost. It would be so much easier, if they were to ask for directions, or get a map. It is the same way in the world of illusion. Most men think they

*know where they are going, yet, in reality, they are lost and have
everyone with them lost. They fail to realize that there is a map to
manhood that they need to follow, a map that will take them all the
way back to the unification with the ultimate Self.*

Student: Where is this map?

*Master: You just experienced it, but it has to be brought out of the
cosmic world, put into a practical application so it can take you back
to the cosmic world. All human life must travel through stages and
manhood and womanhood is different at each stage.*

Student: I thought it was always the same.

*Master: No Dear One, that is the problem in the world. They think
that everything remains the same and it does not change, but everything is always changing. You must go through stages; the stages
are: birth, childhood, youth, adulthood, eldership and death. Each
stage has seven doors that you must journey through; therefore,
many native people still understand that every seven years you go
through a door.*

Student: Why seven doors and seven-year cycles?

*Master: Seven is the number of the mystic; seven is the number of
the spiritual adept. Every human begin is a mystic, whether they
want to realize it or not. You see, it is in walking the path of the mystic that you learn these universal principles. Now, let me introduce
you to the path to manhood that we gave to the masters of the Institute of TransMutational Healing. Here, at the Institute the motto is,
"Many Paths, One Truth". Just as you just experienced the unification with the ultimate self, the oneness, that is the mission and goal
of the institute, to show the initiate their individual path back to the*

ultimate Self. There are three phases: Know Thy Self, Cleanse and Purify, and Living in Alignment With Absolute Truth.

Student: Is this way a difficult way?

Master: Nothing is difficult, all requires work. The work required at the Institute, is mostly, internal work. You have to work on self to know self and to be able to realize the ultimate self, while still in the human body. Most are not willing to work. Most seek the prize, without having to work for it, or earn it. That is why so many men hide behind excuses.

Student: What type of excuses?

Master: Everything, from racism to their mothers' dresses

Student: Master, please explain.

Master: Most men are full of talk and insightful conversation, with little action. When asked why they have not produced, they come up with all kinds of excuses. Why? Because facing self and the short-comings of self is a difficult thing to do. That is one reason why most men run from responsibility. Responsibility is the cornerstone of manhood.

Student: Why?

Master: Responsibility means one will respond to the challenges in life. The challenges in life are designed to bring out the divine in you. It is all about evolving.

Now, let us look at each phase and its contents.

KNOW THY SELF:

a. Excavating the real man – divination and incarnation objective

Here, we are talking about learning why you came into this world and the tools that you brought with you for the journey.

Student: That is so very interesting, because this world seems to think that everyone should be doing the same thing in the way that those in power think they should be doing it. If you try to walk a different direction, then, you are crazy or weird. If you get others to follow you and you become what appears to be powerful, then, they will destroy you.

Master: We all come back into this life with a different purpose, and once you know YOUR purpose for being here, then you can walk YOUR road and not get caught in someone else's drama. That is why we do a divination and incarnation objective on each male that becomes part of this journey back to manhood. Each man needs to know what are his purpose and the tools he has. One of the causes of envy is failing to utilize your own tools and gifts. So many men are not aware of their gifts and where they should be going.

Student: Could this divination and incarnation objective be the road map you spoke of, earlier?

Master: That, it is. The Chief Priest of the Institute, along with other priests and neophytes, consult the divinities on behalf of the initiate to determine their incarnation objective. Then, the initiate is given knowledge to assist him in this journey towards manhood. As such, every experience through the seven doors will be different for each man, but designed to put them in touch with universal truths.

Student: After the initiate receives his road map, what is next in the phase of Know Thy Self?

Master: Then comes, " Balancing Act" – man of steel and velvet. However, before giving you information concerning this aspect, I feel the vibrations of someone very special that I want you to meet.

With that, the master closed his eyes and went into a deep level of trance. There appeared, before the student, a cloud formation and seated in that formation was a female master, the likes of which the student has never seem. She was adorned in yellow, with eyes a deep walnut brown that looked through you into your soul. She was perfumed in self-esteem and spoke in a voice that did nothing but sooth and comfort the startled student. Every word seemed to flow from her mouth, like a peaceful river cascading through a sunlit meadow. Her words were soft, like butterfly wings and her face was aglow, like a fully mature sunflower. There was a peace about her that spoke of her divinity as she addressed the student.

Female Master: Do not be mistaken by my female form, for I am the same as you and the Master, I just chose the feminine form. This is something you will learn of later. For now, I want to give you a message from the Great Mother and the Goddess Oshun. They say, "All the spiritual traditions are chapters in the great book of life. That is why the Institute's motto is "Many Paths, One Truth." They understand that you, like so many, are looking for the thread that unites the different phases of rites-of-passage, or journey to man-hood. However, they say that you must seek the thread that links all the spiritual traditions together. That is why you are here, to link it all together. You must stay focused on this, link it back together. You must keep it simple. As the master spoke to you of the road map, you must identify the universal blue print for rites-of-passage and initiation and the thread that ties it all together. This is your quest, of this you must always be aware. I am honored by your presence here and strengthened by your determination to re-member manhood. You must lead others to the light of this master, that they too might re-member.

With that, she took leave of the student, leaving, in her wake the sweet smell of honeysuckle.

Master: Do not take her words lightly for she very seldom speaks unless instructed to do so by the divinities that she channels. Now, to the Man of steel and velvet, her appearance was very timely for that is the essence of the man of steel and velvet. It speaks of the different aspects of a man. Some say, male and female aspects, however, we know it is all one aspect, which manifests in different ways. However, this is a lecture that the initiates receive in their induction meeting at the beginning of the journey. This is a two-hour lecture, after which, the initiates will receive study guides and questions to carry them further into the process of self- discovery.

Student: Would you say more on the Balancing Act?

Master: As you know, there is a balance in the universe, a balance in all of nature, the same balance is found in you. Balance is what the equinoxes are all about. During the fall and spring equinoxes, there is equal day and equal night. Each equinox is preparation for the next phase, or season. There is the spring equinox, with its equal day and night, which precedes the spring season of planting, the time of rebirth, renewal and new beginnings. Then, there is the fall equinox, with its equal day and night, that precedes the fall season, the time of harvest and time of maturity. Thus, you see in the equinoxes a balance, a balance that precedes a time of renewal and maturity. In the human, you have these two aspects, male and female energies that have to be brought into harmony, in balance, in order for the human

to have a time of renewal, new growth and beginnings, as well as be-
ing able to mature properly. One of the complaints that females have
with males is the lack of maturity, that males are immature. We think
this is because of the lack of balance between the male and female
energies. This is showing us that, if a man is to produce and grow
to maturity, then, the internal energies must be balanced. There has
to be equal balance between the male and female of self, before one
can properly produce and mature.

Student: Are you saying, in order for a male to grow and accomplish
anything in this life the male and female energies of self must be
balanced?

Master: Look around you look into the world in which you live. You
see men who have amassed great wealth, power and fame. Yet, most,
if not all their lives, they are empty. They all continue to search for
more, looking outside of self for it. Look at the games they play, how
they play with human lives. Does this not remind you of immature
little boys, seeking to see who has the most? I think, in urban lan-
guage, it is called "a peeing contest".

Student: I have heard it called that.

Master: This is nothing more than a man manifesting how unbal-
anced he is. Once the male and female energies of self have been
balanced, then, one is comfortable with self and has no reason to try
and prove anything to anyone. You love self, you honor self, and you
can do the same with everyone else. Also, just as you have everything
you need in this universe, once these energies are balanced in self,
you realize you have all you need in you. However, this does not hap-
pen until you have balanced the male and female energies of self.

Student: Master, I look forward to the lecture. Now, what of the stage, Warriors Time Out – recognizing and healing our wounds?

Master: The recognition of wounds is so very vital to the path of manhood. Men carry deep wounds, yet, never realize how deeply they hurt and how these wounds have affected their lives. Do you recall the great hall of books?

Student: Yes, it is a most fascinating place.

Master: Do you recall the vibratory frequency that you have to reach in order to access the great books?

Student: How could I forget, for they are not physical books, but the universal impressions made by the authors on the fabric of time. It requires stilling the mind that it might become like paper, so the impressions of the books can be imprinted on it.

Master: That, is it. I want you to go to the great hall and access the frequency of the book, "Men and the Water of Life" by Michael Meade. There, on page 13, he will tell you about wounds and the path to manhood. Then, return to me and we will go further.

Student: Yes, Master.

With that, the student proceeded to the great hall of books. The hall contained no physical books, only crystals. The student sat in the middle of the hall and began to meditate on the book his master spoke of. There appeared, in the student's mind's eye, the book by Mead. The book opened to page 13 and he heard the voice of Meade coming from the book, in essence, the book spoke to him.

Book, page 12: "Tribal initiations include intentional wounding that leave scars which mark the initiate physically and concretely. Often, the scars are visible and remind everyone that the marked one has entered a new stage of life, for initiation changes a person's relationship to everyone. Through a mixture of reality and artifice, a line is drawn that ends one stage and begins another. From this, a new person emerges who is growing further into life and also moving a little closer to their knowledge of death."

Student: Wounds and scars are important.

Book: "Modern initiatory experiences may leave a physical mark, or they may only be located through psychological scars and emotional traumas. In the psychology of initiation, experiences that change a person's life, and mark the person as an individual, are opened up and re-examined to learn who a person is and who they are trying to become. The wounds work as thresholds between inner and outer realities. Seeing into the wounds and scars reveals that everyone is wounded, and teaches one how to see the person coming out of the wound. Without reopening and re-visioning of the events that mark a person's soul, life seems chaotic and more disorderly than it actually is. You could say that those feelings of chaos, within life, are actually calls from areas of unfinished initiation. Initiatory experiences inhabit the same deep psychic ground of birth and death. When the stages of life and the radical occurrences in the life of an individual are not marked, old age becomes confusion and chaos. Dwelling with the little deaths in life changes the size and shape of the big death. Seen through the eye of initiation, death is not the opposite of life, death is the opposite of birth. Both are aspects of life."

The student turned this information over, and over, in his mind, trying to get a clear understanding. In the mist of trying to understand, he heard the Master's voice; do not wrestle with this, allow it to flow to you. The book is getting ready to reveal something to you that you touched upon in your own book, "Tradition and Transformation"

Book: "The process of initiation also gets activated when there are shocks to a group or culture. Major breaks and changes open a culture to past and future, at the same time. At the threshold, where one epoch ends and another begins, initiation becomes the dominant style of the psyche. Change can erupt like a river, un-dammed by the shifting of psychic ground."

The student thought to himself, yes, here was a piece of the answer to the riddle of slavery in America. Slavery was a shock to African culture and to the group who experienced it. It was an initiatory experience of which the group must continue to reopen the wounds to help make sense in the present life. Just as the holocaust is reopened as a means of making sense in the lives of those who experienced it, it seems that both slavery and the holocaust were initiatory experiences for a cultural group.

Book page 13: "Seen through the eye of initiation, the scars of initial woundedness and of life-changing events turn out to be the openings to imagination and the heartfelt experiences of life. When these experiences are contained in art, in poetry, story, song, and dance, the limits of the individuals and of time are shed, and the timeless territory of the heart and the imagination opens."

Student: That is why we must allow our wounded experiences to express themselves through our arts, song, dance etc., in order to access the heart.

Book: "We enter the territory of the heart by going into our wounds and reliving them. By 'wounds,' I mean those blows from life that stun and injure one's spirit or lacerate and mark the tissues of the soul. There are three major sources of wounds for men: the hurts suffered in childhood, the blows received in initiatory circumstances, and the losses in life that become the cloth of the cloaks of the elders.

The eye of initiation sees darkly and sees in the darkness of suffering the glint of survival and the glimmer of emerging wisdom. "

Student: Men must come together over their wounds and losses, not over their gains and wealth, if they are to heal and move forward.

With that, the student took leave of the Great hall of books to return to the feet of his master.

Master: Now that you have the information from the book, do you have any questions?

Student: Master, that was such a rich experience, I need time to reflect on it all and how it applies to my life.

Master: That is what all initiates must do. Take this information, reflect on it, write about your own wounds and the initiatory experiences that it opens for you.

Student: What of the stage: Rites-Of-Passage?

Master: The booklet that the initiate received at the beginning of this journey contains the rite-of-passage information. However, the name, rites-of-passage, says a lot, the right to pass to the next stage of life. This implies that this is something that must be earned. One cannot go to the next stage of life, without learning lessons and being tested on the lessons. Most want to just drift along and try to get to manhood without earning it. Most are the T.V. version of men; others are their mother's version of men. In reality, only men can make men. Read the book, answer the question and reflect. Dear One, pay close attention to what we are about to say to you: How can you become a man unless someone teaches you of what it con-

stitutes? It is those men who have walked the road that you have to walk who are better qualified to teach you of manhood. They have walked this road; they have made their mistakes and had successes, of which you can benefit, if only you would listen. This media presents to you an image of manhood that is nothing but an illusion, the fantasy of those who write the stories. When, in reality, it is God who has written the ultimate story on manhood and there are men who have given their lives to understanding this story. It is these men who are qualified to preside over rites-of-passage, those men who have walked the path, those men who know the way of God, those men who have the light of God in their eyes and heart. These are the men who are qualified to take you to the next stage, the stage of manhood. This is the work that must be done, if the world is to see the new man. This world gives you the image of a man who has conquered others, who has material goods and power. However, the same man has not conquered his base desires, this same man is controlled by his material goods and is a prisoner to his ego. Dear One, this is not the man of God; the man of God is God. As you know, God stands behind this material creation and is the material creation. God is the totality of all that you can comprehend and more. Such should be the same with a man of God, he should be more than you see and greater than you think. Are you like that? If your answer is no, then, you need rites-of-passage and it does not matter your age. Even your physical body is nothing more than a vehicle for the expression of God on this earthly journey. This you need to understand and be taught, however, it is only those men who have walked and talked this path who can teach you of these things. So, are you ready to earn your right to pass to the next stage?

Student: Yes, Master, I am ready.

Master: Then, look deep inside of yourself and ask your self from whence I come? It is the place that you come from that is the door-

way to rites-of-passage. While on the other side of this reality, you earned the right to come into this life and walk this earthly plane. You earned the right to a physical body; this is not a gift to take lightly. We want you to listen to the call of your ancestors from long ago. Listen to their call, calling you to come home to them and the way that they sacrificed for you. You are caught in this world of illusion and, as a result, your life is a living hell. You walk around blindly, looking for manhood, and there are men in your midst who are more man that you could ever imagine. Men who faced struggle each day, men who faced death each day, men who had little or no education and, yet, made a way out of no way. We say to you, look to these men for courage and strength. However, go back, even further in your mind, and think of the men who laid the foundation for the very civilization that you worship today. These men were in tune with something higher in themselves. They had transcended the ego, personality, and knew they were God, lived like God, and as a result God walked the earth. Yet, today, YOU walk the earth, the you I mean is personality, ego and limited accomplishments. Marvel not at that which you see, for one flood can wash it away, one tornado can blow it away, nature can call it all back to her whenever she chooses. Yet, there were and are men who talk and walk with Mother Nature who can calm the winds and turn back the seas. It is these men that you need to know. Rites-of-passage you ask about? We say, the right to pass on to the next stage is not free.

Student: How does this tie to the Phase Spiritual Baths?

Master: At each stage of the Seven Doors to Manhood, Male Rite of Passage, the initiate is given a spiritual bath. The bath is designed to cleanse the initiate's aura. Just as the physical body picks up dirt, so does the aura pick up spiritual impurities? The bath is designed to pull out those impurities and open the initiate up to receive messages from the divinities.

Student: Messages from Divinities?

Master: Yes, after the bath the initiate is instructed to sit is the shrine room among the shrines and listen with the inner ear for guidance.

Student: What kind of spiritual bath is it?

Master: We go to the Oracle and determine the nature of the bath, based on the initiated vibration. The bath is made with herbs and oils at a specific time of the day and week, all determined by the Oracles. As the student learns to listen to the inner guidance, he is now ready for the next stage, Mirror of Truth – identifying your masculine archetypes.

Student: What is the Mirror of Truth?

Master: Go to any mirror look and seek to understand that which lies behind that which you see.

Student: I do not understand. When I look in the mirror I see an image of me.

Master: You see your physical body, but, as we know, the body is not you, it is only the vehicle that the YOU uses to travel on this earth plane. Thus, looking in the mirror causes you to look deep into the pool of self and try to understand the ultimate SELF, the SELF that is really you.

Student: If there is an ultimate SELF, then, why the need for masculine archetypes?

Master: The ultimate Self has to find expression on this earth plane. You are the Self that chose to manifest in the male form. Well, your male form carries, or channels, a certain type of male energy for the work that you have to do as a male on this planet. Each male channels a different type of energy, which needs to be understood. One of the problems of the world, is that all men are viewed alike, or the world is constantly trying to make them alike. While all males are aggressive, some have more aggression than others. While all men are physically strong, some are stronger than others, some use their minds more than others and the list goes on. It is important to understand the differences. The energy in the universe has different degrees of manifestation.

The male energy of the universe may manifest in different ways, in different men. That energy is portrayed as an archetype. The energy may manifest itself as being very athletic and martial, as a result, you have men who become career military, or police officers, and the like. The energy may manifest itself as being introspective and intuitive, thus, you have men who become sages and the like. Then, you have the energy that manifests as caring and sensitive, producing men who become healers, doctors, etc. The ancients had names for the different ways the male energy manifests itself; such names as Ogun/ Herukhuti (the war lord) Shango/Heru (the King) Orunmila/Tehuti (theSage & Prophet) Obatala/Ausar (the Wise one) and the list goes on, even the female archetypes will manifest in the man form.

Student: Does that cause the man a problem?

Master: No, why should it, we are talking about the manifestation of energy, nothing more. It is because the world of illusion is lost that causes all of the problems of identifying with a particular energy. That gets back to what I said earlier, trying to make all men the same. Thus, we think, because Heruhkuti is all male, then, all men wanted and should have that energy. Such is not the case. While we have all the energies in our bodies, one is more dominant than others. A male may manifest the energy of Oshun/ Het-Heru who is a female archetype. Does this make him any less a man? No, we think not, it makes him the creative male, the musician, the artist, the seer, that is all it means. Now, we can go into this much deeper, but, that is part of the Seven Doors to manhood, the initiate will be directed where to go and look for deeper insight. We didn't give you everything, did we (smile)?

Student: No, I had to search, ask, study and experience.

Master: That has been the way with all those before me and before that. Experience is the best teacher. Now, it is time for the last stage of the first phase – Turn up the heat.

Student: The sweat lodge?

Master: That is right, time for the journey into the great womb of our mother.

Student: Why do you call it a womb?

Master: What else would you call it?

Student: I do not know

Master: There is much about the womb that you do not know, so prepare to enter the great womb of the mother that you might understand why it is called a womb and why all females' wombs are sacred.

With that, the student bowed before his Master, and returned to waking consciousness.

1. Excavating the real man – Divination & Incarnation Objective

With the Name of God, Most Gracious, Most Merciful and in the Presence of Our Ancestors, Both Seen and Unseen.

January 19, 2001

As the student sat in meditation, the sun began to rise, bringing with it healing rays of light and warmth. It was the students practice to rise before sunrise and greet the new day with new expectations, for he understood that, with each day, we have another chance to express and experience the God of self. With each sunrise and sunset, we are blessed to have a complete cycle in the birth and death process, for when we awake from a nights' sleep, it is our resurrection. So, each morning he gave thanks for his resurrection and would pray to always have clear vision.

However, as the student continued to rise each morning, he would notice that much was rising in him. He noticed insecurity; jealousy, vanity and greed would pop up in his mind. From where did such demons arise and for what purpose? He also noticed his desire for attention; this was the most pressing demon of all. Why, and from where, did they come? With that, he sat off to sit with the Master, to inquire of demons and blocks to self-realization.

Student: Master, teach me of the source of human suffering.

Master: Human suffering is the product of ego, for God caused none of its creation to suffer. In order to have suffering one must have a standard with which to make a comparison. Now, what is the standard with which you compare?

Student: I do not understand what is meant by standard to compare?

Master: In not understanding this, you cannot understand the source of human suffering. Someone, or something, had to tell you what suffering was, thus, it was that someone or something, which set the standard. They showed you the standard and made the comparison. Now, Dear One, relax and let us take you on a journey through the cycles of your mind. Let us take you back, in what you call time, and show you that you have lost sight of you who really are, if you ever knew who you were at all!

Here, you sit, starving for attention and success, yet you are attached to the standard of this world of illusion in your quest for recognition. You have lost sight of the fact that you are a vehicle for the manifestation of divine and your frail ego wants attention. When others about you receive attention, you get jealous. Are you still looking for daddy to approve of you? Are you still looking for mother's love and attention? We think that this may be the source of your problem, however, like everything in the universe, there is a purpose for it.

The attention that you seek is really not from other humans, like yourself. You seek the attention of the divine. Yet, that divine is to be found in you, you must go within and realize the divine of self. It is your self that is crying for you to pay attention to it, calling you to come and discover a world that is so full of riches and joy. You have spent enough time in this external world. Yes, it is your Self that is calling to you to remember your connection to all of creation, for you are only a part of a much larger whole.

It is in not recognizing unity that you get caught in the separateness.

Student: How does one account for the different races and the racial confusion?

Master: Look about you at the flower garden; you see such a wonderful variety of flowers, each with its own path, its own color, fragrance, etc. Yet, each flower begins its journey, beneath the surface of the earth, as a seed placed in the ground. As that seed begins to germinate in the warmth of the earth's womb, it begins its journey towards the surface and sunlight. Now, that journey towards the sunlight is difficult, for the roots must push into the ground as the stalk battles to break the surface of the earth. This is the struggle of all life.

Each race of humanity is but a seed beneath the earth of awareness, and each race must struggle towards self-realization, each race must break through the earth of awareness and come into the light of full realization, just as the flowers come into the light of the sun. Dear One, do you not see that the flower does not show its beauty until it has come into the light of the sun. In the light of the sun it grows and the flower comes out. In the light of Self-realization, all of humanity will blossom. However, it must first struggle and break through.

Student: Are you saying that all races have their path to development?

Master: Yes, just like every individual has a particular path for its development.

Student: So, the struggle of Africans, born in America, is about breaking through, like flowers, to come into the light?

Master: Yes, that is so.

Student: Yet, it seems so unfair that Africans born in America, suffer the way they do.

Master: All are suffering, yet, to what are you comparing this suffering to? Them not having what others have?

Student: Yes, I think that is it.

Master: Dear One, when one comes into total self-awareness, they see that all are the same, there is no difference in the self. All races are seeking to, collectively, break through to self-realization. However, it is when you get caught in the difference and the illusion of the world that causes the pain and illusion of suffering. If all is God, and all is the play of God, then, God is in control. It is in the seeking of oneness with God that we all should be striving.

Student: That seems to be a very difficult lesson for me to learn.

Master: It is a difficult lesson for most to learn, but, learn it you must, if you are to ever attain spiritual liberation. All of mankind must get beyond this notion of separateness and realize that it is all one divine source, manifesting itself. It appears that you are now ready to journey to the Temple of the Mystic Light.

Student: I have heard so much about the Temple of the Mystic Light, but, I thought there was a special admission requirement?

Master: After all these years in the Temple, you should know that when the student is ready the teacher will appear. Most times, it is not our desire that alerts us masters to the student readiness, it is the questions that the student brings to us that tells us of the readiness.

Student: Do you mean that my raising the question of human suf-

fering, and my inability to break through my limitations regarding the different races, was a sign that I was ready for the journey to the Temple of the Mystic Light?

Master: Yes, by all means, for we masters are watchers of the soul, not ego driven desires. When one's soul reaches a certain level of vibration, it begins to seek that level in the manifest world. It is in the questions of the student that we learn of the soul's readiness for the physical manifestation.

Student: Master, I understand. It seems, that in the world of illusion, there is so much feeding the ego until desire is running us crazy.

Master: That is how it should be, for all cannot walk this path. So, those who have submitted to the drives of the ego will not reach spiritual liberation in this life. Dear One, all are called to spiritual liberation, but only a few will answer that call. Most are to content to be at the level of vibration where their ego is fed with the material things of this life. That, again, is all the play of God and we appreciate that. Yet, the point we seek to make to you is that your vibration has reached a point where you are ready to go to the next level.

Student: Master, what and where is the Temple of the Mystic Light?

Master: The Temple of the Mystic Light is that place within YOU that when reached, will allow you to open up to the God, or Goddess, that you are. It is that place within You which will allow you to experience, and then live, the ONENESS.

Student: How do I access this place?

Master: It requires Ase Initiation.

EL-HAJJ RAY RITES OF PASSAGE
7 Doors To Manhood Initiation

Student: What is ASE INITIATION?

Master: Ase Initiation is our helping students to open themselves to THEIR Temple of the Mystic Light. We open the gateways to bring them into alignment with their own divine truth and master within.

Student: Do you mean, I have a master within me!!!!???

Master: Who is it that you think I am? Ha! Ha!

Student: I thought!

Master: That is the problem, you think too much, and experience so little. I am but a manifestation of God who is the same God as you. Yes, it is time for you to have Ase Initiation. It is time for you to receive your OWN truth, and be in direct communication with your Orisha, Deity, or Angel, which will activate your life force energy to a much higher level. Now, Dear One, we want you to relax and think of the wonderful flower that you are and the path that you must take towards your own self-realization. We need for you to understand that all is God and all is with God. You are chosen to walk this path and God will care for you, however, you have to have faith. Without faith, all is lost, for you see how limited your ego is and how you cannot even control your thoughts. So, we say to you, it is time for you to return to full faith in us and allow us to guide you towards your greatest level of self-realization.

At this point, it is necessary for the initiate to understand what is meant by Divination and Incarnation Objective. The following discussion on Divination was taken form my book, "Tradition and Transformation , A Philosophical Treatise Based on the Ifa Religious System":

Divination

We all come into this life with a purpose. In his book, The Healing Wisdom of Africa, on pg.3, Malidoma Patrice Some' says:

> The Dagara believe that everyone is born with a purpose, and that this purpose must be known in order to ensure an integrated way of living. People, ignorant of their purpose are like ships adrift in a hostile sea. They are circling around. As a result, tribal practices emphasize the discovery, before birth, of the business of the soul that has come into the world. A person's purpose is then embodied in their name, thus constituting an inseparable reminder of why the person walks with us here in this world.[58]

Many of us will spend a lifetime seeking to learn and understand this purpose. In this quest for understanding, we will journey down different paths, some of which are unnecessary. Think of the many wasted lives that we see each day. Lives wasted on a search to define oneself, based on a standard that is anti-nature. We all come into this life attuned to a specific vibration, yet, we find ourselves seeking to function to the vibration of another. Take, for instance, a radio band, it goes from 87 – 108 and the different radio stations have a set frequency. Some stations can be found at 96.3 and others at 102.1, we will never find station 96.3 at 102.1, it will always be found at 96.3 because that is its assigned frequency. Such is the same with us, as we come into this life, attuned to a certain frequency, and as long as we function in accord to our frequency, we will be successful. However, it is not that easy. We are pulled, each day, to seek to function at a different frequency, pulled to the allure of this material world. We all want the fame and riches, this is not to say this is bad, it is only to say that, in most cases, we are seeking it at the frequency that is not our frequency. As a result, our life seems to be out of harmony with the divine forces of creation. We try, and try, yet we make no progress towards the realization of our purpose for being here, and we make little progress towards the fame and riches we seek. It is divination that can assist us in understanding that we are not functioning in accord to our frequency. In short, divination is the process of communicating both internally, and externally, with the divine forces of creation, and Oracles are the tools that facilitate such communication.

One may come into this life attuned to the frequency of 96.3 and, as long at they stay attuned to that frequency, the divine forces of creation will bless him/her. It is when one strays from that frequency that things begin to go astray. It is via divination that one learns that they are way down at 102.1 frequency and that is why things are not going correctly. The divination will reveal the necessary steps to move the individual back to their frequency of 96.3, and thus, success. Baba Karade writes:

> It is through the process of divination that seekers come to know of themselves and the forces that are shaping their past, present, and future lives. Through the process of divination, seekers come to understand the need for alignment with their most heavenly of selves and how to overcome the opposing forces that disrupt their efforts.[59]

Thus, divination can, and will, be revealing, allowing you to know that which keeps you from fully becoming. It is divination that will show you how to turn the divine dial of heavenly forces, so we might get back to our original state of harmony at 96.3. This turning of the divine dial, generally, takes the form of rituals, sacrifices, and prayer. It is through prayer that one petitions God to turn the divine dial back to your frequency. It is also through prayer that one comes to the realization, and gains the conviction, that God will turn the dial, back to his/her frequency. Ritual is the technology that allows the turning of the divine dial and sacrifice carries with it the power to alleviate the cause that turned the dial from the frequency in the first place. Essentially, it is through divination that one can learn their purpose for being here and how to stay in harmony with that purpose. In the book, African Divination Systems, on pg. 2, Philip M. Peek writes:

A divination system is often the primary institutional means of articulating the epistemology of a people. Much as the classroom and the courtroom are primary sites for the presentation of cultural truths in the United States, so the diviner in other cultures is central to the expression and enactment of his or her cultural truths as they are reviewed in the context of contemporary realities.[60]

An example of this can be seen in how the Dagara view material and physical problems from a cultural view and the role of the diviner. Malidoma Some' writes on pg. 23 of his book, The healing Wisdom of Africa:

The indigenous understanding is that the material and physical problems that a person encounters are important only because they are an energetic message sent to this visible world. Therefore, people go to that unseen energetic place to try to repair whatever damage or disturbances are being done there, knowing that if things are healed there, things will be healed here. Ritual is the principle tool used to approach that unseen world in a way that will rearrange the structure of the physical world and bring about material transformation.[61]

The ritual most commonly used to access the unseen world is divination. It is, as Baba Akinkugbe Karade writes in his book, Path to Priesthood, The making of an African Priest in an American World on pg. 32:

The Divination Process: For the Ifa devotee, divination sits at the center of belief and practice. It's intent is to consult Orunmila in regards to the spiritual nature of our circumstances. By looking into the spiritual nature of a situation, steps can be taken to ensure the most positive and elevating outcome. Divination has as it's root word "divine". This is the true purpose, to bring out the divine nature of all involved; from that, goodness can come into the world. At the heart of that goodness, is the Creator, Olodumare.[62]

Thus, the cultural truths for the Ifa devotee are found in the divination process. This process allows one to understand the nature of their material and physical problems, and gives the steps to be taken to bring about positive changes. It is divination that sits at the center of our cultural belief systems. It is divination that allows us to access the unlimited knowledge of the Creator, and bring our lives in accord with our divine purpose for being.

At this point, the initiate is advised to develop a "Personal Profile" that consists of a destiny divination (consult with local Priest or Priestess), Incarnation Objective Divination which can be performed by a Priest or Priestess of the Ausar/Auset Society, Astrology and/or Numerology Chart, Hindu Astrology chart, I Ching reading and any other Divination that will give the initiate deeper insight into self and their reason for being. During this 30-day process, the initiate should review this information on a daily and weekly basis, to imprint it into the subconscious to help facilitate change at deeper levels in the psyche. Another advantage of this exercise is that the initiate will begin to learn their "center", who they uniquely are. They should be encouraged to find their center and not the center of their father, or mother, family, or ancestors, but their center and their center alone. Once the initiate understands their center, they can join the balance of humanity, confident and comfortable with their place in society and willing to walk their road.

2. Balancing act – Man of Steel and Velvet

For this section, the initiate is advised to purchase the book, Man of Steel and Velvet: A Guide to Masculine Development, by Dr. Aubrey P. Andelin. Not only is this book an excellent treatise on masculine development, but it lays a base for our journey into the deeper metaphysical aspects of self and how we carry both energies, male and female. In the book, Dr. Andelin raises and answers the question, "What qualities within shapes a man's destiny, impels him to success as a husband, father, and builder of society?" In the book, he describes these qualities as Steel and Velvet. He says the Steel aspect of a man, makes a woman, children and others feel secure. It arouses the admiration of all and it makes a woman feel womanly. He describes the Attributes of Steel as:

1. Guide, Protector, and provider
2. Builder of Society
3. Masculinity
4. Character
5. Confident
6. Health

Notice how women and children respond when a man of steel walks into a room. However, a man cannot be only steel, for there is another aspect which Dr. Andelin points out which is just as important, that is the velvet aspect. He says the velvet aspect promotes good human relations among all people and it awakens love in women and children. The Attributes of the Velvet are:

1. Understands women
2. Gentleness
3. Attentiveness
4. Youthfulness

5. Humility
6. Refinement.

These qualities bring balance to the man. In fact, this Steel and Velvet concept has been compared to a skyscraper. The inner steel and concrete are the foundation and support of the building. In a like manner, the steel aspects of a man are his foundation and support. In fact, one can look at the concept of manhood in any culture and you will find these attributes are a fundamental part of the manhood definition. The velvet aspects relate to the landscape, the décor and artwork of the building, all of which adds softness and beauty to the otherwise stern and hard mass of the steel and stone building. These aspects of velvet add beauty and softness to the steel aspects of a man, and when both are properly blended they compose the ideal man, a masterpiece of creation.

In fact, this in one of the reasons the Egyptian Pharaoh wore the Royal Uraeus. Not only does it represent, among other things, the unification of Upper Egypt and Lower Egypt, but the balancing of the male and female energies, harmony of the steel and velvet aspect of a man. Again, we will explore the metaphysical aspects of this later, for now it is necessary for the initiate to understand that, in recent times, the unchanging truth of the masculine role has become blurred and there is a need for it to be brought back into to clear focus. It is necessary for us men to understand the need for us to be noble, caring and loving, these qualities will cause the women in our lives to treat us differently; they will bloom into their femininity and develop a sincere desire to please.

There is a need for us to understand that women respond to nobility, kindness, and gentleness in a man, especially when backed up by masculine self-confidence and courage. And when women respect and admire a man his self -confidence and masculinity is enhanced even further. Thus, we see, the more we move towards balancing the steel aspect of self with the velvet aspect of self, the better it is for everyone.

The need not to be too steel-like in our character is seen in the Ifa story of Shango, Ogun and Orunmila. For those familiar with Ifa, both Shango and Ogun are strong male archetypes. In short, Shango represents the warrior King and Ogun represents raw courage and fearlessness, while Orunmila represents the wisdom, the Prophet. It is said that, one day, Shango and Ogun found the women, but they ran from them, they were too strong. Then, Orunmila came with music, gifts and sweet talk and he got all the women. In this, we can see, if we as men come too strong and hard, it runs the women away. Yet, when we come with a balanced nature, steel and velvet together as typified in Orunmila, then women are not frightened. This is seen, each day, as young women choose strong robust males (the jock type or ruff necks) only to beg for tenderness and attention later on. What they are really looking for is a man of steel and velvet. This problem could be solved, were we men taught to recognize and develop both aspects of our nature i.e., the steel and velvet.

This example is not only relegated to the physical realm, between men and women, but also to the metaphysical realm. In our efforts to access the higher realms of spiritual insight, it requires tapping into the right hemisphere of the brain, the part that governs intuition and holistic thinking, this has been identified as female, or velvet. It requires leaving the rationalizations and linear thinking behind, which has been identified as male, or steel. Being able to balance the two is what is necessary, being able to go into the velvet aspect of self to access the higher realms is what most sages are able to do, while remaining fully in touch with the steel self.

Every man should seek to develop the steel and velvet within himself as a means to reach his full potential as a man. On page 13 and 14, Dr. Andelin delineates on the qualities of a man of steel and velvet. He says:

A man of steel is a masculine man. He is aggressive, determined, decisive, and independent. He is efficient in a man's world, demanding quotas of himself in reaching his objectives. He is competent in a task, fearless and courageous in the face of difficulty, and master of a situation. He has convictions and steadfastly holds to these convictions. He sets high goals, goals which require dedication and patience. He is not afraid of strain and diligence. He rejects softness and timidity. When he has to make a decision based on his best judgment, he is unbendable as a piece of steel. These qualities set him apart from women and weaker members of his own sex.

A man of steel has a sterling character. He remains steadfast to his convictions even under pressure. He is a man of honor and integrity. He is fair, just, and honest in his dealings, possessing moral courage and self-dignity, and those diamond traits which make a strong character. He is master of himself because he has learned to discipline himself. When subjected to pressures, he stands firm.

In addition to all of this, he has achieved a feeling of confidence and peace because of victory over himself. And physically, the man of steel has a body of strength and skill.

The velvet qualities include a man's gentleness, his tenderness, kindness, generosity, and patience. He is devoted to the care and protection of women and children. He understands and respects their gentle nature and recognizes it as a complement to his masculinity. He is chivalrous, attentive, and respectful to women and has an ability to love with tenderness. He has an enthusiastic and youthful attitude of optimism, which he maintains in spite of increasing years. Humility is also a part of the velvet, subduing the masculine ego as his rough nature is refined.[63]

147

It is the blending of these two qualities that makes a man a balanced man, and the crown of creation. This is the balancing act that we speak of, to be able to fully develop both the steel and velvet aspects of self, and know when to use them, being comfortable in doing so. It matters not of the social injustices in the world; this should not be used as an excuse to stop a man from developing his character. In fact, as you look down through history, it was and will continue to be men of steel and velvet who seek to correct the wrongs against humanity. It is time for more men of steel and velvet to step forward and lead humanity into the light day.

3. Warriors time out – recognizing & healing our wounds

Living in the west, we men are raised to be tough and to never give in to the emotional pain and hurt we might feel. Many of us carry wounds from childhood that affect our present lives; yet, we never really take time to understand this, or to heal these wounds. Even in our romantic relationships, we fail to really understand that we, also, hurt. A man can get into a deep intimate relationship and give his all to the young lady. If she, in turn, hurts him, what does he do with the pain? Unlike the young lady who can turn to her girl friends for support and comfort, in the west, the young man has no one to turn to. He will not turn to his partners and say how bad he hurts, discuss the pain. What happens? He will internalize it. For to turn to your partners and discuss the pain and hurt, let alone cry, is to run the risk of be called, "a little weak bitch, etc." So, we internalize the pain and when the next woman comes along, no matter how well-meaning she is, we take our pain and hurt out on her. I realize this is a major generalization, but, never-the-less, from personal experience and discussions with countless men across the country, I am finding this to be the case. What do we do with the pain of not having a father there when you need him? What of the pain of not receiving mother's love? What of the pain of

148

being ignorant to who you are and where you fit in this society? These, and so many more, are examples of suppressed pain that men carry which must be faced.

Another major cause of pain and confusion among men is trying to live up to the standard that has been set by this society, yet not being given the equal opportunity to do so, nor the resources. The cloak of racism is spread so neatly over this society until we have become comfortable in our misery. Each time the thought rises up in the mind of a man to do something positive and progressive, the negative mind comes up with several reasons why it cannot be accomplished. At the top of the list is, " they will never let a Black man do this!" So, we never, really, live our dream and we suppress the pain of dreams deferred.

Little attention is given to what it takes to wake-up, in this country, as an Afrikan man. Each day, all over this country, black men wake up with nothing to look forward to, no matter their station in life. We know, all too well, the reality of the glass ceiling and what it takes to get there. Most men must silently ask themselves, how much of who they are and who they are aspiring to be will they give up today, in an effort to reach the so-called goal of making it. We live in such a deep state of denial and suppressed pain until it is manifesting in ways we never thought possible.

Our desire to be other than who we are is so great, we live in constant cultural conflict. On the job, we must be docile and meek, not be a threat to the individuals in power, then, we go home and try to be strong and powerful, knowing that we are living a lie. As a result, we take out on our families what we are afraid to say at work. Most of our homes are a cold artificial imitation of the corporate elite, yet, when we look in the mirror, we no longer recognize who it is that we are looking at. We see black skin that does not agree with the white mind.

This pain manifests, in drug and alcohol abuse, infidelity and broken families. This internal pain becomes so great until most black men never live long enough to collect their social security!

We must also take into consideration the pain that has been passed on from generation to generation, the psychic trauma of slavery, the memory of which is carried in our cells. It is important for the initiate to understand slavery and the various techniques that were used in making a slave. He will find many of those techniques still being employed today. Instead of using a physical whip to lacerate our skin, we receive blows that lacerate our self-esteem. Blows that puncture our sense of grandeur poison our confidence and pollute our enthusiasm. To heal such wounds will take understanding, caring and patience. There is no quick fix or simplistic answers.

Take, for example, the argument that 'black men' will not commit. Now, I am not trying to make an excuse for our ignorance, lack of responsibility or, "Tom Foolery". However, could this be a carry over from slavery, which is the result of lacerated self-esteem? Among the enslaved Africans, they lived with the reality that marriage among them could never be held sacred. One could be sold off at any time, or the master could take a liking to your mate, thus, it was best for one not to get too attached. Can you imagine the internal pain associated with knowing, and at times being forced to watch, as the master had his way sexually with your wife, or daughter? This was a major blow to the male's self-esteem. Can you imagine the feelings of impotence and sense of powerlessness, not being able to protect your mate or your daughter? We must understand that, historically, men have used sex as a weapon of war, a symbol of authority, victory and conquest. The conqueror would always take the riches and the WOMEN, while the conquered men were forced to submit. We will not even begin to mention the effects rape had on the women and what was passed on to succeeding generations of women! For now, this is about men, African American men and their need to heal.

In her book, <u>Against Our Will: Men, Women and Rape</u>, Susan Brownmiller on pages 24,25,27 writes:

> War provides men with the perfect psychologic backdrop to give vent to their contempt for women....The sickness of warfare feeds on itself. A certain number of soldiers must prove their newly won superiority – prove it to a woman, to themselves, to other men. In the name of victory and power of the gun, war provides men with a tacit license to rape.

> Among the ancient Greeks, rape was also socially acceptable behavior well within the rules of warfare, an act without stigma for warriors who viewed the women they conquered as legitimate booty, useful as wives, concubines, slave labor or battle camp trophy.

> A simple rule of thumb in war is that the winning side is the side that does the raping...Rape is considered by people of a defeated nation to be part of the enemy's conscious effort to destroy them. In fact, by tradition, men appropriate the rape of "their women" as part of their own male anguish of defeat ....Apart from a genuine human concern for wives and daughters near and dear to them, rape by a conquerer is compelling evidence of the conquered's status of masculine impotence.[64]

This state of impotence can be seen, today, in the commercial rape of our women and how we men stand back, impotent, and even join in the process. It is something to hear the cry for female equality, yet watch videos and see the commercial rape and exploitation of our women. I sometimes wonder if our silence to such is nothing more that the resurfacing of our slavery wounds and pain?

We, as men, must face the truth of being a conquered people, there is no way to rationalize it otherwise. We have a love affair with the culture of our conqueror. We worship the God of our conqueror. We wear the names of our conqueror. We speak the language of our conqueror. We dress like our conqueror and treat our women with the same contempt as our conqueror. In fact, we will not buy anything unless it is made by our conqueror. We must realize that no conquered people were liberated without the assistance of their men! We men must face our situation and then decide what we are going to do about it. This is not a call to take up arms to over throw the system, nor is it about demonstrations, far from it. It is about being able to liberate oneself from the gravitational pull of materialism and step outside of this illusion. It is about recapturing one's dismantled manhood and becoming a light in this world of darkness. It is about seeking to reclaim the traditions of our ancestors! They, our ancestors, had a religion, they had a God, they knew how to honor and treat their women. Today, we have no excuse.

It is ignorance, defeat, and gross denial, not to understand where we come from and what we are about as a people. We live in a country with constitutional guarantees. When we reach back and pick up the faith of those great Africans, when we declare that we are Yoruba, Akhan, Muslim, Hebrew, Fon, etc., we are protected with 'Freedom of Religion!' When we stand in the world and declare with a strong voice their ways, we are protected because of 'Freedom of Speech.' Our Ancestors did not have such protections when they were stripped of everything! I thank our ancestors for their sacrifice that we might come up in this country to enjoy such constitutional guarantees, as we seek to heal and reclaim who we are. Healing our pain and wounds will be the first step towards liberation. This pain, which has been passed on from generation to generation, must be faced and healed.

Facing the pain of slavery and its effects, today, is very important, for the shackles were taken off our hands and feet and placed around our minds and hearts. If we, as men, are to truly become spiritually liberated and free, then, healing the wounds of slavery is a place we must start. If one were climbing to the summit of Mt. Everest, one would reach a halfway point. In fact, it is said that many have made it to the halfway point and turned back. Others make it to the halfway point, rest, regroup and go the final distance to the summit. If our goal is to reach the summit of spiritual truth, that we all are one, with the same consciousness manifesting itself, then, for me the issue of slavery is the halfway point. Many have chosen to stay here, to fight here and remind the world of the pain. For them, I give thanks. Yet, I seek to go on to the summit, knowing I cannot get there without making it to this point. In his book, Spirituality Transformation within and without, on page 119, 122, 123, Swami Rama writes:

The more we understand the realities of life, the more we transcend the limitations of racial vanity, communal identities, and affiliation with a particular religion. When we rise above these limitations, our consciousness expands. We become part of the universe and the universe becomes part of us.

The human race is suffering from ego-born narrow-mindedness. Discrimination exists, based on religion, color, and nationality. In the same locality, people are being discriminated against just because they are European or Asian, black or white, Hindu or Muslim. As long as these man-made divisions exist in our society, there is no hope for peace and happiness. We must understand that we are born humans and all other identifications are superimposed on us later. Loving others and receiving love form others is our birthright. True freedom means loving all and hating none. In order to cultivate our humanity, we have to reach out to the hearts of our fellow beings. Political treaties and alliances are of little value unless there is a desire in every heart to overcome mutual differences, which have been artificially imposed by selfish political, social, and religious leaders.

Removing differences and moving from diversity to unity are the
essence of real spiritual practices. This process has to occur at every level of our individual and social lives. By realizing one reality
within all, we will be able to purify our hearts and minds. This purification can lead us to the experience of the divine light within. Once
we experience this inner truth, we will find ourselves to be part of
the universe, and the universe part of us.[65]

In order to transcend the limitations, of which Swami Rama
speaks, requires recognition of said limitations, and he implies that the
divisions among us are man-made. Therefore, it becomes necessary
to examine these divisions and seek to move beyond their limitations,
to transcend into the oneness of it all! Many would like the reality of
slavery to go away, or to suppress and not discuss it. However, that is
a man –made limitation, which has devastating effects on a people,
and humanity for that matter, and it must be addressed by the world,
in general, but primarily by African American men. If we can heal
ourselves of its effects, then, we can heal the world!

We chose to manifest as Black Men, knowing full well what that
carried with it. This was the path we chose towards our spiritual liberation. This is a reality that we must try to understand, confront, heal
and move through. We cannot go around it; we cannot suppress it,
paint it a different color or make it something that it is not! Our ancestors went through it, that we might be here to take full advantage of
this day and time. This is not a time for us to do nothing, other than
stand on the shoulders of our Ancestors and bring in a new day.

Let us continue to look at the effects of slavery on our psyche.
Many often wonder why is it so hard for Black men to open up and
talk. I have often wondered about this myself. There would be times
when my mate would question me, where upon I would totally shut
down and truly not be able to respond, even though I wanted to. I am

not a professional psychotherapist; we have many great therapists who are better qualified than myself to answer this question, however, I would like to offer the following. In her book, <u>A Life of Balance</u>, on page 11, Maya Tiwari writes:

> In the formative stages of life, when the ego is defenseless, protection by parents and teachers is necessary. When these primary guardians falter, the young mind, exercising its singular defense, insulates itself and blocks its natural outflow of expression. The result is the beginning of a weak ego, and oftentimes a lack of self-worth. As this life reaches early adulthood, certain patterns of defense and isolation have already formed. It is immensely difficult for this person to initiate the process of opening painful childhood wounds. These inflictions remain raw and unhealed, within the gray shelters of the mind until that individual finds the courage to expose the damaged self, or is forced by providence through a difficult passage, like a deadly disease, to face and accept the fragmented ego. This arks the beginning of the healing process.[66]

Now, let us take this statement and apply it to our capture in and around central Africa, with no protection by our parents, being held in the slave dungeons with no parents to protect us, in the bottom of the slaveships with no parents to protect us, our being sold on plantations with no parental protection and bring it all the way to today, 2003, with no parents to protect the majority of us. I would say, our young minds have insulated, over generations, and we have extremely weak egos, which is manifested in our preoccupation with superficial things to boost the ego. The wearing of designer clothes we cannot afford, the driving of expensive cars, and the like etc., while all the time being closed-up and sealed off from self. Therefore, we, as men, must find the courage to face our damaged self.

Yes, we have been damaged and it is time that we face it and heal the self. We must be willing to admit our fears, weaknesses, and, in turn, do what is necessary to heal. We must develop the courage to walk into the night of our own despair and find the light of God within. We must be willing face our own demons and not place the blame on anyone else. We must also be willing to forgive those who did not, or could not protect us, for they were victims of their own unfortunate circumstances. It is in the forgiveness that true healing begins. If we are men, then, we must understand that God has given us all we need to liberate ourselves. We have all that we need to step from under the shadows of psychological oppression and step into the world of universal ideals with a new vision for humanity. We have stood on these shores waiting for the return of the savior; little did we know that we were the saviors ourselves.

At this stage, the initiate is taken into self and asked to look at the pain he carries. This must and should be done in a safe, comfortable, ritualized setting. The following is but one example: If working alone, it is suggested that the brother take a bath with 2 lbs of Epsom salt and add to it eucalyptus oil. The reason for this bath is that Epsom salt draws the impurities out of the physical body. It, also, draws out the impurities from the aura. Eucalyptus oil is associated with the Yoruba Orisha Ogun, or, in Kemet, the deity Herukhuti. Both deal with cutting through obstacles and getting to the bottom line. They also both stand for raw masculine courage. Thus, this bath is designed to assist the brother in developing the courage to cut through his own illusions about the pain he carries.

He should soak in the tub for no longer that 11 minutes (Herukhuti's number) in water as hot as he can stand. Then, he should allow the water to drain out of the tub, while still sitting there, and envision all of his anxieties going down the drain with the water. He should put on lotion that contains coconut oil, which is associated with the Orisha Obatala or Ausar, both of which are associated with the God in us. Also, Obatala was the Chief of all Orisha. He stood for morality and wisdom and all the negating forces feared him. We want the brother to be protected from his own negating forces. After the bath, the brother should dress in white, sit in front of his shrine, if he does not have a shrine, he can take a white cloth, and place it in a safe spot. He should place and light a white candle on it, along with a white flower in a vase and a glass of water. He should pray to his God, and call to mind his ancestors for assistance in facing his pain. The brother should then sit in meditation and listen to the answers that come, take note, face them, then, lay out a plan of action for healing.

Healing can take many forms, so, the brother should take pride in seeking professional help. Today, there is a host of professional, spiritually sensitive, counselors available to assist. This ritual can be modified to accommodate a group of brothers, and, in fact, it even helps men to bond. The notion of facing our pain individually, and collectively, is frightening. That is why, from a ritual stand –point, we call on the energies of Ogun/Herukhuti and Obatala/Ausar. Most importantly, an understanding mate is the most important asset we can have. A woman who is open to spirit, comfortable in her womanhood, can do more in assisting us to heal than most doctors. The power of love can never be underestimated. There is a Yoruba saying, "the man is the head but the woman is the neck that turns the head." In our efforts to heal ourselves, at times, it requires that we take our heads and put them in the loving hands of our mate.

Another great aid in helping us to heal and bond is the sweat lodge, which is something that I cannot give enough value to. For those who are familiar with the sweat lodge ceremony, you know that you generally do four rounds, one for each of the directions (west, north, east and south.) Normally, when we are in the lodge, with only men, during the first round I will call on the Great Mother and invoke the spirit of the matriarchal mothers. I will, then, go around and have each brother give thanks for the women in his life. It never fails. Before we make the complete circle, a brother will begin to apologize to the females in his life for the pain he has caused them. Some men will begin to cry, open up and offer their own apologies. The energy, at times, becomes so strong, until we all are crying, purging and healing. This opens the door for further discussion regarding our pain once we complete the sweat and are back in the cabin or around the campfire.

It is amazing how the support, encouragement, and love the men offer each other, and how the presence of spirit is felt by all. Besides being the domain of spirit, another reason I believe the sweat lodge is so effective in helping men to heal is it challenges them. The intense heat is a tremendous challenge, therefore, if we are looking for a test, the sweat lodge provides it!

We cannot fear partaking in ancient rituals, following spirit and making the necessary modifications to meet our needs. As I said earlier, my sweats are a blend of Native American and African spirituality. The base will always be Lakota, with the spiritual essence of Yoruba and Kemet, and whatever else spirit guides me to with validation from the oracle. It is not that we seek to go off half-cocked, doing our own thing, no, far from that. We should always be open to healing and allow spirit to guide us, for I believe, with all my heart, that spirit is bringing to us Africans, born in America, healing rituals designed for the unique conditions of this country and our situation. The initiate is strongly encouraged to seek sweat lodge ceremonies in his area. The ceremonies are very sacred and private and most Native Americans are very reluctant to invite strangers. However, I am confident in the saying, "knock and the door shall be opened." If you are sincere, open and prayerful, the universe will open the door.

Want to do a little deeper healing? A healing that is trans generational? Then, the initiate is asked to read the following words of Ra Bena Saa Tur and heal:

With the Name of God, Most gracious, Most Merciful and in the Presence of Our Ancestors Both Seen and Unseen.

February 1, 2001

Over the years, the student had walked many paths and had seen much. He was ever on the alert, looking to experience different spiritual expressions. As a result of his initiation via death experience, he was not limited in his outlook, yet, there were times when he would get caught in the worldly illusions of limitations and staying on one path. This, at times, bothered the student greatly because he wanted so much to be stable, yet his spirit called him to experience life.

Pained from his going to and from different expressions of belief systems, the student knew it was time for him to make the journey to sit with the Ancestor of Ancestors, Ra Bena Sa Tur. This ancestor had come to him, years ago, and was always giving him guidance and direction. The student knew that going to see the great Ancestor was no easy undertaking, for he knew that Ra Bena Sa Tur, like his masters, would make him face the truth of himself. However, being an Ancestor of his made it just the more unsettling, for Ra Bena Sa Tur would make him look in his ancestral lineage for his answers and that was, sometimes, difficult to face. Like most people, the student had an image of himself, which was, at times, false and out of touch with reality. He knew that it was only through introspection that he could grow into the spiritually liberated being he desired to be.

The journey to the abode of Ra Bena Sa Tur was a pleasant one, filled with such wonderful natural sights. Deep in the forest of his mind was the dwelling of this great Ancestor; thus, it was an inward journey. The student had to pass the clutter of his mind, he had to get past his own illusions of self, his ego had to be surpassed and

REACHING BLACK MALES THROUGH SPIRITUALITY

his personality had to be subdued .The path to Ra Bena Sa Tur was one in which he knew he could not carry his worldly conditionings, for they were too heavy and of no use. So, deep into the forest of his mind, he journeyed, seeking this great Ancestor of Ancestors. Getting past his jealousy, his envy, his greed, and need for recognition was such, that kept him from getting to the abode of this ancestor. Struggling with these vices, fighting them, facing them and then allowing them to not control his life, was the hurdle that he had to get over in order to find the place of this great Ancestor. Over the years, the student had come to know that Ra Bena Sa Tur was the evolved Ancestor of his which was working and moving in his life. So, he knew it was time to go to this Ancestor and submit before him.

Finally, the student was able to get beyond his mind and its distracting activities to reach Ra Bena Sa Tur. Once in the presence of this Ancestor of Ancestors, the student laid down before him in full prostrate position in a show of submission and humility.

Student: Ancestor, please forgive me for being away for so long.

Ancestor: You have not been away, for we have always been with you, it is just that you have been so caught in the world of illusion until you failed to pay us any attention. Dear One, the universe is always here. It is when we get caught in the separateness that we think we are away.

Student: Ancestor, I come for assistance, for I seek to become spiritually realized, yet the thought of racism continues to bother me and I know it is holding me back.

Ancestor: How, so?

Student: When I think of what was done to our ancestors and how they suffered, it gets to me, makes me feel their pain, and I get angry.

Ancestor: That is how it should be, for that is what it was for. However, you must not allow your emotions to keep you for the point of this lesson.

Student: What is the point?

Ancestor: That all of this life is nothing more that God expressing itself, that this world is a place of karma and that we come here to pay karma for past deeds. Yet, you are looking at it through the eyes of the world and not through God's eyes. For all in this manifest world of illusion is paying karma. No matter how it looks to you, it is still the will of God.

Student: Then, why does it make me angry and upset?

Ancestor: Emotion and victimization. You are looking for someone to blame for your failure and your lack of effort in bringing about a change in your life and the universe. We, your ancestors, had to pay a price for the betterment of the world and ourselves. Yes, by the standards of this world of illusion, it was a terrible thing, but it all looks terrible when you look at it through your un-evolved eyes. Remember all must pay their karma, it is out of your hands, and all you can do is change you. Look into our lives and learn and seek to make yourself a better person. If you change your thoughts, you change the world, your world.

Student: I get so caught up in my thoughts and emotions. I think I am supposed to be mad about this, but, what do I do with the anger?

Ancestor: The anger is what destroys you. It produces poisons in the body and you actually destroy yourself. You must learn to release anger.

Student: How do I do that?

Ancestor: With Love!

Student: You mean, I am to love those that committed atrocities against my ancestors!!!? I am to love those who seek to keep me down!!!?

Ancestor: What is all of creation a manifestation of?

Student: It is all a manifestation of God.

Ancestor: Are you sure it is all a manifestation of God?

Student: Yes!

Ancestor: Then that means those who did this to your ancestors are a manifestation of God also ?

Student: Yes!

Ancestor: Are not we to love God as Our self?

Student: Yes!

Ancestor: Then, we are to love it all, for it all is a manifestation of God.

Student: Yes, I see, but it is a very hard lesson.

Ancestor: Yes, but that is the lesson you must learn in order to reach true spiritual liberation. Look at it, you hold white people responsible for what happened to us, but who was it that sold us into slavery in the first place?

Student: We did?

Ancestor: That is right, just like you stand around today and watch our young people kill each other for a few pieces of gold and money, your ancestors stood around and watched as we were sold off for a few pieces of gold and trinkets.

Student: This truth is hard to take.

Ancestor: Yes, it is because you like to exist in a world of make believe, a world of romanticism. Oh, your great ancestors. Yes they were great, but they were human, caught in the same illusions. They had their challenges to overcome. Besides, if nothing happens without the permission of God, then, who, in reality, should you be mad with?

Student: God?

Ancestor: That is correct, you should be mad at God. Yet, you have been too conditioned to face the truth. You are afraid of God. You will not go to God, for you do not know God. Now, go and seek to really understand God and its working in the universe.

With that, the student came back to consciousness of this reality and began the process of seeking to really understand God. How does one become aware of God, really? If God is everywhere and in everything, then, that means that God is in me, yet who am I? Am I this individual who exists in this world? Am I this body? Am I this mind? Or am I spirit, part of the Great Spirit? These are questions that the student pondered and searched himself to understand. What is the self?

As the student thought on these things, it came to him, if I am part of the Great Spirit, then everything must be a unity! I am part of that unity and my problems lie in my thinking that I am separate from everything. Oh! That is the illusion that is the trick, thinking that one is separate from all of creation. Yet, it is so very easy to get caught in that way of thinking because the I, the I, wants attention. It pains one to think that they are nothing more than being part of a greater whole. I want attention; I want to be somebody! Who is this somebody that I want to be? With that thought, the student could hear the voice of Ra Bena Sa Tur:

Dear One, such is the challenge of life, seeking to transcend the I and become conscious of the we. For it is all a manifestation of God, you are a part of it all, and it is found in everything. You are that tree, you are that flower, you are that bird, you are the wind, you are one with all that has taken on form, for beyond the form, it is all God. One of the challenges that manifested creation faces is begin caught in identifying with the form. Most think that they are the form, the form is only the vehicle God uses to express itself on this material plan. Yes, you are conscious, but conscious of what? You are conscious of the difference; the quest is to become conscious of the unity. Once you become conscious of the unity you will attain spiritual liberation. You see it is being caught in the form that you lose sight of the unity, it is in the unity that you find peace, peace of knowing God as God is, a divine unity that is expressing itself in a multitude of forms.

Dear One, do not get caught in the form, do not get caught in the separateness, for that is what is wrong with religion today.

They are all looking at the religious form, all trying to make their expression of God greater than the next. Just as you want to be somebody, all are trying to make their religion somebody. Ha! Ha! When in reality, it is only a form that spirit is trying to use in an effort to guide humanity to the oneness. Yet, you get caught in the form. For you who are un-evolved, it is all about form, my body, my ego, my personality, my profession, my religion, and my material things. So little time, do you devote to the unity. Even in your thinking of the races, you are caught in the illusion of form. While you are housed in this body, it is only the vehicle the spirit uses to travel on this earth plane.

Look at how there is such a wonderful variety of cars, or, as you say, automobiles on the earth plane. All are used to transport you around this earth. In fact, there are so many different forms of vehicles used as a means of transportation. Why should one argue as to what vehicle is better than the next. Some people will chose a Ford, others will chose a Honda, who is to say what person's choice is better than the next. It is the person's choice, the free-will of the person being expressed.

Such is the same with the races. You chose the vehicle, called body that you will use to transport you around this earth plane. The problem comes in when you get caught in the form of the vehicle. Spirit chooses the African body, spirit chooses the European body, spirit uses the Asian body, and spirit uses the Native American body, and so forth. You, as spirit, have chosen that body to transport you around. Just has each car had different instruments; your body has different instruments, however, the fundamental nature of the car is the same. Such is the same with you; the fundamental nature of humans is the same. Yet, they have a different path to travel towards the manifestation of the unity. You, as Africans born in America, with the bloodlines of so many others, have a particular path to walk and it is that path, your path that you must understand. You cannot compare your path to anyone else's path. It is like trying to compare one car to the next. In doing so, this sets up competition and identification with the difference, separation. In the identification with separateness comes the pain, confusion and the whole host of problems that keeps one from spiritual liberation. Dear One, we say to you, learn your path, follow your path, be happy in your path, for it will lead you to spiritual liberation.

Student: Ancestor, am I to follow one religious path?

Ancestors: Do not get caught in the form, for there is but one religion, it is seeking God realization. The different forms are but the different vehicles used to get to God realization. No matter what the form, no matter what the religion, it is to bring you to God realization and the understanding of the unity. It matters not if it is Christianity, Hinduism, Islam, Yoruba, Akan, Jainism, or whatever, it is all a form to bring you to God. However, just like you get caught in the difference of bodily expressions, you get caught in the difference of religious expressions. Think of it as being in a flower garden, all the flowers are beautiful, they all are wonderful and together they make up the garden. The different smells coming together make up a common smell in which you cannot identify one smell from another. All the religions are the flowers in the garden of God that will lead you to God realization. Dear One, we say to you, enjoy all of the flowers, do not choose one over the other. However, if you prefer a rose over a carnation, then it is ok, but one is no better than the other, they all are flowers. Come, enjoy God's religious garden. Sit with the flowers of Christianity, smell the roses of Islam, enjoy the carnations of Yoruba, dwell among the lotus of Hinduism, breathe the sage of Native American spirituality and walk the path of divine unity.

Dear One, we say to you, rest from the confusion of this world of il-

lusion, rest from the pain of difference and enjoy your manifest life in the unity, not the separation. Come to us; let us hold you in our love, keep you from being caught in the confusion that is driving mankind to such pain. For everything is moving so very fast, now, it is moving fast and so many are not able to keep up. Dear One, we say to you, follow your spirit, know your spirit, for there, in your spirit, will you find God. Dear One, we close now saying to you, it is the unity that brings the peace you seek.

4. Rites-of-Passage – Pathway to Manhood

While rites-of-passage is the central theme of this book, at this point, the initiate must begin to examine his inner thoughts about manhood and what he thinks manhood is. He must begin to look at his entire life and examine the models of manhood he had, who were the significant males in his life? Was there a father in his life? What effect did this have on him and his image of a man? How much of his current behavior has been shaped by these models? These are the questions that he must begin to ask himself. In those deep introspective moments he must ask himself "How comfortable am I with my manhood?" How comfortable am I on the job? How comfortable am I with my mate and others? Am I always seeking to prove myself to others? Am I in a covert, and overt, war with my mate, concerning my manhood? Am I threatened by her and her power? Do I fear my sensitive side? These are many of the questions we must ask and answer for ourselves.

If we approach these questions honestly, then the answers will determine our direction. It is said, "The first thing a seeker after truth must do is be truthful to themselves." The initiate should keep a journal on those questions, and his reflections, working with his innermost feelings, he will soon hear the voices of his ancestors, calling him to the initiatory experiences of old. He will begin to not fear the uncomfortable feelings of insecurity, but will embrace them and allow them to lead him to the rite-of-passage experiences. He will search out new models, make a commitment to change his behaviors, form strong bonds with like-minded men and he will no longer fear the power of his mate.

The deeper he journeys within, the further removed he becomes from the external definitions of manhood; he will begin to discover within himself, his reservoir of male energy, which has been waiting for his acceptance. He will discover the need to walk in balance with both aspects of himself (male and female). He will discover his true nature, yet he must walk in truth, never lying to himself. For the African American male, he will see that the men we think we are, is not who we are. He will discover the he is the product of centuries of dismantled manhood. He will hear the cries of the ancestral males, who hung from trees, calling him. He will hear their voices, saying, "we could not define ourselves as you can, we sacrificed ourselves that you could evolve in this time and define who it is you are in this day and time. It is time that you stand on our shoulders, reach back in our ancient past and bring forward models of manhood which will change the world." He will hear the ancestral males who were broken, calling him to stand tall, straight and strong as a new day sage, committed to living manhood as his ancestors lived it.

The student will understand, from a conscious perspective, that he will have to make progressive compromises in this society, but will make then from a point of certainty in who and what he is. He will, no longer, feel the pain of emasculation, when he makes a compromise on the job, at home, or in the streets. He will feel fresh energy of manhood moving through him and will rise, as a light to the world.

However, the first thing the student must do is go within, and truly examine who he is now, and who it is he wants to be. Therefore, he must answer the questions and submit to a rite-of-passage program. Joining other men in the reclamation of manhood. The student should greet the rising sun with open arms, for as the rising sun heralds a new day, this is a new day for him. This is the first day of his life, when he, with other men, will define manhood for themselves, based on the ways of their ancestors. He will feel the winds of change blowing in his life and, have the courage to follow the drummer he hears. The true seeker will be like the bee, which gathers pollen from all kinds of flowers, searching the different ancient definitions of manhood. Like the deer who finds a quiet place to graze, he will find a quiet place to digest all that he has gathered. Then, like a madman, he will go anywhere he pleases, for he will live like a lion, completely without fear! He will understand that a rite-of-passage is no more than the RIGHT to PASS to the next stage of life. He will understand that our ancestors paid the price that we might earn the RIGHT to PASS to the next stage.

Now, what is that right? The right to be able to express yourself as free men, a right our ancestors could not enjoy! The right to reclaim their religion, their God, and their way of live—a right that was denied to our Ancestors! The right to love and stay with your family, and have a stable marriage. A right our Ancestors did not have! Yes, my beloved brothers, the price has been paid and it is time for us to collect.

5. Spiritual Baths:

The initiate needs to understand that a spiritual bath is different from a regular bath and should be prepared, and administered, by a qualified Priest, or Priestess. Like the physical body that picks up filth, the aura and spiritual body can also become dirty and require cleaning.

Let me give you a working example. We talk about feeling 'vibes', the vibrations that people give off. You can go home and your mate is mad at you, they do not have to say anything, you can feel it. You feel the energy; your aura picks up the energy. Well, if you can feel and pick up the energy of your mate, what of the energy you might pick up at work? What of the collective energy of a town, a state, a country and a world? We are all picking up and sending out energy.

Have you ever been around a person and when they leave, you feel tired, but they feel good? They have dumped their negative energy on you and you are still carrying it. You go home in a bad mood and take it out on your mate, not understanding why? This energy must be removed, for the same reason we remove physical dirt – it is unhealthy! Many of us are spiritually sick and do not understand why? Part of it is that we are carrying negative energy.

Besides being a means of removing negative energy, a spiritual bath can center you, and open the channels of communication with your spiritual energies. Spiritual baths cleanse the soul and the spirit, help heal the wounds the soul is suffering and help to promote the healing of your being. We, as men in general, and African American men in particular, need healing. During this stage of the initiation process, the initiate is encouraged to consult a Priest, or Priestess concerning a spiritual bath. In most cases, the consultation will involve a divination, to determine the nature and ingredients of the bath. We say, enjoy your bath and the insights that will follow.

6. Mirror of Truth – identifying your masculine archetypes:

The Second College Edition, The American Heritage Dictionary, defines Archetype as: "An original model, or type, after which similar things are patterned; prototype."

Now, the question is, what is the original model after which we, as men, have been patterned? We know that we are modeled and patterned after the Creator of this wonderful universe; however, the universe is a manifestation of a multitude of forms. So, what is the masculine energy of God that we, as men, manifest? For that answer, it is necessary to journey back into ancestral history and search the annuals of self. This is a question that each male must answer truthfully for himself; however, he must be equipped with the necessary knowledge. Surely, if our ancestors could survive capture, the middle passage, slavery, segregation, and Jim Crow, we must be carrying some heavy male/female energy.

For example, in the Yoruba tradition, we all have a governing male and female energy known as Orisha. This male energy is seen as an archetypical form, manifesting in our actions. An individual may have the male Orisha, Ogun or Shango, as their governing male Orisha, thus, the person with Ogun energy will be found to be full of courage, quick to go to war, ready to stand up for and render justice. The Shango type will be very charismatic, a strategist, political leader and warrior King. The same can be seen in the Kemetic system of the Ausar/Auset Society, when they identify your incarnation objective, which shows the deity governing your incarnation this time. This is, somewhat, a general description, the initiate can do his own investigation and consultation with a priest, or priestess. Also, archetypes are found in the totem system among the Native Americans. Some men are found to carry the energy of the Hawk, the Bear, Eagle, Lion, and etc., all of which give one an idea of the personality of the man. It is up to the initiate to find out what is his masculine archetype, then find out how to live it in his life.

At this point in the process, the initiate is, again, encouraged to get a divination from a competent Priest, or Priestess, to determine his ruling male Orisha and incarnation odu/objective. Next, he should research and study the attributes of his male archetype, seeking to incorporate the qualities in his life. He must pay close attention to both the positive and negative qualities, for our archetypes are trying to tell us something, revealing to us what we should avoid and what we should seek to develop. It is important for him to understand both the historical and spiritual significance of these figures. Their spiritual significance will serve as a model for the initiates' continued growth and development. However, he must pursue wisdom, and seek assistance, in trying to understand the significance of his Orisha/ Deity archetype. It is a common mistake to take the spiritual symbolism of these archetypes as reality.

Being a priest of both Shango and Orunmila, I sought answers, because it is said that Shango had 435 wives and Orunmila also had numerous wives. My then, God Mother, Shango Obatoyo Olufuni, who first introduced me to the faith, explained it to me this way. She said, "They were not for sex, Shango was/is a warrior King and strategist, each wife had a secret which Shango needed in his battles." I also inquired of my Godfather, Baba Ifa Karade, who initiated me into Shango and Orunmila. In fact, on the eve of my Shango initiation, he explained it to me in his characteristic, wise, calm manner. He said, "Koleoso, maybe Shango is trying to tell you how not to be." That was all Baba Karade said and I got the message clearly.

I often think of the problems I would cause others and myself were I out here trying to manifest this attribute of Shango literally. No, it is about respecting and honoring the female energy in the universe, as it manifests in creation as woman. It is also about honoring the woman in self. I know most of you readers understand that as long as you respect and honor a woman, never seeking to cross the line, you will have a friend for life.

EL-HAJJ RAY RITES OF PASSAGE
7 Doors To Manhood Initiation

The following is a description of Orisha and Deity characteristics, which should serve only as a starting point for the initiated: The following information on Orisa, Spiritual Archetypes Guides, has been provided by Priestess Osunnike Anke:

Orisa
Spiritual Archetypal Guides

In Ifa, it is believed that nature and the Divine Creator (Olodumare) are One, and that all forces within nature are to be honored and revered as reflections of the 400 + 1 different aspects of Olodumare, manifesting within nature. These nature forces *(Orisa)* govern different aspects of the universe, such as the wind, volcanoes, the ocean, the moon, stars, the sun, mountains, trees, the earth, and each **Orisa** is imbued with their own *ase* (consciousness or life force). The word **Orisa** represents – the **Ori**, which means head, or consciousness, and **sha**, which means selected or chosen. So, the term **Orisa** means our selected consciousness and the *ase* of the **Orisas** symbolizes not only their archetypal expressions within nature but can also be found embedded within human consciousness. Therefore, we enter into an interdependence with these cosmic forces that has a direct influence on our very existence. This spiritually symbiotic relationship, is rooted in the belief that one's relationship to an **Orisa** begins even prior to conception. It is believed that the relationship between you and your primary **Orisa** are a part of one's sacred incarnation agreement. So, by being in alignment with one's primary **Orisa** is to honor and fulfill one's destiny. In this way, **Orisa** can also be experienced as emissaries of Olodumare.

This is further exemplified in the archetypal qualities expressed in the different characteristics of a particular **Orisa**. One should also be aware that these archetypes are spiritual forces also, known as angels, deities, and totems in other traditions, and carry many of the same universal attributes and functions. For example, if we say that someone is Omo (child of) Osun, then you will see expressed in their personality many of the different aspects of the **Orisa** Osun. That person's overall expression will be loving, joyful, artistic and seeking to bring harmony and beauty to various situations. You can also see the energy of Osun, expressed in nature, the beauty of different flowers in bloom in the spring, the sweet smell of fresh rain, just to name a few. Taking a closer look, you can see the energy of Osun expressed in human relationships. The attraction between all female and male species is the work of Osun. All of creation functioning in harmony, from the smallest cells to the great universe, is the creative expression of Olodumare, manifesting as Osun.

The **Orisa** also exhibit polarities and these polarities, when out of balance, create disharmony within nature and the individual. When one lives in alignment with the laws of nature, and the emissaries of the forces of nature we call **Orisa**, the balance between the mind, body and spirit can occur.

Earth Spirits	Air Spirits	Water Spirits	Fire Spirits
Ori	**Obatala**	**Osun**	**Shango**
Onile	**Esu**	Yemoja	Agayu
Ochossi	**Osun**	**Olokun**	**Ogun**
Osanyin	Oya		
A) Oduduwa			
Nana Bucan			

Orisa characteristics

The number of Orisa are quite extensive. This is a brief description of the 7 major Orisa archetypes.

Obatala – Color is white. Associated with mountains and the sky. Represents wisdom, purity, ethical standards and morality, calmness and patience. Obatala types need time alone, they prefer small groups, they have a strong sense of honor and justice, and they love ideas, staying at home, and enjoy seeking to understand why people do what they do. They must stay away from alcohol, and highly spiced foods. Obatala is the father, or chief, of all the Orisha and you will find them in leadership positions as well as bringing peace to situations.

Ausar – color is white. From a Kemetic perspective, Ausar carries the same attributes as Obatala. Ausar is the divine indwelling intelligence, the God aspect that is in us. Ausar represents unity, how all of creation is one.

Yemoja – Color is blue and white. Associated with water. Represents emotional caring and nurturance.

Osun – Color is yellow. Associated with water. Represents beauty, fertility, sensuality, creativity, and artistic abilities.

Oya – Color is purple/indigo. Associated with the wind and thunder. Represents change, and transformation through spiritual death.

Sango – Color is red and white. Associated with lightening. Represents male virility, transformation through fire, courage, and leadership. Shango types are very articulate, they look ahead for the probabilities of people's actions and deeds. Masculinity, Kingly, Stately, and protector are also attributes of Shango. His kemetic counterpart, Heru, represents the will, meaning that all his actions should be in accord with the will of God. Heru represents the leader, father , King . These types must avoid arrogance, being stubborn, full of pride, and being dictatorial, to name a few negative manifestations.

Ogun – Colors green and blue. Associated with metal. Represents justice, the law, and energetically clearing the path from obstacles that impede one's progress. Ogun has a warrior nature and represents force, strength, primal instincts and aggression. Ogun types are full of courage, always ready to go to war, sometimes without thinking. They are quick to stand up for justice. They love knives and weapons. They like to get to the bottom line and will make a way when there is no way. They dislike confinement and being bored. Kemetic Herukhuti-seeks to restore the laws of MAAT that have been broken. As a result, he is the judge. These types can be very quarrelsome, arrogant, and full of passion.

Esu/Elegba – Colors are red and black. Associated with being at the crossroads in life and operating from one's free will. Esu offers a myriad of possibilities and offers numerous opportunities to make healthy choices, while leaving us to accept the consequences of unhealthy choices. Esu is about communication and intellectual understanding. These types like sex, having fun, and being always in the know. They have many friends of the same gender. Esu/Elegba is the messenger of the Orisha and the Policeman of the Yoruba cosmology. Esu/Elegba is the one who opens the way and takes our offerings to the Orisha. His Kemetic counterpart, Sebek, stands for communication, being sharp and witty, and learns well from observation. They must be careful of being critical, and getting into people's business when not invited.

The initiate must bear in mind that we have only provided a partial description of the male orishas/deities to get you started on your search. It is as Baba Ifa Karade once said to me, "Koleoso, we cannot give people everything. They must go after it for themselves, that way, they will have the experience for themselves and experience is the best teacher."

So, my dear brother, commit yourself to understand your male archetype. Learn all you can about it and see its manifestation in your life. Welcome the positive and seek to eliminate the negative. Welcome to the world of self-declaration.

7. Turn Up the Heat – Sweat Lodge and Fire Walk:

Involved with any rites-of-passage/Initiation is a test of courage. The initiate is made to endure pain, deprivation and trial, all in an effort to prove himself worthy of dying as a child and being born as a man. He must earn the right to walk among the men of his tribe. The sweat lodge is an excellent mechanism for trials.

We have already spoken of the lodge on pages 15-20. Here, I would like to speak of its transformative power and how it can test an individual. This sacred purification ritual, in many respects, defies description. It has to be experienced, for not only is it a collective experience, but an individual one as well. One must pay attention to everything that is associated with the lodge from beginning to end, for the sweat lodge is the domain of great spiritual forces.

The lodge expands consciousness and allows one to see beyond the veil of their present reality. The heat becomes so intense until one comes face to face with death. In fact, many go into the lodge with one perspective and come out with an entirely new one on life. The lodge brings the initiate face to face with his/her inner fears and joys while bonding them with others in the lodge.

In the past 10 years that I have been conducting sweat lodge ceremonies, we have used the lodge as a vehicle for initiation. I have seen the toughest so-called, OG's, shrink under the heat, darkness, and fear of facing self. Then, I have seen 9 year olds sit and endure until the end with the Elders. This book does not contain enough room for me to express my gratitude to the "Great Spirit" for allowing me to be a custodian of this sacred ceremony. We view the lodge as the sacred womb of our Mother, in which we return to be purified and renewed. It is an experience that cannot be analyzed, or quantified. It must be experienced.

When we are in the lodge with only males, during the first round we invoke the energy of the Great Mother. Each brother is asked to give thanks for the women in his life. Without fail, before we get all the way around the circle, some brother will begin to ask forgiveness to the women he has wronged. Every male in the lodge will bear witness and join in. Before too long, brothers are crying and praying for forgiveness. At this point, you can feel the maternal energy in the lodge and from that point on, we have a wonderful transformative experience.

By the time we have completed four rounds the men are renewed and resurrected. Then, there are those special times when we will do an extra round and chant to Ogun/Herukhuti, the orisha/deity of fire and courage. We reach such a high-energy state until we will leave the lodge and run back and forth through the fire! The men are amazed that they actually do it. Talk about a confidence builder. I recall one young man saying, "I have just completed five rounds of intense heat and ran through the fire. There is no reason I cannot pass my final exams!" He went on to pass his exams and graduate. Several of our local fraternities have used the lodge as an initiation experience. I recall several of them commenting, "this was worse than anyone beating on me because I had to deal with me, straight up."

Whatever the reason, the sweat lodge stands as the perfect vehicle for purification, transformation, and resurrection of the human spirit.

The initiate is strongly encouraged to find a sweat lodge ceremony in his area and take part in it.

B. CLEANSE & PURIFY

1. What's eating you- the effects of food on your nature: It is safe to assume that if you are reading this book then you, more than likely, have a good idea concerning diet and how food affects the body. In fact, many of you can teach me. I would like to say that the body is of the earth and, as we seek to honor Earth Mother, we must give honor to our bodies. The damage we have done to the earth is the same damage we do to our bodies.

It is something to watch, as a man will have a love affair with his car, making sure he puts the correct oil in it, the correct gas and correct inflation of the tires. This is a wonderful thing to see, yet the same man will put all kind of JUNK in this fabulous machine called body! This body is one of the greatest gifts we, as men, can have, for it is our vehicle that transports us through this dispensation. It is our earthly car, designed to carry our spirit in this life. I say to you my beloved brothers, treat your body better than you treat your car, because you can purchase another car, but you cannot purchase another body.

Spend time with your body and learn how foods affect you. Do you have an addiction to sugar, coffee, etc.? Learn what brings the maximum benefit to you and your body. For those who are interested in seeking more knowledge concerning the diet and the body, may I suggest taking a look at Ayurvedic Nutrition.

My wife suffers from Multiple Sclerosis, of which they say there is no cure. Yet, I was guided to take her to the RAJ, an Ayurvedic spa in Iowa, and in four days they had her walking again! After an additional visit she has been able to manage her disease. I know this 5000 year-old healing system works. Ayurveda is a healing system that was given to the world by the Africans who settled in southern India. They gave to the world the Indus Kush civilization. There are so many who do not know the African origins of these great healing sciences, the origins of which are important to this work of reaching black males through spirituality. There are great healing sciences found in India, a place of tremendous spirituality.

The ancient spiritual seers stated that one walking the path to spiritual liberation must observe certain ethical and lifestyle principles, among them are cleanliness, contentment, non-violence and truthfulness. Therefore, those of us who claim to walk the spiritual path must always seek truth and uphold it. This seems to apply to all aspects of human existence and all areas of knowledge; thus, seeking the truth of history must be a part of this quest. It is one thing to walk this spiritual path and seek to be in harmony with creation, yet quite another thing to walk this path and deny history. Doing so causes so much pain and destruction, because we effectively destroy the history of a people. It seems also to deny history, particularly the history of spiritual truths and origins, which means one is walking this spiritual path in a lie. We are delusional. Along this path we are cautioned against self- delusion. If one of the ethical principles of this path is 'non-violence' then it is possible that denying the history of a people could amount to an act of violence. According to the <u>Second College Edition The American Heritage Dictionary</u> the meaning of ' non-violence' is "1. Lack of violence 2. The doctrine, policy, or practice of rejecting violence in favor of peaceful tactics as a means of gaining esp. political objective." Violence is defined as: "1. Physical force exerted for the purpose of violating, damaging, or abusing. 2. An act or instance of violent action or behavior. 3. Intensity or severity, as in natural phenomena; untamed force. 4. The abusive or unjust exercise of power. 5. Abuse or injury to meaning, content, or intent." Violent; is defined as, "1. Marked by or resulting from great physical force or rough action. 2. Showing or having great emotional force; 3. Severe; intense. 4. Caused by unexpected force or injury rather than natural causes. 5. Tending to distort or injure meaning, phrasing or intent."

Now, one could argue that by 'non-violence' the ancient sages meant ' lack of violence', as it relates to physical violence. This is well and good, but I do not consider myself qualified to interpret what state of non-violence the sages were speaking of. I am just taking the concept of non-violence and juxtaposing it with the denial of history, for we should not forget, there is also mental and spiritual non-violence and violence. One can see that it is an act of 'violence' to deny historical fact.

As African American men, struggling to gain a healthy self-image and concept, and in light of the great healing wisdom found in yoga, Ayurvedic sciences, meditation, etc., it is truly a violent act for us to distort history. Violent here meaning, "5. Tending to distort, or injure meaning, phrasing or intent."

As one reads the works of today's authors on the subjects of yoga, mediation, Ayurveda, etc., as they write of the history of these great sciences, nothing is mentioned of the people who gave these sciences to the world. Nothing is spoken of the Africans who inhabited the Indus Valley. As Ra Un Nefer Amen states in his book, Metu Neter Vol.1 on page 39:

> Very few people realize that the yoga teachings that are being dis-seminated throughout the world are fundamentally a creation of Africans. Hinduism, as we know it today, is a blend of prehistoric Western European religion, with many systems extracted from the original African cultural base.

> The earliest evidence of yogic practice date back around 3000 B.C. Figurines of men seated in the Lotus pose, and symbols of Shiva and Shakti,- the main symbols of ancient Black Dravidian spiritual culture were found in the excavated ruins of the two oldest centers of civilization in Indus Valley; Harappa, and Mohenjo Daro.[67]

Perhaps, if the meaning of 'violent' is, "5. Tending to distort or injure meaning, phrasing or intent." Then, is it a violent act to write volumes of books on the history of these sciences and make no mention of its African origins, or distort the meaning by saying the systems were brought to India by the Aryans? Is it not a violent act to distort, or in-jure meaning, in relation to spiritual history? If so, and in light of such historical falsifications, how can we say we are walking in the path of the sages in reference to being 'non-violent and truthful?'

In their book, Ayurveda Nature's Medicine on page 9, Dr. David Frawley and Dr. Subhash Ranade write:

By the third millennium BCE, Ancient India contained the world's largest urban civilization, evidenced by such large cities as Mohenjodaro, Harappa and Dholavira. These sites extended from the Ganges in the east to Afghanistan in the west and from the coast of Iran to the region of Bombay. Originally called the "Harappan " or "Indus" civilization, it is now being renamed the "Sarasvati" or "Indus-Sarasvati" civilization because the great majority of its many sites occur on the banks of the long defunct "Sarasvati" river.[68]

We know, according to Ra Un Nefer Amen and numerous other scholars, that the inhabitants of this large urban civilization were black. It makes one wonder if the move to 'rename' the area carries with it the same intent that placing Egypt in the so-called Middle East carried? By placing Egypt in the so-called Middle East, it took it out of Africa, thus, no association with Africa. By renaming the Indus civilization Sarasvati, it would further disassociate it with the black Dravidians. Doing so could be classified as a violent (abusive or unjust exercise of power) non-violent (peaceful tactic as means of gaining esp. political objective) act. It is all designed to write Africans out of history and deny us our legacy.

Why is this truth so important in the context of this book? In a perfect world, a world predicated on spiritual unity, we would all know that we are the same consciousness manifesting itself on so many different levels and forms of creation. However, this is not a perfect world and the affect of racism has taken its toll on humanity. We cannot hide behind spirituality and pretend that all is well, for it is not. Racism rears its ugly head time and time again in the most subtle forms and in the most unexpected places. One would never expect to find it among spiritual seekers and healing practitioners, but it is there. In the book , Dalit The Black Untouchables of India, by V.T.Rajshekar on page 43, he writes:

The Dalit were the original inhabitants of India and resemble the African in physical features. It is said that India and Africa were one land mass until separated by the ocean. So both the Africans and the Indian Untouchables had common ancestors. Some portion of these came to found the Indus Valley Civilization. These original inhabitants of India put up a strong fight against the Aryan invaders. However, the latter, working through deceitful means, defeated the innocent but hard-working original inhabitants who had built the world's most ancient civilization in the Indus Valley.[69]

Why is there a persistent need to try to write Africans out of history? If another ethical principle of this path is to 'speak the truth', then why is not the truth told regarding the African presence in this part of the world and Africa's contribution to these great sciences? What is the fear? Is it the same fear the former American or Western Hemisphere slave masters had regarding allowing the slaves to read? That they would one day learn who they really were? For those of you who are familiar with the Kemetic story of Ausar and Set, you may recall that it was Set who used deceit to defeat Ausar. Also, the Honorable Elijah Muhammad told us our Ancestors were tricked into coming to this country; the traders deceived those who sold us into slavery. We are living in a time when the truth must be told and the record set straight. V.T. Rajshekar goes on to say:

The original inhabitants who fought and were enslaved were kept outside village limits. They became Untouchables (Scheduled Castes). Those who fled to the forest and hill became tribal (Scheduled Tribes). The invading Aryans were nomads, barbarians, without a civilization. It was they who enslaved women and destroyed the Indus Civilization, introducing patriarchal gods to the, previously matriarchal, original peoples.[70]

Thus it seems that the Biblical passage, "The people who walk in darkness have seen a great light," has more than one application. This can be applied to the Dalits as well as Africans born in America. On page 54, V.T. Rajshekar says "So, the Indian Untouchables are languishing-unsung, unwept. This is the real picture of the original black inhabitants of India, the rulers of India who founded the world's most ancient civilization (Indus Civilization) of Harappa and Mohenjodaro."[71]

It seems that no matter where you look, people of African heritage are isolated and denied their place in history and the world. While many may read this and become upset, when truth is hidden for so long, it causes a paradigm shift in which many care not to engage. It would mean that history would have to be rewritten. Let's look at an example of what is taking place. In the book , In Search of the Cradle of Civilization, by George Feuerstein, Subhash Kak and David Frawley, page 140, it says:

> Furthermore, scientifically speaking, there is no such thing as an Aryan and a Dravidian race. Strictly speaking, the so-called Aryans and the so-called Dravidians are members of the same Mediterranean branch of the Caucasian race. The darker skin color of the peoples living nearer to the equator may be no more than an adaptive mechanism in response to the hotter climate.[72]

With all due respect to these great scholars and their work, are we to believe such an adolescent explanation? To take their reasoning would mean that the Eskimos should be pale white, due to climatic adaptation to the snowy climates. Alternatively, why is it that Africans born in America, living in theses climatic conditions, are still producing dark skinned offspring? To follow the same reasoning, can we conclude that the Africans would also be dark skinned Caucasians? No, we need to look at the truth and have the courage to stand on it. It is important to look at the damage that is being caused and the continued division that exists today, as a result of our taking spiritual truths and clothing them in our own personal agendas.

There is a need for so-called spiritual scholars to come together and agree on the truth. In the book, <u>African Presence in Early Asia</u>, edited by Ivan Sertima and Runoko Rashidi, on page 83, Wayne Chandler writes:

> At this juncture, clarification must be made as to the racial stratifications arranged within Indian history. As previously noted, the original layer consisted of Ethiopian Blacks known as Negrito. The second element, later introduced, was that of the Proto-Australoid. Bharatiya describes these people as black and platyrrhine (having a broadnose with widely separated nostrils). With the Negrito, this race may once have covered the whole of India; a genealogical offshoot would later generate the aborigines of Australia. The merging of these two culturally diverse but monoracial groups- the Ethiopian Negrito and the Proto-Australoid- produced the people of the Indus Valley civilization.[73]

In fact, Chandler goes on to identify a total of six racial groups in India.

Therefore, it is important for us to revisit the truth and accept it. This truth would also mean that Africans, born in America, would have to continue to stand up, take responsibility for their lives and stop blaming others. We have a grand and glorious history. The more we accept this, and seek to live it, the less time we have to blame others. I give thanks for our scholars and historians who have paid the price that we might read their works and once again understand who we are, and the responsibility we have to live the ways of our ancestors. There is much truth in the phrase of Jesus, "the truth will set you free." Knowing that we have an ancestral tie to these great civilizations and healing systems is personally liberating for me. As with most seekers and African American males, we like the heavy sciences, the deep stuff. Well, when you begin to dig deep into the Vedic, Yogic, Kemetic, and other spiritual sciences, it can do nothing but humble you, causing you to fall on your knees and give thanks to God for opening your eyes.

These are great spiritual healing systems, which can assist in the healing of African American men, and all men for that matter. If African American men knew and understood their historical connection to these sciences, maybe they would study and become practitioners, thus, helping to heal themselves and the world. Also, if we are going to walk in the footsteps of the ancient sages, then we must promote the truth. As the Native Americans say, "I come to you with open hands and straight eyes." I have nothing to hide. Let us no longer hide the truth!

On the subject of Ayurveda, Dr. Vasant Lad writes in his book, The Complete Book of Ayurvedic Home Remedies on page 1:

Ayurveda is the art of daily living in harmony with the laws of nature. It is an ancient, natural, wisdom of health and healing, a science of life. The aims and objectives of this science are to maintain the health of a healthy person and to heal the disease of an unhealthy person. …Ayurveda is a profound science of living that encompasses the whole of life and relates the life of the individual to the life of the universe. It is a holistic system of healing in the truest sense…As a science of self-healing, Ayurveda encompasses diet and nutrition, lifestyle, exercise, rest and relaxation, meditation, breathing exercises, and medicinal herbs, along with cleansing and rejuvenation programs for healing body, mind and spirit.[74]

Again, in their book, Ayurveda Nature's Medicine, Drs. Frawley and Ranade write:

Ayurveda is based upon a deep communion with the spirit of life itself, upon a profound understanding of the movement of the vital force and its manifestations within our entire psychophysical system.

We are not simply an accident or a design of chemistry but an expression of a living consciousness that is universal in nature, which is inherently wise and which has the power to balance and transform itself once its nature is understood.

Ayurveda is a humanistic and person-centered medicine that shows us how to find our own natural health and unfold our deeper energy potentials for the fullness of life, in which drugs and hospitals can become peripheral not primary.

However, Ayurveda is not only a system of medicine in the conventional sense of the methodology for treating disease. It is a way of life that teaches us how to maintain health and improve both our energy and our awareness- how to live life to our full human and spiritual potential.[75]

The major premise of this writing has been about healing the male spirit and seeking to understand our place in the grand scheme of things, giving us the motivation to strive to live our lives to the full human and spiritual potential. It appears that a healing system, such as Ayurveda can assist in the process.

To get a general understanding of the basic philosophical principles behind Ayurveda and how it relates life to the universe, I have attached an outline developed from the book: A LIFE OF BALANCE, by Maya Tiwari. The majority of the quotes are taken directly from Maya Tiwari. At this point the initiate is encouraged to research and write about each aspect of the outline. This will help to develop a deeper understanding of the philosophy behind Ayurveda and inspire additional research.

OUTLINE:

AYURVEDA: A LIFE OF BALANCE   by Maya Tiwari

CHAPTER 1: COSMIC ROOTS

i. Ayurveda is rooted in Veda scriptures; which date back to 1500 b.c.

   A. Of the four Veda; Rig Veda and Atharva Veda give
      information concerning healing, surgery, and longevity.
   B. *Rishis* compiled the Vedas- they received this information
      and instruction internally.
      1. *Rishi* means 'seer'
      2. They would 'see' the truth via contemplation and
         meditation.
      3. They received this information from the cosmos

   C. Ayurveda arose from the microscopic examination of the
      macroscopic; the silence which contains all knowledge and
      sacred memory of all time- our cognitive memory.
      1. Ayurveda is also a science of living
      2. Ayurveda cures by removing the causes of disease.

   D. From the **Rishis**, we are learning: transgression against
      Nature's laws against our wisdom is the cause of all disease.
      Wonder if the oracles can be used to let one know which
      natural and spiritual laws have been transgressed?
      (emphasis mine)
      1. Disease may be physical or karmic in origin.
      2. Physical disease is the result of: improper diet,
         engaging the senses too much, ignoring the cycles of
         the seasons or our age.

3. Karmic disease results from incorrect actions in this or previous life times.

E. The Physical body is the only part that dies.
   1. Our psychic instrument/*Antahkarana* is composed of intellect, mind , and ego/*ahamkara*.
   2. They all travel with us, from life-time to life-time, until we reach final liberation/*Moksha*.
   3. Physical and karmic transgressions cannot be separated;
   4. As long as we ignore a Karmic condition, we cannot be whole
   5. As long as we ignore a natural Law, we will remain fragmented.
   6. Ayurveda removes the cause of disease by righting or correcting these transgressions (ignoring Karmic conditions and natural law) and reestablishing balance to our system.

F. To treat our Cosmic nature we must address all the component Parts.
   1. They are three according to Ayurveda; physical, astral and causal in western terms, they are the body, mind and soul.
   2. The *Antahkarana*/ psychic body exists in the astral/mind body
   3. The physical body is a vehicle for practicing *sadhanas*, or wholesome activities.
   4. Food contains the memory of all time; it is a very potent medium for bringing balance to our being.

G. From Pure Consciousness arose the sound 'OM'
   1. In turn, the Five Great Elements took birth; space,

earth, water, air and fire.
2. These five elements took the form, in the human body, of the three **Doshas**, or body humors
3. It is from these three **Doshas** that our individual constitution / **Prakriti** is formed.
4. In identifying with these three primal elements, we create a bridge back to the sky.
5. According to the Veda, human birth is the most difficult to attain in the karmic cycle. *This is why we must appreciate this life, honor and value it.*
6. Human birth is the greatest act of transformation that a human being experiences.
7. Free will, self-reflection and distraction are divine birth rights.
8. Distraction is the cause of confusion and chaos. *Distraction from our purpose of being.*

H. Presently we are preoccupied with our individual selves and external pursuits that distance us from the throb of planetary harmony.
1. The universe is a cohesive entity, held in majestic motion by space and her magic grasp.
2. To be obsessed with our quest of personal uniqueness and excellence, while ignoring this life giving space and all she contains, is to behave like immature adolescents.
3. To be obsessed with the woes of our planet and lose sight of the true self, which is **Consciousness** and **Awareness**, is equally immature.

I. According to the Vedas – the entire body is renewed every seven years:
1. Disease persists beyond these cycles of renewal

because we cannot make the transition from separate
and experiential selves into the whole state of
cognition.
2. We are prisoners, trapped by the concepts of time and
space; living in the past and future and not the
PRESENT.
3. Endless and timeless present is always with us and
filled with possibilities.

J. According to the Vedas – The conscious self is referred to as
ATMAN, or the Indwelling Spirit *(Ausar?)*
1. This conscious self, or atman, is a source of true
balance
2. Health is the solid union of mind, body and spirit.
3. Health is also the integration of self with nature,
family and all living beings.
4. Fragmentation is the source of all illness; we must live
a holistic life.

K. Dosha – " that which has a fault", a system quick to change.
This is the definition given by the Ancients to our
experiential nature.
1. We are not meant to be perfect; *consciousness* is the
only perfection.
2. Every manifestation is essentially endowed with
change.
3. Aspire to live a life of balance, not perfection
4. Through our state of fragmentary, imperfect existence,
we can learn how to invite the cognitive self.
5. Via cognitive self, we can approach the conscious self,
or Atman.
6. Aspire to knowledge of self as being unified with the
nature of the absolute. *IT IS ERRONEOUS AND*

*BURDENSOME TO ATTEMPT TO MAINTAIN
A PERFECT BODY, PERFECT LIFE AND
PERFECT HEALTH. THE DOMAINS OF SUCH
STRIVING STEAL THE VITAL FORCE FROM
LIFE.* **WE ARE TOO BUSY TRYING TO 'BE'
PERFECT UNTIL WE NEVER JUST 'BE'
PRESENT IN LIFE IN THE NOW.**
7. Ayurveda is the pursuit of balance. A life of balance
has no extremes and very little fragmentation.

A HEALTHY AHAMKARA (EGO)

A. The Vedas define Ahamkara (ego) as the individual self, the
vehicle bestowed on each of us at birth to facilitate our
particular life's journey.
   1. It is referred to as EGO, but not in the Freudian sense
   of the word.
   2. Ahamkara (ego) is the essence of remembering self,
   as an aspect of Antahkarana (psychic instrument), that
   is refined through the process of multiple births.
   3. The Ahamkara (ego) contains, both the individual self,
   with its experiential memories of this life, and
   cognitive self, with its collective memories of all time
   past, present and future.
   4. Each life is a journey towards the Atman (indwelling
   Spirit). It is the Ahamkara (ego), through the cognitive
   memory, that is the bridge to the knowledge of Atman.
   5. Meditation, or practicing sadhanas, particularly food
   sadhanas, help to invoke cognitive memory which
   opens the doors to the timeless past and future and an
   intrinsic knowing of the past.
   6. Ahamkara (ego) is conditioned, from life to life,
   through conception in the womb. Ego's identity is

influenced by
   a. maternal ovum
   b. paternal sperm
   c. time and season of conception
   d. state of mother's womb
   e. foods and emotions of the mother
   f. seasons through which the embryo grows
7. The core of Ayurveda science of health is based on our inborn constitution/Prakriti;
8. Karmic, or causal, factors also affect our individual birth.
9. Ahamkara(ego) registers each & every behavior, conscious or unconscious, from the inception of each life.
10. Ahamkara (ego) controls the million of cells of the immune system.
11. A clear, fresh, experiential and cognitive memory helps to safe-guard the organism against the invasion of mental and physical disease.
12. When the Ahamkara (ego) is displaced, fragmented, or shifted from its primal source of universal at one-ment, it leaves the immune process vulnerable and volatile, which is the cause of ill health.
13. The ego is defenseless in the formative years, thus it needs the protection of parents and teachers. *This is seen in the African concept "it takes a village to raise one child." The entire village provides protection for the defenseless ego.(emphasis mine)*
   a. when the primary guardians falter, the young mind exercises a primary defense of insulating itself and blocking its natural flow of expression.
   b. the result is a weak ego and lack of self worth
   c. it is difficult for the person to face early wounds;

they must find the courage to do so, or are forced by providence, via deadly disease, etc., to face and accept the fragmented ego.

    d. Facing the fragmented ego marks the beginning of the healing process.

14. The practice of reparative sadhanas and a meditative life are necessary to become conscious and alive to each moment.

15. Sadhanas can help us attain a constant awareness of the whole cognitive self.

16. Sadhanas mean: wholesome, everyday practice observed in accordance with cyclical rhythms of nature; spiritual practice that awakens the power of awareness; healthy, joyful response to life.

17. The process of healing may take many lifetimes

18. External pursuits of health are a waste of time and energy

    a. There is no alternative to the process of achieving salubrious well-being. However, this is hard work.

    b. Our healing begins with our forgiving our protectors, who were also helpless prey to their own difficult circumstances.

    c. The greatest health of all is acceptance of ourselves, as we are.

    d. The accomplishment of inner quiet, signifying peace of mind, removes years of aging.

    e. Nurturing the wounds of the ego can cause time to reverse itself.

    f. Immortality is maintained by living in the present, without moments or minutes. This is the foundation for holistic health.

EL-HAJJ RAY RITES OF PASSAGE
7 Doors To Manhood Initiation

It is important that the reader understand the information presented represents only a minute fraction of a fraction of the body of knowledge known as Ayurveda. It is a lifetime of study and well worth the effort. I am a beginning student. I give thanks for the great seers and sages of the past and present for giving to the world such profound wisdom, for placing in our hands the very tools that can assist in our total liberation from the shackles that continue to hold us in bondage. It is wisdom such as this that opens the initiate to a new way of viewing reality and gives them the opportunity to take full control of their lives.

It was once said by Prophet Muhammad, (God be pleased with him): "If you have your health and peace of mind, then you have heaven." It is so important for us to be in the best of health, that way, we can channel the higher vibratory frequencies which allows us to bring back such profound wisdom. It is my firm belief buried beneath the physical, mental and spiritual oppression, suffered by Africans, born in America, is a wealth of spiritual knowledge waiting to be born.

Think of it, what great spiritual systems were conceived in the hulls of the slave ships? What spiritual systems have been incubating in the psyche of African Americans? The work of Ra Un Nefer Amen attests to this as well as the work of Baba Ifa Karade of the Yoruba tradition. Both men have reached deep within their ancestral memory, mastered the traditional systems, blended it with modern-day reality, and have given to the world a new view. How many more are out there, waiting to be freed from, as Dr. Akbar says, "The Psychological Chains of Slavery?"

May God, the Divinities and the Ancestors bless you as you seek to regain your total physical, mental and spiritual health.

2.Who do you think you are? – Your beliefs, values and thoughts.

While there are any number of excellent books available dealing with the subject of the mind and positive thinking, there is a need to seek to understand the mind, in general, and who we really are. Are we our thoughts? Are we our beliefs and values? Or, are these the clothing we wear? On page 7 of this volume, we spoke of the 'Self', the 'Divine Self' and 'Divine Consciousness'. Now, how do our beliefs, values and thoughts tie into this? The answer requires an understanding of the mind, its function and relationship to consciousness. According to Dr. David Frawley, in his book; <u>Ayurveda and the Mind</u> on page 110:

> The mind coordinates the five senses and their data. It functions as the screen on which sensory data is gathered and scrutinized. Through the mind, for example, what the eye sees is correlated with what the ear hears. Otherwise, the data coming from the different senses would remain separate and disorganized.
>
> The mind, itself, is the sixth sense organ because through it we take in ideas and emotions- mental impressions. When we read a book, for example, the mind is also functioning as a sense organ, taking in emotional and mental information. All our sensory inputs involve some mental and emotional component. Similarly, the mind is the sixth motor organ and rules over the other five. As an organ of action, it is our main means of expression in the outer world. Only what we have first formulated as a mention intention can we express through our motor organs...The mind is the central circuit board for both sensory and motor organs. It is like our mental computer, while the senses are its software.[76]

Now, if the mind is the central computer, then a computer can only function to the extent of its programs. How have our mind computers been programmed as men, particularly Black men? If the senses are the mind's software, then, what kind of software are we running in our mind-computers? For the most part, we have been programmed by this western world of illusion, programmed to act and behave in a manner other than self. Our programs contain little or no, knowledge of self. Thus, when we come in contact with self- knowledge, we do not know how to respond or act. If we do act, we act in a manner contrary to our own self -interest.

In terms of the sensory software that we run in our mind computers, all that we see, hear and touch (feel), in relationship to being a black male in this society, is negative. If the mind is gathering and scrutinizing this data, what is the conclusion the mind comes to in regards to being a black male in this society? The data, as given by this world, is telling us that "you are no good and not wanted." Now, if the mind is also an organ of action, our means of expression in the outer world, what are our actions as black men telling the world? Are they saying that we have accepted our programming, which we have scrutinized all the sensory data concerning how no good we are and now we will cut it out!

Knowing this then, we, as men, have an excellent opportunity to change our programs, get new software, and live a liberated life. It is time that we take control of what our senses filter to our minds. We must watch what we see, hear, taste, touch and smell, in reference to black manhood. Decide today that you will reprogram self. In fact, for the next 21days, decide on a behavior that you want to change and seek to replace it with a new and better behavior. Ra Un Nefer Amen says that it takes 21 days to change a behavior.

At this point the initiate is to take inventory of what is fed to his senses concerning black manhood. He should make a list of both positive and negative sensory input concerning himself and black manhood, seeking to eliminate the negative and stress the positive. Look at the company he keeps, the places he goes, what he eats and etc. All of this is having an effect on his mind computer, influencing his external behavior.

3. A Man's Best Friend – Phallic Purification Rituals:

This section grew out of an experience provided to me by my wife, Yoruba Priestess, Osunnike Anke. Following a very difficult and draining sweat lodge ceremony, she informed me that she could sense that I was pulling a lot of energy from my groin area. This was quite true, because the lodge was full of young, aggressive, powerful young males with egos as big as America (smile)! Their energy was like dealing with wonderful wild horses. After the ceremony I was, needless to say, drained. She instructed me to take a bath in Epsom salt. She informed me that she had been given a ritual from Spirit that would help to restore my energy. After the bath, I met her in our shrine-room, at which time she lit some charcoal and placed herbs on it. She instructed me to kneel over it so that my genitals could be consumed by the herb rich smoke. Using a "Hawk" fan, she gently fanned the smoke and warmth around my genitals, instructing me to relax and visualize my energy being restored. Needless to say, it was one of the most invigorating experiences I have ever had. This experience demonstrated to me just how little I knew about my genitals. Yes, I knew what most of us know about our genitals, yet I knew so little of their 'spiritual' sensitivity and the need for 'spiritual ' purification and care.

Think of the need for us to purify our genitals. Think of the places we have taken this highly sensitive organ, in the name of so-called manhood. Think of the unhealthy energies we have emitted and absorbed, in the name of sexual conquest. It reminds me of the scene in *Dances With Wolves* when they came to the area during the buffalo hunt, where the buffalo were indiscriminately killed, skinned, and the carcasses just left to rot. Think of the women we have skinned, destroyed, and left behind as we go off to the trading post of macho stories in an effort to impress other sexual poachers like ourselves.

How many of us really understand the great wisdom of the Ancients, when they instructed us on semen retention during intercourse? Why was the Egyptian God 'MIN' depicted with an erected phallus? Do we know, or understand, the damage we do to ourselves by ejaculating numerous times a night, or week?

According to Muata Ashby in his book, "Egyptian Yoga" page 124:

Horus in the form of Min, symbolizes that stage in spiritual development when sexual energy is controlled and transformed into spiritual energy ...The God Min is usually depicted with an erect phallus, holding a flail in his right arm. Min represents the erectile, creative force of the universe that is latent in every human being (female and male), from which life springs...If controlled and sublimated, this creative, generative force could transform one into the heights of creation, but, if misused, such as in overindulgence of physical sexual activity, either in thought or action, it will erode the higher spiritual capacity. For reasons of physical health and spiritual strength, it is important to aquire the proper amount of sleep, nutrition and to observe the practice of sexual energy sublimation.[77]

For many of us, it is our sexual overindulgence that leads to lack of mental clarity and dis-ease. It is said that sperm is 10 times richer in nutrients than blood; therefore, with our sexual overindulgence, we are bleeding ourselves to death! One wonders, why so much overindulgence? Is this a carry-over from slavery, in which a man's worth was determined by his ability to produce children? Is sex the only comfort and joy we have in our lives? Is our sexual conquest a definition of our manhood in this modern age? No matter what the cause, the negative effects are apparent. Dr. David Frawley and Dr. Subhash Ranade write in their book, Ayurveda Nature's Medicine, on page 112:

> To gain true knowledge, living a self-controlled life is essential. If the sense organs are properly controlled, the mind has clarity, good concentration and good memory. This also means controlling the sex organs, which is another meaning of Brahmacharya...During adulthood, every healthy person possesses the desire for sexual intercourse. However, yogic teachings do not look at this act from the angle of pleasure alone. They compare the sexual act to a ritual or sacrament. This is because the person has to assume the responsibility of possibly bringing a new individual into birth. The sexual act also creates an emotional intimacy that connects people at a very deep level.[78]

It is clear, from the above statements, why our ancestors cautioned against early sexual activity among the young people. They knew there was great power in the sex act and to get involved in it at an early age would be to release a power they could not control. Celibacy was encouraged, until at least the age of 21. However, in our society, young people are engaged in sexual activity as early as 9 years of age. Young girls are having babies at the tender age of 11 or 12! We get involved in sex at such an early age, we get hurt and many never recover from it. This is not to mention our lack of responsibility for the babies that are born from our sexually irresponsible over indulgence! How many enter into the sex act as if it were a ritual, or sacrament? Frawley and Ranade go on to say:

> If the desire for sex is not fulfilled, it can result in physical or mental sickness, and block the person's healthy and happy functioning in life. However, excessive or perverted sexual activity results in loss of strength, weakening of immunity and disease, and disturbs the mind and heart.[79]

Yes, one might be gaining much physical pleasure, but at what cost?

EL-HAJJ RAY RITES OF PASSAGE
7 Doors To Manhood Initiation

If we as men are to evolve along the spiritual path, it is clear that we need to master our sexual urges. It is important for us to exercise discipline, as well as learn the ancient technique of ejaculation control. Of this, Daniel P. Reid writes in his book , The Tao of Health, Sex, and Longevity, page 264:

> Preserving semen lies at the heart of Taiost bedroom arts, as illustrated in the following line from a commentary on the adept Pien Chang's biography, in *Dynastic History of Later Han:*
>
> > The art of bedroom consists of suppressing emissions, absorbing the woman's fluids, and making semen return to strengthen the brain, thereby attaining longevity,
>
> Thus, a man must treasure and conserve his semen during intercourse. Whenever he does emit it, the loss must be compensated by absorbing the 'essence' of women's secretions. That is why ejaculations, through masturbation or homosexual relations, are regarded as being especially harmful to the Yang essence and energy.[80]

By absorbing the 'essence' of a woman's secretions is meant remaining inside of her until one's erection subsides. There is a lot to be said for closeness after intercourse; we understand another reason our women want us to cuddle with them after the sex act. Now, I know many of my brothers are wondering how can I have sexual pleasure without ejaculation? In fact, many of you may think this is B.S.(smile), but journey with me a bit further. Reid goes on to say, this was the same question the Yellow Emperor had, after he was encouraged to regulate his ejaculations. Of this Reid writes on page 265:

> The Emperor's enquiry on this matter sparked the following exchange between two of his closest counselors, Peng-Tze and the Rainbow Girl, recorded in *Secrets of the Jade Bedroom;*

Rainbow Girl: It is generally assumed that a man gains great plea-sure from ejaculation. But, when he learns the Tao of Yin and Yang, he will ejaculate less and less. Will this not diminish his pleasure as well?

Peng-Tze: Not at all! After ejaculating, a man feels tired, his ears buzz, his eyes get heavy, and he longs for sleep. He is thirsty and his limbs feel weak and stiff. By ejaculating, he enjoys a brief moment of sensation but suffers long hours of weariness as a result. This is no true pleasure! However, if a man regulates his ejaculation to an absolute minimum and retains his semen, his body will grow strong, his mind will be clear, and his vision and hearing will improve. While the man must occasionally deny himself the fleeting sensa-tion of ejaculation, his love for his woman will greatly increase. He will feel as if he could never get enough of her. Is that not the true and lasting pleasure of sex?

The last point is a particularly subtle and significant observation: a man who maintains consistently high levels of testosterone, sperm, semen and other male-essence by practicing ejaculation control, will experience an overwhelming enhancement in his love and af-fection for his woman. He will also gain the capacity to act upon that loving urge, over and over again.[81]

In addition to ejaculation control, Reid also speaks of regulating ejac-ulation frequency. On page 295, he gives a suggested schedule, which may be of benefit to the reader. He states:

Thus, a robust male of 20 may ejaculate twice daily, but an emaci-ated one should do so no more than once daily. A 30 year-old male may ejaculate once a day, but only every two days, if he's an inferior specimen. A flourishing man of 40 may emit semen once every three days, but, if he's weak, he may do so only once every four days. A robust man of 50 may ejaculate once every five days, but only once every ten days if he is weak. A 60 year-old man, in good health, may emit once every ten days, or once every 20 days if his health is poor. At 70, a robust man emit once a month, but a weak one should no longer emit semen at all.[82]

At this point, the initiate is asked to begin to pay attention to his own sexual urges, from where are they coming? He is asked to observe the frequency of his ejaculations and the effects on his body, mind and spirit. Aside any physical illness, the initiate is advised to begin to learn the ancient techniques of ejaculation control. Not only will he benefit, but his mate and his relationship will benefit greatly. This is the time when he will need to be open and honest with his mate, asking her for her honest input and assistance. Many of us will be quite surprised to learn that many of our mates have been nothing more than warm flesh for us masturbate in! The majority of our mates will be more than willing to assist us in mastering this ancient technique. In fact, Queen Afua in her book, Heal Thyself page 127 –128, gives our mates a formula to assist us in restoring ourselves. She writes:

"Restore Lost Fluid in Men after Lovemaking"
Women, prepare and serve this formula to him to help prevent premature aging, sexual impotency, prostate gland blockage, loss of hair and mental deterioration. A constant releasing of sacred fluid without replenishing will cause some of the above health imbalances over a period of time.
Formula: 2tbsp. Lecithin
                   200 mg. Vitamin E
                   15-30 mg. Zinc
                   2 ounces Pumpkin seeds (soak overnight)
                   8 oz. Of Water
                   Blend together
                   Raw honey or raw maple syrup, for taste
                   For additional rejuvenation take saw palmetto berries
                   herb (2tbsp. With 2 cups of boiling water). Steep 1
                   hour and drink for extra male potency.[83]

Besides absorbing the 'essences' of our mate during love making, here, one of our Queens, Queen Afua, gives us a formula to ensure our proper restoration after ejaculation. This points to the fact of how willing our women are to assist us in reclaiming who and what we are – Gods! In fact, in her book, Sacred Woman, pages 345 – 351, additional information is given on how men should deal with our organ of regeneration, i.e. phallus. It is suggested that we establish an altar to our organ of regeneration. This speaks to the sacredness of our phallus and who we are as men. Reading Sacred Woman is well worth the time and effort, particularly the section "Sacred Man: Brother-to-Brother Response to No more Lovers," written by her mate, Hru Ankh Ra Semahj. The entire book will leave the initiate with a greater appreciation for our women as well as himself.

At this point I would like to say something about premature ejaculation. These are things we as men never talk about or are never taught. For whatever the reason, be it pride, shame, or ignorance, we never approach this subject. I hold that it is not for us Elders to impress you. We Elders must open our lives and allow you to see the good and the bad. We must tell you of the mistakes we made, so you will not repeat them. I recall my own struggles with premature ejaculation and the physical, emotional and psychological pain it caused me and my mate and how my negative self-image affected my children. In the heat of an argument, my wife brought it to my attention in a not so tactful way of how I was way off the mark. You can imagine how she put it. Any demeaning expression you can think of would not come close to the manner in which she cut me (smile). However, it was a wake-up call and the hard truth of which I had to face. Yet, the universe is so very merciful because I wanted to know why and how to correct it, and was guided to a master herbsman of the Ausar/Auset Society, Shekhem Tepraims Saau of Washington D.C. I recall our first meeting on the campus of Howard University and how matter of fact he was with me. Yet, I could sense an underlying love and concern for men. He asks me how many times a week I was intimate with my wife and did I give up my seed each time. He questioned me concerning my diet, my job and other activities. At the time I was working full time, going to law school at night taking a full load, speaking around the country and trying to be a father to three children and a husband to my wife while being the principle bread -winner. After being open and honest with him concerning my problem, he looked at me and said, " Baba, your problem is you are giving it up at both ends." I was physically run down, mentally exhausted and stressed to the max. No wonder I was misfiring, my engine was out of time (smile). He taught me of the pressures we black men face, particularly conscious black men. He taught me of diet, nutritional secrets, proper vitamins, REST, meditation, breathing, and directed me to additional books to study. I cannot begin to tell you how much I value my relationship with Shekhem Tepraims Saa, for he is truly a Brother's brother. Armed with this new understanding, faith in the Divine and assistance from my mate, I was able to overcome the problem. Brothers, I share this because many of us are missing the mark, we know it, but we will not talk about it. Our mates are just putting up with us and living frustrated lives, you doubt what I am saying, have a heart to heart conversation with her, she will tell you, maybe not in the manner my mate told me (smile). Brother Elders, let us open up more and pass on to those coming behind us the knowledge that will make them greater men than we.

My beloved brothers, we say to you this is an area, ejaculation control, of which if we can master we would be well on our way to the success that we seek. Think of it, think of the power that you experience on your way to orgasm! Here you are in what they call the sexual trance with all thoughts blocked out and nothing in on your mind but the feeling, power and sexual drive. Can you imagine being able to take that level of power, concentration and drive and channel it into your worldly activities? Nothing at all would stand in your way. Here, you are able to merge with your mate at a level you never thought possible, you can feel her at such deep levels and experience her essence. Here, in this sacred act you can balance each other and hold the images of what the two of you want to accomplish in life together. Then, at those times when you want to treat yourself to ejaculation, you must remain inside of her close as never before as she and her essences restore you to your fullness. Oh such a wonderful thing. For those of you who are seeking to bring back ancestors, the two of you, via sex, can stand at the edge of the universe and call back the great ones. The Bible tells us to be fruitful and multiply. Thus, we see in the act of procreation the closest that man and woman together can come to realizing the God force of each. Such a wonderful blessing from the universe. So, my beloved brothers, let us seek to master our sex drive, grow strong, and stay close to our mates.

4. Tell it like it is – the bitch syndrome

On page 21, we first addressed this issue. At this point, we would like to take a different approach to it. We must face it. We have been made other than who we are and all that we do benefits those other than ourselves. We have been so programmed until we want nothing to do with the ways of our ancestors. In fact, the suffering and sacrifices of our ancestors have been so trivialized until, in 2003, they held a Jazz concert in the Slave Dungeons in Ghana!!

The very place that our ancestors suffered and endured all kinds of horrors for us has been reduced to nothing more than a Jazz Club! Yes, we have been made the biggest bitches on the planet. Do you think for one moment the Jews would do such a thing with the concentration camps in Germany? No, they go there to remember and commit that never again, for them, that is sacred ground. Yet, we allow such things to take place because we have been made to forget, we are asleep and like anyone who is asleep, we do not want to be awakened!

EL-HAJJ RAY RITES OF PASSAGE
7 Doors To Manhood Initiation

There is a need for us to remake ourselves; we must go through a metamorphosis. Today, more than any other time in our history as a people, there is a need for us to reach back to our ancestors, for answers to our modern day problems. In fact, that is what this book is about, reaching back to our ancestral ways for a ritual, rites-of-passage, as a means of bringing modern-day boys into manhood. However, we are in the position to take the knowledge of the west and synthesize it with that of our Ancestors, and produce a healing, not only for ourselves, but for humanity.

I contend, it is important for us to learn to listen to our scholars. After I read the works of Amos Wilson, I turned to my wife and told her that I needed some psychological help, because I knew I had been made crazy. We have so many brothers and sisters on the frontier of black psychological thought. Individuals who have the best of western education, but are conscious enough to study, understand, and apply the ways of our ancestors to their practice as a means of assisting us.

What of this concept of metamorphosis? The term metamorphosis means:
1. A transformation, as by magic, or sorcery.
2. A marked change in appearance, character, condition, or function.

Therefore, when we are talking about the metamorphosis of the black male, we are talking about transformation, as by magic, or sorcery, which will produce a marked change in the appearance, character, condition, or function of black men. At this point, it is necessary to state what I mean by magic and sorcery. It is necessary to take these terms away from the superstition associated with them. We want to see these terms in their light and how they relate to our transformation.

In the book <u>Serpent in the Sky</u> by John Anthony West, on page 132-133, he writes:

> Schwaller de Lubicz carefully distinguishes between magic and sorcery: Magic is a summoning- up and utilization of natural cosmic energy by harmonic means. Sorcery concerns itself with influencing the psychological ambiance, thus with an energy emanating from the complex of human life. Both are valid, both 'work'...and there are higher and lower forms of both magic and sorcery.[84]

He goes on to say of sorcery:

> Sorcery works. It works by influencing the will of the victim, a procedure not susceptible of measurement, but demonstrably effective. In the twentieth century, sorcery is called 'Advertising' by the businessman, 'Propaganda' by the politician and 'Suggestion' by the psychologist. All are sorcery, and nothing but sorcery. It is irrelevant that these modern witch doctors and their bewitched victims do not actually realize what they do, or even how they do it; they do it and it works.[85]

However, in my mind, I believe the modern day witch doctors do know what they are doing and we, the victims, are so bewitched, we do not want to know what has been done. One of the greatest tolls at the hands of the modern day witch doctors is the television, and how it has us in its spell. We want to be what we see on T.V., we want to buy what we see on T.V., we want to live the lives that we see on T.V. T.V and the movies, and their power of suggestion, is beyond our understanding at this time, yet, those modern day witch doctors know the power. That is why they keep such tight control. You shape consciousness with the media, and he who controls the media, controls consciousness.

We must begin to address the issue of how we successfully influence the will of Black men to cause a transformation, a marked change in appearance, character, condition or function. We also want to take note of the need for this influencing of the will of the black man's consciousness by the media, and the need to change it. We cannot begin to successfully talk about the influence on the will of the Black man without discussing the work of the Most Honorable Elijah Muhammad.

There has been no one in modern day history who has had the effect on the transformation of the black man as did Elijah Muhammad. Brothers, regardless of what you think of him, Elijah Muhammad was/is successful in transforming boys to men. In fact, the majority of the black men we respect and admire were influenced, in one way or another, by the works of Elijah Muhammad. We must seek to get beyond our religious differences and seek the truth. No one can deny the courage, strength, insight, and leadership qualities of Minister Farrakhan. He is a man transformed by the work of Elijah Muhammad. I make this point for the purpose of showing that we do have models in our community that have demonstrated that they know the way to manhood. The question is are we listening?

Now, let us examine how the will of the black man has been influenced by sorcery and what we must do to counter this influence. Everything in life goes through stages of development and it is no different for us as men. In his book, Visions for Black Men, Dr. Na'im Akbar gives us a working model of this developmental, or transformative, process. He begins with us as males, the coming into Boyhood, and finally, Manhood.

His model of the male is characterized as a biological entity driven by passions, desires, and instincts. He argues that being male by no means makes you a man. You can see how T.V. does nothing but feed us at the male level, it feeds our passions, desires, and instincts.

Everything on BET and the videos is feeding our passions and desires, thus, we are being kept at the base biological level of male.

Dr. Akbar characterizes Boyhood as discipline, reason, sentiment, selfishness and play. The emancipated minds he speaks of is one of educational training, but lacks mental liberation. Like the emancipated slave who did not want to leave the plantation of the slave master, the emancipated mind does not want to leave the plantation of the slave masters' ideas. We want to remain, and be like the slave master, and we devote all of our energies of being his imitation. *At this point, please re-read the title of this section.*

The final stage of this evolution is Manhood, which Akbar characterizes as guided knowledge, which leads to a conscious awareness of seeing what accurately is, seeing things as they really are and not how you want them to be. This awareness enables the man to face the problems of life, accepting responsibility and finding solutions. It is our Elders, via rites-of-passage, that will impart this guided knowledge to us. Ultimately, the consciousness of manhood gives rise to God-consciousness, that sublime state of mental awareness that has only been attained by a few realized souls in this life- time. God-consciousness is that state of mind in which you see everything as God. You live, as if, all is God.

Using Akbar's model, let us examine the work of this modern day sorcerer, and the work we must do to counter this magic and sorcery. Akbar states, on page 3 of his book that "A male is a biological entity whose essence is described by, no more, or no less than, his biology. One need not look beyond the observable anatomical characteristics, primarily the genitals, to determine that he is male." Echoing Dr. Akbar, Dr. Nsenga Warfield-Coppock says, in her book, <u>Afrocentric Theory and Applications, Volume 1: Adolescent Rites of Passage</u> that "Manhood is not the same as maleness, which is dubbed upon a person at the moment of birth. Maleness is a biological definition of human and differentiates them from the female of the species."[86]

Thus, it is clear that being a male does not make you a man. Maleness is a function of your manifesting in the biological body of a male and having the organs to produce spermatozoa for fertilizing the ova. We are born male, with the potential of becoming men. But even at the fundamental level of male, the will can, and is, influenced to retard further development into manhood. Dr. Akbar further states, "Maleness is also a mentality that operates with the same principles as biology. It is a mentality, dictated by appetite and physical determinants. This mentality is one guided by instincts, urges, desires or feeling."[87]

As we said earlier, all of our urges, desires and feelings are fed by T.V. Our young men are growing up on a steady diet of sex, violence, material riches and foolishness, as fed to them via television. While these urges, desires, feelings, and passions are natural for the evolution from maleness to boyhood, they must be guided with wisdom. This is the role of the wise elders.

The next series of questions are: is it possible to influence the will via the passions? Is it possible to influence the will via urges, desires, and appetites? Is it possible to influence the will of the evolving male to the point that he is, forever, in a state of maleness and never reaches true manhood? The answer to these questions is yes. It is nothing to learn of black males competing with each other to see who can produce the most children, yet, they will not assume responsibility for them. This modern day sorcerer is very busy.

His sorcery, disguised as advertisement, influenced our will to the point that we will pay $55.00 - $98.00 for a pair of $7.00 blue jeans or $70.00 - $130.00 for some $25.00 gym shoes made in Korea.

His sorcery, disguised as propaganda, has influenced our will to the point that we will vote for someone who does not care for us, or better yet, we will deny the teaching of a man, Elijah Muhammad, whose work stands in the world as a manifestation of true success in building black men in America.

His sorcery, disguised as suggestion, has influenced our will to the point that black men will lose their lives over nothing, and our women will judge us based on the suggestions of a paranoid white race.

Recalling Schwaller de Lubicz's distinction of sorcery, as influencing the psychological ambiance, it becomes an energy emanating from the complex of human life. Ambiance means, "the special or distinctive atmosphere surrounding a person, place, or thing." Thus, we are talking about influencing the mental atmosphere around the male. If you successfully influence the mental atmosphere, you can, and will, forever retard the development of black men. Proof is seen in the fact that the entire mental atmosphere of black men is full of negative images, thus, we see the negative development of the black man.

Now, magic is defined by Schwaller de Lubicz as "The manipulation of harmonic forces which may lie outside sensory perception and are therefore, beyond the pale of possible measurement." Note, magic is the manipulation of harmonic forces. This implies there must be a harmony, and magic is the interference with this harmony. Following Dr. Akbar's lead, we can see that man is created in harmony with natural laws. If he evolves undisturbed, and in submission to these laws, he will attain manhood.

Our Ancestors were aware of this harmony, this rhythm, but it has been interfered with. They understood that every seven years you pass through a door and therefore, had ceremonies to mark this natural transition. This is one reason why at the age of fourteen, give or take a

EL-HAJJ RAY RITES OF PASSAGE
7 Doors To Manhood Initiation

year, we need to take our young men through a rites-of-passage, to be in harmony with the natural physical transition they are going through. Our Ancestors saw, and understood, this period and how important it was to guide the young men.

Today, the modern day sorcerer uses magic, the manipulation of harmonic forces, to arrest our transition from boyhood to manhood. For example, this transition is arrested by the manipulation of the harmonic forces surrounding our young men. Take for instance, the natural harmony and rhythm of coming into puberty. This is the time of the young warrior, the young men want to express themselves, conquer, and build. By appealing to our base desires, via lewd music, hard driving sound and a constant diet of sexual and violent images, our young men are forever locked at the level of animals, fighting each other for territorial rights to mate with the females. And like many animals, once they have impregnated the female, they walk off!

There is a natural harmonious drive in the evolving male for knowledge. By providing an inferior knowledge, you influence the will of the young males towards negative behavior. Therefore, we, the Elders, must begin to influence the will of our young men in a positive direction. I contend that a solid rites-of-passage program is an excellent beginning. We must begin to provide them with knowledge that will allow them to see reality differently. Again, Dr. Akbar says, in his book, <u>Visions for Black Men</u> that "The force that transforms the person from being a boy to becoming a man is knowledge."[88] Thus, we see that knowledge is important in the transformation from boyhood to manhood. However, a particular knowledge is what we are looking for. As Elijah Muhammad said, "The Black Man must gain a knowledge of self." It is the knowledge of self that will liberate us from the mind, and behavior, of little boys and the male stage of development. Akbar further states:

213

The boy takes his budding rationality and uses it to expand his consciousness. In fact, it is critical that he should be guided in the use of his yet immature reasoning, so that it doesn't get entrapped in the form of boyishness...This is why good teachers, fathers, brothers and uncles, are so important. They are the instruments of guidance which help the boys move toward manhood.[89]

Echoing this call for fathers, teachers, brothers, and uncles as guides, in his article, "Missing Movement, Missing fathers: The Culture of Short Lives and Low Expectations", Haki Madhubuti writes that "I believe, and maintain, that if culturally focused/politically clear and responsible Black fathers were a majority in the African American family and community, there would not be a gang, drug, or crime problem at the level that exists today." Therefore, our young men need to be guided by conscious, committed males. It is time for us to put down our differences as men, and assume the responsibility to being guides and role models for our young men. We have been at war with self, and each other, for too long. Please understand, in the words of John A. West:

The ultimate aim of war is not so much genocide as the psychological conquest of the enemy. Brute force alone invariably provokes violent reaction; tyrannies seldom last long when based solely upon military power. But when the enemy is psychologically helpless, the ruler is secure.[90]

We can either be, or not be. We, as males evolving to manhood, must make the decision. I close with the question: WHOSE BITCHES ARE WE?

5. Spiritual Baths

At this point in the process, the initiate should be taking 'spiritual baths' on a regular basis. However, it is strongly recommended that this be done under the guidance of a competent Priest or Priestess. The reason being at this stage in the initiation process, the initiate is beginning to cleanse and purify this being on all levels, as a result, he is attracting certain energies that may impede further growth and development. Special baths will have to be prepared in accordance with what is revealed through divination. The divination may reveal that the initiate needs special herbs or oils. Also, since this is part of a rites-of-passage program, it may require baths be taken certain times throughout the program. However, this is something to be determined through divination, via a competent Priest or Priestess.

6. Free your mind, body and spirit – cleansing & clearing rituals

The initiate should be aware that there are so many rituals for cleansing and clearing the body, mind, and spirit. That is why we recommend that a rites-of-passage program have a Priest or Priestess to consult with. We are dealing with energies, spiritual energies, and one who has dedicated their life to understanding and appeasing these energies is the best to guide this process. There will be programs that require 'strong medicine' and others that require 'sweet medicine'. For example, if your mate is mad at you, you can feel the energy when you walk into the house. He or she does not have to say a word; you just 'feel' the energy. Well, if you can feel the energy coming from your mate, then think of the energy we pick up from the job, the city in which we live, and the area of the city in which we live!

You can take this concept all the way out to the world in which we live, even the universe. Some programs will take place in cities, in high crime areas, where there is a lot of violence and murder. The rituals required there may be strong, freeing, and sweet. Other programs will take place in the quiet suburbs, or in the country, the medicine there will be different. Yet, how will you know? Yes, you will need divination from a Priest or Priestess to determine exactly what is needed. There are common cleansing and clearing rituals that will work any place or time, those being prayer, meditation, and smudging. Prayer is one of the most powerful tools we, as humans, have to realign self with the divine. To be able to surrender in prayer to the divine is so liberating and freeing.

It matters not how you see the Divine, being able to turn to the divine in sincere prayer is what matters. One thing that has kept us apart as men is how we see the divine. It is said that man will not go up to God, but man seeks to bring God down to him. If you are standing at the base of a mountain you can see only so far, yet, if you climb to the top of that mountain you can see much further. If we seek to go up to God, then our vision will expand and we will lose the need to be dogmatic and dictatorial.

Once upon a time, five blind men were placed at different places on an elephant and each was asked to describe the elephant. The one at the ear said, "an elephant was a fan," the one at the trunk said, "you are wrong an elephant is a hose," the one at the tail said, "you both are wrong an elephant is a rope." Then, the one at the side of the elephant said, "you three are incorrect, an elephant is a wall." Finally, the one at the leg spoke up and said, "you all are wrong, an elephant is a tree!" When there came along a woman who could see, she saw that based on their location to the elephant, all five were correct in their interpretation, but she who could see saw exactly what an elephant was.

My beloved Brothers, none of the Prophets, Seers, and sages ever fell into disagreement concerning God, for they knew well who and what God was/is. Yet, today we want to argue concerning God, even in

EL-HAJJ RAY RITES OF PASSAGE

the name of God, we wage wars to further our own political agendas. We even hold our wives spiritual prisoners in the name of God!

As you all know, there are many roads into your particular city, those coming from the north will take one route, those coming from the east will come a different road, those coming from the west will take yet a different road, and those coming from the south will take a different road. However, we rejoice that we all can meet in the city. You cannot fault me for coming to your city from the north because I live in the north, nor I can fault someone coming to the city from the east because they live in the east. Such is the same with God, you cannot fault someone for coming to God via Islam if that is their orientation, nor can one be faulted for coming to God via Christianity, Yoruba, Judaism, Hinduism, Native American, Ausarian, or any of the many religions. We should rejoice in the fact that we worship God! For it matters not how you see it, or call it, there is but One God, even quantum physics with its unified field theory is saying to us that all of creation evolved from one unified source to which we will return. It is to that one source that we can turn to at anytime, any place, and offer prayer.

The reading of your particular spiritual book, as you know, is a wonderful means of clearing and cleansing.

Meditation is another ritual, which is of great benefit in clearing. There are many different meditation techniques. The initiate is advised to search for one that appeals to them. Ra Un Nefer Amen, Chief Priest of the Ausar/Auset Society, has produced an excellent set of tapes that can guide the initiate in the meditation process and his book, Metu Neter Vol. 1, is one of the best you can find on the explanation of the meditation process. Just remember, prayer is when we talk to God, and meditation is when God talks to us.

Smudging is an excellent way to cleanse and clear one's self. One can use incense or herbs; some of the most common are sage, cedar, pine, frankincense and myrrh, and sandalwood.

While we may have approached these techniques separately, we encourage the initiate to combine them all. Select a special place in your living quarters to place a shrine, all homes should have a shrine, a place to focus your spiritual attention. A place that is sacred and holy. When you have those times that you are feeling off center and need to clear and cleanse, you may want to try this. Sit on a towel, take a bottle of sesame seed oil, and start to massage your entire body from your head to your toes. Sesame seed oil has wonderful healing properties. Allow the oil to soak into your skin for about fifteen minutes. While the oil is soaking, you can light the candles on your shrine and burn your favorite fragrance.

Next, take a nice warm shower with black soap. Towel off and put on special clothes, preferably with some that are only for prayer and meditation. Sit in front of your shrine, offer prayers to God, while you have soft music playing in the back ground. After prayer, pour libations to your ancestors. Then, sit quietly and open yourself to messages from the Divine. They may come from your Higher Self, Divinities, or your Ancestors. Keep a pencil and pad nearby to take notes. However, the most important thing is for you to reach a point of total relaxation and peace. Forget all the pressures and stress of the day, and just be in the moment. You should sit as long as your body will allow without trying to push yourself. Your body will let you know when it is time to end the session, listen to it.

After you have finished writing notes, then, go to your Holy Book, kiss it, place it to your forehead, then open it to any page. On the right hand side, count down seven lines and there will be a message for you. Take this message into mediation and it will give you additional guidance. Brothers, this is just one technique that may be helpful. As you continue this rites-of-passage process, the universe will bring you in contact with so many more wonderful healers, guides, sages, shamans, gurus, Priests and Priestesses who will offer you so much more. You will discover a whole new world. Enjoy your journey into Self and give thanks to God as you know it.

7. The other side of daylight – introduction to feminine mysteries

It was said by Prophet Muhammad, "When God loves a Man, he gives him a good woman." I consider myself extremely blessed, because I have one woman who is the mother of my children and my heart, and another who is the mother of my soul. Mama Rashidah, who has journeyed with me for well over 31 years, is the mother of my children. She has battled Multiple Sclerosis for 25 years and has managed to cross many seas with me. To her, I give honor and respect.

Then there is Iya Osunnike Anke, who came into our family bringing with her the healing energy of Osun/Het-Heru. However, not only did she bring a healing to my family, but to my spiritual family as well. She came walking on clouds, carrying a gourd of honey, which has sweetened the lives of all she has come in contact with. This woman, who has dedicated her life to this spiritual path and healing others, has turned my head in a most skillful manner to the other side of daylight. She introduced me to the sacred feminine mysteries and caused me to love the feminine in me. As a result, my love for both her and Mama Rashidah is without equal. I will forever thank God for the day, that Shango and Osun took my offering at the Osun spring, here in Lexington, Kentucky, and then two weeks later brought this Moon Goddess into my life. It is she who is qualified to introduce you, my beloved brothers, to this section. For not only must we accept the woman in us, but we must truly learn to accept, honor, and respect our woman and the man that is in her. However, I will let her speak on this;

The Sacred Feminine Mysteries Initiation
Destiny Revealed

Several months prior to my pilgrimage to Peru, I began to realize that I was in the midst of an intense shamanic spiritual life crisis. Everything I had come to know about who I AM was being unraveled, thread by thread. My whole life was filling up with doubts about myself, from a – z. I felt like an empty shell, totally disconnected from whom I believed I was. The very things I valued were being shattered, leaving me to stare blindly into the cosmic mirror of my own eyes, which reflected the scattered fragmented images of my soul.

After what seemed to be decades, but perhaps was only a few months, I began to experience somewhere deep inside, yet far from access, a strange sense of being brand-spanking new, and ancient at the same time. It was a very familiar, un-grounding yet solid, feeling that I somehow remembered having experienced during many of my other lifetimes. But, what exactly was I remembering, now? I mean, I knew I was stuck like a distressed fetus trapped inside the birth canal within my mother's womb, and I also knew I was on the threshold of another major rebirth. When and how I had no clue and I didn't even know how I knew all of this. Frightened and helpless, numb, I desperately searched in agony for the spiritual answers to the same question, who am I, that I began *consciously* asking over twenty-five years ago.

Well, the answers began to come, slow but sure. Returning to the ancient whispering echoes, nurturing womb, and nourishing bosom of Peru liberated my spirit and reawakened, once again, the dormant memories of the *Sacred Feminine Mysteries Initiation* that I began thousands of years ago in *Mu, Lemuria*. During the first couple of days in Peru, I experienced my spirit detaching from my body. Panic stricken, I searched for the remnants of that lifetime in the mirrors of nature and in doing so, was amazed when I began to see myself in a collage of supernatural forms perched high upon the Andean mountains which were beckoning me to fully embrace my return. Then, it all began to come together on the night before going to Machu Picchu, the highly advanced pre-Incan civilization where I once lived as a high priestess, shaman, and seeress. That night was one of the most significant nights of my life. It was the turning point for me and the beginning of total blissful surrender.

That night, I witnessed an ancient aspect of myself, which was part human, insect, extraterrestrial, and multidimensional, and with its enormous dark wings it swooped down and drew me into it high upon an Andean mountaintop. I experienced all of these different aspects of myself merge and my whole body vibrated with the intensity and speed of our union, as we traveled at the frequency of sound and light through the agonizing screams of the underworld. Which, like thousands of years before, gifted me with the opportunity to embrace the darkened shadow of my soul while slowly, through the mercy of many lifetimes, piercing through the veils of my illusions, antiquated conditionings and self-defeating limitations that clung desperately to my flesh. As I surrendered to the full remembrance of this truth, in the rush of what felt like an eternity, I felt my rage, pain, jealousy, sorrow, shame and the disappointment of so many failed reunions with my Higher Self, now being cellularly cleansed from the bowels of my mind while purifying and healing those painful memories of my tragic lifetime as Vonnia in Lemuria and Mama de in Peru that were embedded within the cellular memory of my womb. Liberated from the emotional pain of the olden memories of Mama de, wise seeress and spiritual oracle for humanity, the features of her life now began to unfold like a panoramic movie before my eyes. In a whirlwind of stillness, I could see and recognize her strong broad face with my sharp keen inner eyes, the same inner eyes that allowed her to traverse the three worlds in the blinking of our deep brown eyes. As our souls merged, I carefully slipped into the body temple that once enclosed her spirit. I remembered how I could feel their angry breath of raw fear breathing down upon my heels way before my capture and long before they brutally severed my tongue to silence the prophesy of the sacred oracle that effortlessly passed from my lips and gutted out my womb in hope of extracting and eradicating the power of *The Sacred Feminine Mysteries* that I and the other *Ancient Mothers of Mu* had vowed and devoted our entire lives to safe-keep. I could hear my silent screams echoing in the wind as they violently and viciously tore from the inner sanctum of my womb my innocent baby girl whose tormented soul would be lost in the fibers of bewilderment, endlessly searching for its completion lifetime after lifetime. Reconnecting to those memories has allowed me to release the torment of being fragmented and to finally embrace the unifying circle of wholeness that contains the medicine to fully integrate all of my lifetime experiences into one truth. The truth of Unconditional Love.

Being energetically immersed in the mystifying womb of Africa, cradle of civilization and home of the goddess Osun, suckling the rich nutrients of unconditional love flowing from the bosom of Peru and the many spiritual paths I have been guided along, have drenched me in the sweetness of universal balance and unifying multidimensional solidarity. However, most importantly, these journeys have allowed me to reclaim my divine inheritance as the *Keeper Of The "Ase" Serpent Wisdom* and devotee to the *Sacred Feminine Mysteries*. I now reseal my divine covenant as one of the seven *Ancient Mothers of Mu* by honoring their legacy, which will always vibrate on the echoes of their ancient wings soaring inside my heart and throughout my cellular body.

My entire journey toward home, so far, has challenged me to surrender to Truth and to freely fall back into the maternal arms of loving energy that I so desperately desired for eons. And, to trust in my ancient knowing that I could safely soar to the top of her steepest mountains, travel down into the core of her being and be suspended in the radiance of her love and the love of my biological mother and father, ancestral mothers and fathers, universal teachers, guides, sisters, and brothers. Each day, the petals of my heart continue to open even wider to love. Reminding me that unconditional love is the thread that weaves together the Tapestry of My Soul.

Mojuba Great Mother, Mojuba Iya Naomi Jace Drayton Scott, Mojuba nana Iya Sara Fickens Drayton, iba se, Mojuba Clarence Kennon Drayton, iba se, Mojuba Baba William Robert Scott, iba se, Mojuba to all of my African, Cherokee and European egun whose names I do not remember, iba se, Mojuba Ye Ye Osun, Mojuba Iya Mi, Mojuba Ancient Mothers of Mu, Mojuba spiritual midwives Iya Jean Lawrence, iba se, Iya Felicia Abimbola, Iya Omoladun Anke, Iya Olorisade Adunni, Iya Sidikatu Anke, Baba Steve Quintana, Baba Wande Abimbola, Chief Ogundiya Iroko and Baba Ogunyeye Akangbe . I say Modupe, Modupe, Modupe. Ase, Ase, Ase O. I remember....

Sacred Feminine Mysteries Initiation Passage into the Great Mother

The Sacred Feminine Mysteries Initiation - Passage into The Great Mother, is a nine- month initiatory pilgrimage traversing the labyrinth of Self. This inner spiritual journey is uniquely designed to rekindle and excavate the dormant memories of the *Serpent Wisdom* of the *Ancient Mothers of Mu (Lemuria)* from the belly of your soul. The *Ancient Mothers of Mu*, are the keepers of the *Serpent Wisdom* and the spiritual guardians of humanity who represent and uphold the integrity of our planet. They are the spiritual midwives who make possible the passage through the sacred womb of *The Great Mother*, the cosmic womb that births All Humanity.

Many ancient mythological legends refer to the lost sunken continent of *Mu (Lemuria)*, as a highly spiritual motherland, which physically existed approximately 104,000 years ago and greatly influenced the dualistic rhythmic patterns that govern our universal cycles of time. During the civilization of *Mu*, this ancient passage into the *Sacred Feminine Mysteries* took a lifetime to complete. It begins again for you in this lifetime with your conscious desire to *remember* your divine covenant with *The Great Mother, the Ancient Mothers of Mu*, who still exist today within the spiritual realm, and with their guidance, reactivating the *Serpent Wisdom* within you. The *Serpent Wisdom* is deeply embedded inside the cellular memory nestled within the cavern of your womb, and contains the blueprint of the mysteries of *birth, life, death and rebirth*. This timeless cellular umbilical cord is not only the divine link between you and your birth and ancestral mothers, but to the *Great Mother* and to the remembrance of your spiritual lineage, legacy and divine purpose.

Your spiritual journey, this lifetime, has been designed to activate your innate knowledge of who you truly are. Perhaps you've sensed the whispered echoes of an ancient voice calling to you. Or possibly you've had flashbacks of past life memories involving ritualistic initiations as a high priestess accomplished in the art of sacred sexual union and alchemy. Maybe you've experienced present lifetime out of body sensations and situations where your natural innate knowing from your lifetimes in the ancient temples as a midwife, herbalist, shaman, energy healer, dream interpreter, seeress and oracle reader continues to surface. Better yet, what about those numerous "other worldly" spiritual readings you've had that reveal your natural and perhaps still dormant abilities in the visual and performing arts doing sacred dance, writing, drawing, sculpting, and painting. Finally, there are those vaguely familiar daunting images of being a warrior priestess, or just a subtle knowing that you once reigned as a queen in leadership of an empire, or simply that there is something ancient longing to come forth from inside the darkened calabash that contains your soul.

The Sacred Feminine Mysteries Initiation is designed to ignite the divine spark of higher consciousness within you and pierce, illuminate, and transmute your darkened states of illusion into enlightenment and transcendence. *The Sacred Feminine Mysteries Initiation* exists as your souls answer to the call of the *Ancient Mothers of Mu* and to trigger your dormant memories of who you truly are sketched within the cellular blueprint of your womb. *The Sacred Feminine Mysteries Initiation* is a medium for the restorative seal of the divine covenant between you and the *Great Mother*. *The Sacred Feminine Mysteries Initiation* presents you with the sacred key to unlock the gateway to your *Ase*, housed within the sanctuary of the Queens chamber, which will ritualistically usher you into a mystical re-membering and re-unification of your feminine and masculine energies uniting you with *The Oneness of All Creation. That's the Ase of feminine power!*

In the West African Yoruba spiritual tradition of *Ifa*, one of the meanings for the word *Ase is Life Force Energy*. However, the fuel that ignites the *Ase*, is the mystical *"kundalini"*, the coiled serpent laying dormant at the base of our spines. This powerfully potent, yet un-manifested reservoir of *feminine* energy when skillfully aroused and awakened, will propel primal sexual expression into Divine spiritual ecstasy. In *Ifa*, the orisa (deity) known as *Osun*, experienced as the primal erotic feminine magnetic force of attraction in nature, is the essential ingredient in the triangular equation of *Creation and procreation.* In her mythical role as *leader of the Iyami, primordial feminine power, Osun* also symbolizes the *Creatress and the mystical vessel of Creation.* This *feminine power* not only reproduces her-self but the male form as well. That's the *Ase of feminine power!*

Ultimately, The Sacred Feminine Mysteries Initiation propels you into a rhythmically spiraling sacred dance between the magnetically powerful *feminine* force of *contraction* and the electrifying *masculine* force of *expansion.* While the spiritual midwives, the Ancient Mothers of Mu, guide your spiritual rebirth by weaving the fragmented threads of your spirit through the alchemical womb of *The Great Mother. The Sacred Feminine Mysteries Initiation* finally culminates in a tapestry of your soul's remembrance and honoring of the *Serpent Wisdom. Welcome home to the Sacred Feminine Mysteries - the Serpent Wisdom...the Ase of feminine power!*

In the Spirit,
Iya Osunnike Anke
Ancient Mother of Mu & Keeper of The Serpent Wisdom
Ase (May It Be So)

Be ye therefore wise as serpents and gentle as doves......
Matthew 10:16

C. LIVING IN ALIGNMENT WITH ABSOLUTE TRUTH

With the Name of God, Most Gracious, Most Merciful and in the Presence of Our Ancestors, Both Seen and Unseen.

August 8, 2000

NOTE TO THE READER: The information contained herein is from the "In Search of the Self" course produced by Siddha Yoga foundation in Fallsburg NY. Unless otherwise noted, whenever Ram is speaking, it is Ram of the Siddah Foundation who authored the course. Should the reader desire the course, they can call (914) 434-2000.
The play between the student and Ram is a personal way for me to gain a greater understanding of this walk along this path. It is my prayer that you, the reader, will enjoy it as much as I.
Peace & Love
Koleoso

This was a time in the life of the student that required him to examine his commitment to the spiritual path. For much had taken place in his life, causing great introspection. Off- balance and knowing that he was off-balance, the student made his way to the valley of the masters. This was a place that only those students who had reached the crossroad of commitment were allowed to go. For being in the presence of the masters required an emptiness that only the crossroad of commitment could provide. The student was fully aware of his emptiness because he had nothing to say, nor could he feel his own presence in this life.

He could feel all of this coming on, as a result of a sweat lodge experience this past weekend. He had given all that spirit would allow him to give. Empty of ego and intellectual ponderings, the student knew he was at the crossroad of commitment and, thus, began the journey to the "Valley of the Masters." After several days of journeying, he had made it to the door of the palace. Now, did he have the strength left to go through the door? The journey had required that he empty his mind and body of physical and mental impurities. He walked up to the door and was met by a master clothed in the orange color of renouncement, for these were masters who had renounced the world of illusion and devoted themselves to inner enlightenment.

Student: Greeting master

Master: Greeting to you Master

Student: Why do you refer to me as master?

Master: We are but reflections of each other

Student: If that is the case, then why not greet me by saying, greetings God?

Master: In your answer you now understand why I said greetings Master.

With that exchange, the student was a bit confused but never the less he was too tired to carry the exchange any further. As he sat there thinking of the exchange, it occured to him, how could he see himself as God, if he did not see himself as a master? Now, he understood, the master was only trying to elevate him. Could it have been that the Master could sense his emptiness and began to fill him? With that, he prepared himself for his meeting with Ram, the Siddha Yoga Master, for this was a meeting that he had the feeling would be of great value to him. Once inside the great hall of meditation, among the smell of flowers and the soft feeling of candles burning, the student sat in the presence of this wonderful being.

Student: Greeting, master

Ram: Greetings to you, master

Student: Thank you for allowing me this time with you.

Ram: Such is not necessary, for you have come to the crossroad of commitment, a time of spiritual emptiness, of which we must fill you with divine love.

Student: Why is such emptiness necessary?

Ram: If a glass is full, can you add more to it?

Student: No, it will only overflow the glass

Ram: If that happens, then what?

Student: The contents are wasted.

Ram: So, you empty the glass in order to refill it.

Student: I am beginning to see what you are saying.

Ram: You will understand better, when you realize that there is nothing to empty from the glass, ha ha.

Student: How is this?

Ram: "Throughout the ages, there have always been great beings-

known as saints, sages, or Siddhas- who have taught that this entire universe is the manifestation, or expression, of one universal Consciousness, and that this divine Consciousness exists within every individual as his own Self."

Student: Could this be what Ra Un Nefer Amen of the Ausar/Auset Society meant when he said, "Most people are caught in the quandary of knowing, on one hand, that all men are integral parts of one whole, yet on the other hand, do not know how to acknowledge that oneness in action, because of their need to defend themselves against others whose attitudes to life are in violation of the oneness of life."

Ram: Yes, this is so, but before we can understand that concept, we need to lay a foundation. The great ones that I speak of "have taught the same Truth in many ways-always in a style and terminology suitable for the people of their particular place and time. Still, the Truth is always the Truth, and the essence of the teachings of all the great saints remain the same."

Student: Is this why it is said, "Today as Yesterday, Tomorrow as Today, is Truth!"

Ram: Yes, because "Siddha not only gives the highest teachings, but also transmits the experience of the Truth to those who are open and receptive."

Student: Thus, in my being empty, is that like my being open and receptive?

Ram: To realize that you are empty means that you are open, and receptive to being filled, you realize that you need filling.

Student: Yes, I understand. I am sitting here taking in all that you say as if I am eating a wonderful meal.

Ram: A meal for the soul. The concept of which I spoke, moments ago, "it is similar to a lighted-candle, passing on the flame to an unlit candle. This transmission is possible through the spiritual power, or SHAKTI, which spontaneously flows through all of Siddha's words or actions. It is a mysterious and fascinating process."

Student: Is this Shakti the same as the Ashe of the Yoruba?

Ram: Before I answer that, what do you know of the Ashe?

Student: Baba Ifa Karade says that "Nature is viewed as the manifestation of Oludumare's Essence, through degrees of material substance. That essence, translated as ashe, is the inherent force of all creation."

Ram: Yes, that is the same as the Shakti. Now, you can see what we mean when we say all the great ones taught the same truth.

Student: Yes, I can see and I feel the personal need to see the same truth in all that I see. It bothers me greatly, to see how everyone is trying to say that their way is the only way and trying to control others. Master, this is why I have come, I come to be filled with universal understanding. I no longer wish to participate in the game of separation and difference. I seek to understand the whole. I believe that there is a unity running through all of creation and it is in living that unity that we find peace.

Ram: That is good. Tell me more.

Student: I have grown so very tired of looking at everyone seeking to gain a following based on separation, being different. We seem to pride ourselves on being different, yet we talk about unity. All of this sounds very flowery and nice, but we are so insecure until we find comfort in being different. The reality is, we all come from the same source and we are the same essence – GOD! This goes back to what Ra Un Nefer Amen said, "Most people are caught in the quandary of knowing, on one hand, that all men are integral parts of one whole, yet on the other hand, do not know how to acknowledge that oneness in action, because of their need to defend themselves against others whose attitudes to life are in violation of the oneness of life." Most of us who use spirituality to get a following, or to enslave people, are in violation of this oneness. The minute we stop teaching unity, we fall into separation and violation of the oneness, thus the defense, this group against that group. Master, I tire of this game, I seek to live in unity, in the light!!

Ram: It seems that you have become open and receptive, "when an open and receptive person comes in contact with the Shakti of a living Siddha, it can cause a spontaneous spiritual awakening within the individual. In the Eastern scriptures, this awakening or initiation is known as Shaktipat. Once this occurs, the individual begins a process leading to total transformation."

Student: I see what you are saying, because that is what I am experiencing, I want to move to another level of acceptance. Baba Ifa Karade says, "Oludumare, the Creator, must be seen in all things. Humans, devoid of oppressive ego, must see themselves as also part of the creation, and behave accordingly." With that statement, I can see the unity in what he is saying, what you are saying, what Ra Un Nefer Amen is saying, I can truly see the unity. Yet, I find that I get caught in the illusion because I want to live and be accepted in a community. Yet, I realize that I cannot be accepted in a community that does not realize the unity.

Ram: Maybe this will help, for there is a greater community out here, to which you are being called. "The Self is Consciousness. That Consciousness is all pervasive and eternal, without beginning or end. Consciousness is unmodified, formless, undifferentiated, and ageless. It bestows light on all that is seen; it knows all that is known. From this pure Consciousness, we believe, springs a grand and divine play. Although we are this pure Consciousness, we believe ourselves to be individual, separate and apart from the whole. The feelings of being finite, limited, unworthy, impure, and lacking in love arise from this sense of separation. Through wrong understanding of our nature, we create endless pain and struggle. As long as we remain ignorant of our true nature, true happiness is unlikely. The search for the Self leads to the recognition of our own inner Truth."

Student: Could it be that I tire of being separate? I truly desire to break free of this inner division that I experience. I want to commit myself to living and spreading the unity.

Ram: Before you can do that, you must realize the unity within yourself. "Once a person recognizes the light of the eternal Self within, he finds supreme contentment. Established in her/his own serenity, such a person is beyond being disturbed by situations or circumstances- she/he participates in them, like a game, while she/he continues to play their appropriate role in life. Love continuously arises from within such a person, and they naturally radiate that love and joy to those around them, through whatever one says or does."

Student: So, I got caught in thinking that I was the game, instead of playing the game.

Ram: Yes, that is why your frustration is so great, you, like many, loss sight of who you really are. Now, as I was saying earlier, "a per-

son who lives established (established in their own serenity) in such a state is known as a free, or liberated, being. He is also known as Self-realized. One who lives in this state at all times is a Siddha. The Siddha Yoga process leads to being firmly established in the state of perfect Self-realization."

Student: Is Siddha Yoga full of rituals?

Ram: "Siddha Yoga meditation is not a system of beliefs or rituals, but a process leading to direct experience of the Truth. There is nothing complicated about the Truth. The truth is very simple. One who knows the inner Self lives in a state of divine love – love that is unconditional, pure, and ever new. It becomes their natural feeling. That love is the Truth, and it exists within everyone, all the time, and everywhere. The reason we practice Siddha Yoga meditation, the reason we participate in this course, is to recognize and become established in the Truth. In a sense, the Siddha Yoga process is the process of being totally true to ourselves."

Student: Now, I understand what they mean by the saying, "The first thing a seeker after truth must do is be truthful to self."

Ram: Yes, "In the realization of one's true nature, there is great joy."

Student: What is one's true nature?

Ram: The Self, or GOD. "In this understanding of the Truth, one becomes naturally cheerful. One is lighthearted about the details of life and enjoys the humor in things. For a Siddha, laughter and joy arise spontaneously."

Student: How do we get to this understanding of the Truth?

Ram: "Ordinarily, we don't recognize how the conditioned mind prevents us from directly perceiving the Truth. If it were not for this mental conditioning that distorts our experience and perception, the nature of the Self would be immediately obvious. Participating in this course is a process that gradually exposes and expels this conditioning, to prepare us to see the Truth as it is."

Student: As I understand it, then, the Self is the unconditioned and unlimited aspect of God that manifest as us. I recall Ra Un Nefer Amen saying, "Man's Self-Identity, the perfected (fully evolved) Man has his identity with the fact that his Being is unconditioned, and unlimited in its creative capacity. In other words, there is no identification with any personality complex that is characterized by specific human preferences (likes, dislikes, inclinations), abilities or inabilities, etc. At this level the Self-Identity rises beyond class, race, occupation, nationality, etc. There are no conditioned reflex patterns in the spirit that can force the individual to respond in a determined manner. In everyday life, this means that the person will not be controlled by conditioned responses. He will be totally free of the control by likes, dislikes, love, hatreds, fear, anger, and the whole pattern of conditioned ways of thinking and emotional responses to given situations." Can Siddha Yoga assist us in overcoming these conditions?

Ram: Yes, however, you do not have to take my word for it. In fact, "There is no reason to take anyone's word for anything. In the Siddha Yoga process there is nothing to blindly believe or accept on faith. It is the yoga of our own experience, of our expansion. The only reason anyone practices Siddha Yoga meditation is because of what actually happens to them. The validity of the Siddha Yoga process is that it works; it actually transforms us and our lives."

Student: How does this work? As I sit here, I hear you speaking of a course, a course of study?

Ram: Yes, a course of study, in a different sense. "This course is not like reading a book. There is an actual process that takes place from lesson to lesson, and from volume to volume. It is that process, more than written words, which makes the course so powerful. People who participate in the course often share that after having profound insights, they feel like, OF COURSE, I ALREADY KNEW THIS. I WAS JUST NEVER ABLE TO PUT IT IN WORDS. This is the way Truth is conveyed. The Truth always come from within – never from without. A true teacher doesn't try to drive knowledge into us like a nail, or fill us with knowledge like pouring water into a cup; a true teacher awakens knowledge already intuitively inside us. It is an ancient Truth we have already always known somewhere deep within. A vivid clarity of this highest Truth reveals itself, and all its wonders, through the guidance of a Siddha."

Student: It is so good to hear you say that a true teacher brings out of the student what is inside. As I have traveled, I have come in contact with so many teachers who have fallen into ownership of individuals. They try to make you into clones of themselves and seek a great following. They seem to hold their followers captive, with the use of fear and guilt. I guess that is the effect of seeing self separate from the higher Self, or God.

Ram: Yes, that is a good observation. That is why we say "This course is a course on opening the heart, and learning to truly see, hear, understand, and relate most openly to others, while maintaining a genuine love for our own Self."

Student: So, I can truly relate to others, and yet, maintain my Self? I find that so many of us lose sight of self as we relate to others.

Ram: That is because we do not know Self. Open up to the process, allow yourself to experience the process of Siddha Yoga, allow the

Shakti, or the Ashe as the Yorubas' say, to flow through you and assist in your development. It is always present, you just have to become conscious of it and tap into it. If what you have heard in this session with me has resonated with you, then there is a good chance that you will enjoy the balance of your time here with us in the Valley of the Masters. You must understand that your, I repeat, YOUR own inner experience is the only way you will know the Truth about this or anything else.

Student: Master, it resonates well within me. After my last initiation as a Yoruba Babalawo (High Priest), I was given the charge to open a Temple as most masters have done in the past. However, having seen so much confusion and different approaches to the truth and all claiming to have the ultimate Truth, I did not want to get involved in that circus. Now, since you have shown me that there is only one truth and that Truth is universal, it is my desire to build a Temple, dedicated to the motto of "MANY PATHS, YET ONE TRUTH." Master, I want all to be comfortable to come as the masters here have made me to feel. I want to convey this love to all and seek my own personal liberation as I assist others. I find that there is much spiritual sickness in this world of illusion and I pray not to become a part of if, but to offer a cure for most of it. It is to the showing of the unity and one Truth that I seek to dedicate the temple. Master, I give thanks for you allowing me to come to the Valley of the Masters.

Ram: You are most welcome, yet the process of which I speak is a twelve-year process, your life will be changed and the lives of all you touch will be changed. All that you will be given can be understood, on any level. Apply it in your life and allow others to experience it for themselves. Now, go, rest, reflect, and prepare for your first lesson with tomorrow's sunrise.

Peace & Love

1. Can't live with her/can't live without her – the spiritual significance of male/female relationships

"The Beloved asked the Lover, do you love me more than you love yourself? The Lover replied, I have died to myself and now I live for you."

RUMI

"Men and women can be examples of love. They can transform their materialistic notion of love from "having" to "being". They must love themselves and fulfill themselves and be as complete as possible unto themselves. They must stop playing the tug-of-war game of emotional giving and taking."

On the Breath of the Gods
Ariel Tomioka

Central to a strong community is strong families, thus, strong male/female relationships are a must. There must be harmony, independence, and interdependence in the relationship if both parties are to grow and evolve as true spiritual beings and as a spiritual couple. However, this quest must and should be taken from the proper cultural perspective, for it is culture that shapes our behavior. For African Americans to pursue healthy relationships following the relationship model of a society with a history of racism and oppression is to insure the failure of that relationship. At some point, it becomes necessary to reach back, examine and reclaim our cultural heritage in all aspects of our daily lives, particularly in our relationships.

There is a need to recognize what the war is that continues to take place in our lives and relationships. While we may want to forget, we must look back with a clear head and analyze the past. Our failure to analyze the dynamic of white supremacy is a tragedy, because it is this

237

dynamic that is the fundamental cause of our failed relationships. We must remember, it prevented marriages of African American males and females during slavery and it is essentially doing the same today. In the love affair with this world of illusion, we fail to realize that the very cultural patterns that we attempt to imitate are the same cultural patterns that were responsible for our enslavement. Our Ancestors did not have the storybook weddings. We were property and were treated as such, and were sold at anytime – thus destroying bonds and family. This is something we should never forget; it should be a guiding light in our efforts to establish strong relationships today. While we do have the opportunity to establish stable relationships today, it seems that the war continues; yet the war continues not only from the outside but also from within the relationship. It seems that we are at war with each other, struggling for power and control following the European model of patriarchy. Our relationships must be defined as an ongoing struggle to reclaim our lost manhood and womanhood, in light of our cultural legacy. The same squabbling, struggling, and fighting we do with each other as a people, we do in our relationships.

At this point the initiate should spend time reflecting on all the time and energy he spends struggling with his mate in their relationship, struggling for control, searching for the myth of "living happy ever-after." We can never live happily ever-after until we reach across time and reclaim our lost legacy. In so doing, we might be pleasantly surprised to find that our relationships were not about inter struggles between the couple, the relationships were of mutual respect, cooperation, and harmony. We must begin to uncover the pattern on which our African and Native American Ancestors built their relationships. We contend, if a divorce is to take place, it should be a divorce of Western culture, and a marriage to African and Native American culture. In the book, An Afrocentric Guide To a Spiritual Union by Ra Un Nefer Amen, on page 8, he writes:

If 3% of the population comes down with an illness, you look into the constitution and lifestyle of the sick individuals. On the other hand, if 50% of the population comes down with the same illness, you must then look, not at the individuals, but for some social, or environmental cause of the problem. According to the statistical abstract of the United States for 1991, published by the U.S. Department of Commerce, the average duration of marriages in the U.S. from 1970 to 1987 was 7 years. The average age at divorce was early to mid 30's. The average rate of marriages for 1980 to 1989 was 10 per 1,000 population, while the divorce rate- not including most annulments, legal separations, and unofficial separations – was 5 per 1,000 population (50% of the marriage rate).[91]

If 50% of our marriages are ending in divorce after 7 years, then, it becomes necessary to look beyond the individuals, the problem has to be with what we are taught regarding relationships. When there is a problem or failure in a relationship, it will always be the fault of the man or woman. However, we never stop to think that it might be the fault of the society that gives us our values? Again, Ra Un Nefer Amen writes on page 7:

> The fundamental cause of marital problems in the Western world must be laid at the feet of the institutions – religious and educational – in charge with shaping (cultivating) the behavior of people, as well as the other main social institutions (government, economical, etc.) as they act as reinforcers of the negative behavioral patterns that create the social framework that dooms interpersonal relationships to failure.[92]

One must understand that, an individual's actions are mostly the logical results of the values, customs, and norms programmed into them by society. Again, take the bathing suit example of programming, if you walk up to a woman on the street and ask to see her underclothes (panties, bra) you would receive much opposition, and rightly so. However, were you to follow the same person to the beach, or public swimming pool, you would see the same person in panties, bras and much less. Why is this? Because society says, it is a custom for us to go to the beach, or pool, in panties and bras, disguised as swimsuits, but we are not to do it on the street. Thus, society has programmed our behavior, and we accept it. Society has given us our values regarding male/female relationships, and it is time to question these values. Together, both men and women must question the values, that govern their relationships and change them, if necessary. We must recognize the war that is taking place, both within and without on our relationships.

While speaking with Ur Aua Hehi Metu Ra Enkamit, the Paramount King of the Washington D.C. region of the Ausar/Auset Society, he said, "in the word 'marriage' you find 'mar', or 'MARS.' Mars is the planet that rules over 'wars'. It is also the planet associated with the Kamitic Deity, "Herukhuti", who is known as 'Ogun' in the Yoruba tradition. This is a very martial energy, for Herukhuti/Ogun is the warlord, fighting to establish truth. The majority of our marriages are WARS, fighting for control as we seek to replicate the Eurocentric standard of marriage i.e., men fighting to dominate and women fighting to survive. In his monumental work, <u>Metu Meter Vol.1</u>, page 281, Ra Un Nefer Amen describes the personality portfolio of hot and dry energy of Mars and its action on our animal spirit as:

Emotional traits:
(+): Courage manifesting as lack of fear of bodily harm, energetic, prudent, magnanimous, forceful, enterprising, constructive, muscularly skillful, zealous, passionate; delighted and motivated by situations involving challenges, or hard, and dangerous but relatively short work.
(-): Quarrelsome, antagonistic, pugnacious, arrogant, impetuous, rash, choleric, destructive, violent, forceful, excessive, irritable.

Overzealous, and excessively passionate, inclined to tobacco, alcohol, murder, treason, cruelty, etc.[93]

For those of us who have experienced separations and divorce, I am sure we can look back and see the negative aspects of Herukhuti/Ogun working in our relationships. Think of the countless passionate quarrels fueled by emotion, over nothing, or our arrogance in the face of being wrong, too proud to admit that we are wrong. We could go on and on, however, our purpose was to show that the majority of our relationships are wars. We are warring against each other and not ignorance or societal imposed values.

However, it is possible to call on the positive energy of Herukhuti/Ogun to face the challenges of our relationships. Herukhuti/Ogun enjoys a challenge and goes about establishing justice with a passion. We must become passionate in our efforts to establish a 'just' relationship. This brings us to the central point of this discussion; the root word of relationship is 'relate'. How can you relate to someone else and be just to him or her, when you cannot relate yourself. Seek to understand self before you can understand someone else. It is the relating to self that will insure that healthy relationships will develop. If one learns to love and honor self, then one can love and honor someone else without them becoming a projection of all of our fantasies and desires.

It seems we are looking for someone to love us, yet it is in the quest to realize the Divine self that one learns self-love. It appears that any other efforts are only centered in ego. We enter into relationships with baggage, generational. We expect our mate to unpack our baggage, and if they don't, we think they don't love us. We must develop the courage to recognize and unpack our own baggage. In a very symbolic sense, the quest to realize the Divine Self is in unpacking our own baggage. Meditation, prayer, rituals, yoga etc., all take one into one's self. It is this internal journey that one must take before one can take or appreciate an external journey with a mate. However, one will soon find out that the journey with a mate is both external and internal, and the relationship will bring you face to face with your baggage.

We must learn to face self – face our pain, and develop the courage and determination to heal our relationships and ourselves. Most, if not all of us, have been hurt in a relationship; and we have packed that hurt away. So we enter into new relationships, we unpack the hurt and seek to get even. However, we take it out on the new person. If she is hurt badly, then the next man will pay for the hurt caused by the previous man and the same with men, hurting her for what some other woman did. At some point, we must face the hurt, heal the pain, and realize that the present person you are with did not cause the pain. Females are good at voicing their pain, sharing and healing with other women. However, we men will not face the fact that this woman hurt me, let alone get with another man and discuss it and seek ways to heal. We walk around with so much pain, because we are afraid to go to our partners, our boys, and discuss the pain. We believe they are subject to say to us, "Ah! Bitch stop crying," or "Stop acting like a Bitch." As a result, we walk around full of pain and we never heal. It is time that we, men, recognize that we have pain, we hurt, and we should and must help each other to heal.

From a spiritual perspective, it is pain that causes us to grow spiritually, however, I realize this is difficult to understand when you are hurting. Yet, pain is one way that spirit can carry a strong impression into the inner body to trigger understanding and growth. Instead of taking it out on the other person, you should seek to understand the lesson of the pain. Learn, heal, grow, and evolve. What understanding has one gained from the pain? Realize that everything is distinguished by its opposite. Were it not for pain, we would not appreciate the experience of joy. We do not seek to suggest that the essence of all relationships should be painful. This is far from the case, yet we realize that pain is associated with growth. It is our desire that the reader should look for the lessons learned and not for revenge that the reader grow from the experience and not die in the darkness of self- pity. For we understand that one's self image can become distorted in a relationship; and if one enters into a new relationship with a distorted self-image, then the relationship itself will be distorted. This is another reason all the sages and seers taught self-love and self-acceptance that we should seek to realize the Higher self.

How do we make our relationships work? How many of you reading this book have ever taken a course at a college, or even in high school, on relationships? What about a course on understanding men or women? Look at any college catalog and you will, more than likely, not find any courses of this nature offered. There is a need for us to be taught regarding all aspects of relationships. While one can attend some of the most prestigious universities in the world, it is doubtful that one will find classes on manhood, womanhood, or marriage. In the Western world, we are left to discover for ourselves how to establish good relationships; so we turn to TV, movies, etc. Yet, it was the way of our Ancestors to teach manhood, womanhood, and marriage via rites-of-passage. Such teachings were central to our culture and nothing was left to chance.

It is through initiation and rites-of-passage that our people learned of their roles in the society and the important role that relationships play. Now, as then, we must be taught by our Elders. Our places and roles as men, women, husbands, and wives must be shown to us by Elders, via initiation. Think of the times you have attended a wedding and overheard someone say, "I don't give them a year!" Instead, we should hear, "They are going to do well because they have the community behind them and they are going to spend time with Elders who have been married for 35 years or more. The Elders will pass on to them all of their years of experience and learning."

Yes, we must return to our Ancestral traditions; we must be initiated into the knowledge of relationships. One of the principle purposes of the initiation rites was to introduce the young people to matters of sex, marriage, procreation and family life. The initiation, rite-of-passage, ritual is a sanctification and preparation for marriage. Only when it was over could one marry. In fact, rites-of-passage and initiation was/is the door to marriage. The entire community takes part in the ritual, the community prepares the young people for marriage and family life. Thus, it is the community that takes part in the teaching, regarding relationships. The young people are not left to find the way for themselves as we are in the west.

Today, young people look at the appearance of a person, what they drive, and how they respond in bed. Based on these superficial things, they make the decision to marry, and within 7 years the marriage is over! Today, more than ever, there is a need to employ the traditions of our Ancestors in regards to our relationships. We all must get involved with the process of building strong stable male/female relationships. Our young people must start to sit with the Elders, profit from their mistakes and build on their successes.

Among our Ancestors, it was during rites-of-passage that the young men and women were separated from their communities, and each other, and given full instruction of manhood and womanhood. It is time that we do the same, our young people are dying for lack of knowledge which we Elders possess. It is vital that we heal our relationships, that we understand our roles, because the foundation of any society is strong families. If the family is not together, then any attempt to solve social, individual, and international problems is doomed to failure.

The lack of strong family values has led, and continues to lead to many of the problems we see in our communities. Due to the lack of fathers in their lives, our young men are desperately looking for models of manhood, sometimes finding it in the wrong places. It must be borne in mind that young women who grow up without a father in the home generally end up having problems with their relationships. Girls learn how to negotiate reality with a man from their fathers. Today, many young ladies are using their bodies in an attempt to experience male closeness, which they missed by not having a father present. As a result, we have a never-ending cycle of fatherless children, looking for daddy in the wrong places.

While we all come into this life with challenges that we must overcome and face, it is not about taking it out on our mates. We are at war with each other, mainly because we are at war with self. Self -hatred is so great until we project individual self-hate on our mates and make life a living hell for each other. This is not to say that mistakes are not made in choosing a mate, however, this is where the oracles and Elders come into play. The oracles can see what we cannot see, that is one reason it is strongly advised that the person get an oracle consultation before taking a step in a relationship. Seek to know the background of the perspective person and consult the Elders. In many cases they are living oracle systems who can look at a person and give you their life history.

Seek to understand why the universe brought this person into your life, what lessons have they come to teach you?

We cannot place enough emphasis on the need to be connected to Elders who have gone over the road that we are yet to travel. During the various wars, troops would come upon a minefield. They would send a man through and you would have to watch where he stepped. If he made it through safely, then you would know where to walk. By walking in his steps, you could get through the minefield a little faster. Such is the same with Elders; they have made it through the minefields of marriage. Sit with them and allow them to tell you their experiences and the mine that they have stepped on (smile). Brothers, sit with the Elder men and listen to stories of heartache, as well as triumph, in the face of tremendous adversity. Look deep into the eyes of these old sages and open your heart to be taught. Walk with these old men as they show you what life is about, allow them to place you on their shoulders that you might see a greater future. In many cases allow them to experience their deferred dreams through you. It is our prayer that we will open and ask our Elders for guidance in family matters, that we can avoid their mistakes and build on their successes. Brothers, sit with the Elder mothers and allow them to lay those eyes on you and look through you. Allow them to tell you what they see, and most of all, act on what they tell you.

My beloved brothers, take time to look at your mate and lay down the weapons of war. The two of you should seek to understand that you and your relationship is a product of the society that made you. Gain the courage to look for something new to mate you, look to God, Divinities and the Ancestors to assist you in making a relationship that will withstand the test of time. Open your hearts, and allow each other to truly see each other. We understand that opening the heart means allowing yourself to be vulnerable, this means that you would have to trust the person that you are with. If you cannot trust your mate to open fully to her, then, maybe you do not need to be with her. Seek to become more than a talking "dildo" for her. In her nature she carries all the healing energy you need if you would but allow yourself to open and trust.

It is said by the Yoruba, "The Man is the head, but the woman is the neck that turns the head." Allow your lady to turn your head, for she sees what we do not see. However, this requires a level of self-confidence. We are so unsure of who we are as men, that we fear listening to a woman. However, the Holy Quran says, "You are the two halves that make the whole," in another place it says, "that you are clothes for each other." Recall when you were a small boy trying to dress yourself, your clothes would be half buttoned, your pants unzipped and your shoes untied. Now that you are a man, you can walk through the house, shaving and dressing at the same time. Such is the same with your relationships, in the beginning it will be difficult and you will need the help of the Elders, but 25 – 30 years down the road you will know her and she will know you so well that you will be able to give advice to others.

She is strong where you are weak and you are strong where she is weak; assist each other in realizing the God/Goddess of self. Enjoy your relationships, for you have a chance to make your relationships a thing of great beauty. Spend time with each other in the presence of nature; allow nature to speak words of love to you both. Allow the vibrations of that which is natural to stir memories of the natural harmony that can exist between the two of you if you follow spirits' guidance. Speak to each other of dreams deferred and assist each other in realizing your goals. Get to know each other deeply, clean up your body, mind, and spirit, so when you embrace each other in sacred union you will be able to reach across time and bring back great ancestors.

Allow your children to grow in an environment of love and understanding. Yes, we understand that you did not come up like that, but we as men are duty-bound to give to our sons and daughters what we did not get. Let not your relationship become weighted-down with the politics of sex, etc. Make it not, business 101, I do for you and you do for me. No, *give*, give from the heart expecting nothing in return.

My Beloved Brothers, let us learn to respect and honor the wombs of our mates. Her womb is the causeway to heaven. Let us not pollute it, or seek to destroy it, for she is a co-creator with God and from her womb comes our future. Likewise, always honor your penis, for this is your tool of procreation. This is your means of piercing the unlimited darkness of heaven, filling the night skies with cosmic nectar for the production of an ancestral vehicle. Honor the gift that has been granted to you.

It is with much love and respect that I write these words for it is time that "men guard the door while the women work the magic."

2. Walking the walk & talking the talk – next steps

My beloved Brothers, I want to take time to thank you for taking this walk with me, for my quest to find manhood has been the same as yours. Thank you for reading the words. I pray that they have helped you and will serve only as a reminder that we are blessed to be alive and able to reach back home for our ways to manhood. Now, what are the next steps? It is said, that you can only be shown the path, you have to decide whether you want to walk it or not. Should you decide to walk it, then, we can only stand here and welcome you when you return. This is your life, it is a subjective experience of such great pleasure and mystery until you do yourself harm, by not placing your feet on the path to reclaim your lost manhood. Your spirit knows what to do and the universe stands ready to provide you with all you need for the journey. It is with these words that I welcome you to a path of healing. Come, let us together go into the expanse of the universe, reach across time, and reclaim our lost manhood.

Much respect

Babaji

VIII

CONCLUSION

It has been said that some people forget their culture as a means to survive, while others **remember** their culture as a means to survive. I believe that it is time that we remember our culture as a means to survive. It is time that we reach back and bring forth those ancient systems of initiation to ensure our survival as a people and the survival of humanity. Cleary, we all can benefit from a clear definition of manhood and womanhood. Many of us, grown adults, (grown in age) are in need of an initiation. We can no longer identify ourselves by our material goods. If we are to be true to self, we must acknowledge an inner pain that seems to grow stronger each day. With the passing of each minute our inner emptiness grows deeper and deeper to the point that no alcohol, no reefer, no crack, no amount of sex, and no amount of money can fill. Our souls are crying for something more; our Ancestors are calling from the other side, they are calling to their children that we remember their ways and pick them up again, that found in their ways are the healing that we seek, the healing that humanity is in need of. This is no time for us to allow racial, sexual, or religious differences to keep us for this cosmic healing. All children of today are in need of guidance. White young men are just as lost as African

American young men. In fact, while African American men may kill each other over a beef, white young men will seek to kill everyone, including themselves!

Most men in America are insecure and frightened of the woman in themselves. As a result, they will attack anything, or anyone, that reminds them of that fear. We are seriously homophobic! It is not my intention to speak to homosexuality, but to address the issue of men dealing with the woman in themselves. It is, as Carl Jung noted, that men have so many female hormones and women have so many male hormones, men have a woman in them and women have a man in them.

It is rites-of-passage that allows for the grounding of one in their sexuality, while allowing for the expression of the male or female qualities. Our Ancestors knew that every seven (7) years you go through a door, 7- 14- 21, etc. If you will notice, it is around the age of 14, give or take two years, when a young woman has her first cycle and young men produce sperm. It is around the age of 12 – 14 that young men should be taken through a rites-of-passage and grounded in their manhood so the woman in them can come forward. By woman in them, I mean those female qualities that are nurturing, caring, sensitive, devoted, and allows us to go into trance. Once a man is grounded in this manhood, i.e., he knows he is a man, then there is no need to prove to others that you are a man. You know you have a penis and you do not feel the need to pull it out and show others every chance you get. There is no need to get into urinating contest with other men who are also unsure of their manhood. Today, guns are but symbolic penises in the hands of insecure men just as the atomic bomb is a penis in the hands of the world's insecure power elite.

Once grounded in your manhood, you can allow the woman to come forward and BALANCE you. To take a phrase from the Bible,

CONCLUSION

"Let Us make Man in our Image." If this is God speaking, then God is both male and female. In order to be a balanced man you must allow the woman in you to take her place. In order for us to be a balanced society, we must allow our women to take their place BESIDE us, not behind us. We must not fear following the lead of a woman, and we must not fear following the lead of the female aspect of self. It is the female aspect of self that takes us into the deeper regions of the self and helps us to unlock the mysteries of the universe.

It was in the dream state that Einstein saw himself riding on a beam of light; as a result, he came up with the theory of relativity. Dreaming is associated as female. The point here is that being a balanced man is what led to the great discoveries of the past. It was balanced men and women who built the great civilizations of the past. Rites-of-Passage serves to ground and balance the individual as one learns then knows that he is a manifest man. Thus, when the woman in him asserts herself, he allows her to come forward and thus balance himself. Look around you today, most single mothers are balanced women, why, being alone has forced them to develop male qualities, they must be aggressive, protectors and providers for their families. Now most men are not caring, sensitive nurturers, as a result, a lot of single mothers get involved with unbalanced men and end up realizing that they are raising another little boy! We need Initiation and Rites-of-Passage to balance us.

In America, when the average young lady has her first cycle, there is a mother, grandmother, aunt, or some knowledgeable woman there to walk them through this most important door in their life. As a result, many pass through this door confident and secure. To the converse, when the average young African American male has his first 'wet dream,' there is no father, no grandfather, or knowledgeable uncle, to assist him in walking through this most difficult and sensitive time in his life. As a result, he walks through this door INSECURE, insecure of his manhood. He joins other insecure men, and if he is looked at wrong there is a fight! You know the story all-too-well. Yet, he fully accepts the ways of one who is culturally blind, he seeks to become a model of European manhood and runs from the African and Native American model. Most men walking the streets today are frightened and insecure due to the lack of initiation and rites-of-passage conducted by their elders. We have come to that point in time that we, Elders, (42+) must bring our young men and women close to us and teach them of secrets long forgotten. We must bring them to us with love and caring and usher them through the doors of manhood and womanhood, that they might go forth thankful for the sacrifices and knowledge of their Ancestors as they seek to heal humanity.

I pray that God, the Deities and Ancestors will continue to move us all towards the realization that it is spiritual cultivation that will bring us into our humanity. I pray that God will bless you who read these few words to reach back and bring forth our great systems that will heal humanity and us.

Peace & Love

IX

ADDENDUM
Rites of Passage: The Metamorphosis of the Black Male in Higher Education Administration; There is always free Cheese in a Mouse Trap

Many African American educators have directly inherited the benefits form the Black consciousness movement of the 1960s. Those recipients include professionals, who work in higher education, either as faculty, or as administrators. African American faculty and administrators have received those accommodations, as a result of the Black men and women who, spearheaded the Black Power and Civil Rights Movements. In response to these political-social campaigns, predominantly white colleges and universities gradually increased the enrollment of black students and later added the recruitment of black and other non-white faculty and administrators to their efforts. Chishom (1987) in his article, "An Assessment of the Role of Black Administrators at predominantly White Colleges and Universities ", highlighted Morris'(1972) assessment of the Black student's struggle and the connection to Black College professors. Chishom declared that:

Black student protest of the 60's, calling for more relevant role models at white colleges and universities, caused a Black 'brain drain' form black colleges to white colleges. Morris concluded that Black professors were being sought because of pressure from government and campus militants.

It was the bravery of the black militant men and women of the 1960s, and government legislation such as the 1964 Civil Rights Act that opened the doors of higher education to black faculty and administrators at predominantly white colleges and universities. Young blacks formed partnerships, and found support in the local black communities, that fueled their organizational intensity and propelled the movement, adding to its strength on a national and international level. As Haki Madhubuti writes in his article, <u>Missing Movement, Missing Fathers; The Culture of short Lives and Low Expectations:</u>

>...the struggles to share local, state and federal power; the opening up of public facilities to all on an equal basis; the empowering of the disenfranchised with the vote; the recapturing and redefining of the Black/African image in the American/World mind; the equal participation in the educational process by the underserved; the enlargement of living space for people of color; the redefinition of what it means to be a woman in a male dominant society; and the open and raw disclosures of the worldwide destructive powers of racism (white world supremacy) in maintaining a Nazi like world form South Africa to South Carolina is what the Black Movement of the 60s and early 70s was about.

It was this recapturing and redefining of the Black/African image that led myself and other young Black men to search for a new meaning of manhood. Organizations such as the Nation of Islam, Black Panthers, Republic of New Africa, Black Christian Nationalists, and many others, provided the motivation, social guidance and teachings to capture this new Black Male identity. For instance, the Honorable

ADDENDUM

Elijah Muhammad, Minister Louis Farrakhan, Don L. Lee (Haki Madhubuti), Maulana Karanga, Dr. Ben, Dr. John Henry Clark, Stokely Carmicheal (Kwame Ture), Huey P. Newton, H. Rap Brown (Jamal El-Amin) and many others served as professionals who shaped this new young black manhood. They offered the young Black campus militants the motivation and strength to organize and demand change. These demands included the call for black studies, black faculty and administrators. As Madhubuti writes "The Black movement provided young African Americans of that period a context for discovering identity and purpose, and it also provided serious proposals for the future."

This movement among young black males and females, and their courage to initiate change, is the reason black faculty and administrators are part of the white university hierarchy today. But in their/our hunt for tenure and other academic and administrative positions, many of these individuals failed to recognize that they have been reaping the benefits of the 1960s movement. We in higher education administration must realize how we got here and based on this realization, we must decide on a future direction that is centered on the liberation of the African American mind.

Black males are in higher education administration as a direct result of the 60's civil rights and liberation movements. The question is, do we see Black Men? I use the term Males and Men with a distinction in mind. In his book, <u>Visions for Black Men</u>, Dr. Na'im Akbar, defines males as the biological identification of the entity and Man (men) deals with the conscious liberated mind in total control of his destiny. To use the phase of Dr. Evelyn Reid of Ohio University, " Anglo Males Cybernation" (white male control), I raise the issue; can, or will, American colleges and universities (predominantly black, or white) that are managed via Anglo Male Cybernation (administration and board-controlled) tolerate, or accommodate, BLACK MEN as

255

defined by Akbar? This question of tolerance is directly related to the Black Male Rites- of-Passage in Higher Education Administration.

There is a definite rite-of-passage that occurs in higher education, but it is not of the type and function practiced by our African ancestors. As stated earlier in the book, Rites-of-passage were used to take one from a passive state to an active state. In many cases, they marked the transition from passive childhood into the active world of adult responsibility. After 25 years in higher education, it is my position that the majority of black males in higher education administration on white campuses remain in the childhood state of passive participation; they have little, or no, decision-making power, not to mention major budget control. Hoskins (1978) points out that Black Administrators at white institutions held lower ranks than their counterparts at black institutions.[94]

According to William E. Sedlacek of the University of Maryland, "In addition to the usual school pressures, a Black student must typically handle cultural biases and learn how to bridge his or her Black culture with the prevailing one at the white university."[95]

It is the bridging of the black culture and that of the University (black or white) which is the fundamental issue for black males in higher education administration. Janice Hale-Benson writes

"One of the challenges the Black man must face is the conflicting images of masculinity, that predominate in the Afro-American community, against the images in the broader society."[96]

Thus, a black male enters higher education with a dilemma. How much of his manhood must he give up to get tenure, Vice Presidency, or the Presidency? As Madhubuti points out:

ADDENDUM

...most of the Euro-American systems and sub-systems are structured to systematically keep conscious Black men out. However, if Black men wish to become imitation white men, there exists, within the political-industrial-military complex, significant token positions (Gibson,1978) – which are used to legitimize the system and to cloud its true relationship to Black people, a relationship of slave master to slave. In fact, the "Slave" position is the major rank that Black men, regardless of the title and income, are allowed to occupy.[97]

Therefore, if the black male wants to progress in the system, he must become an imitation white man. He must give up any hope of mental liberation and independent identity, deny his culture, Ancestors, and most of all, his manhood. As Haki further states:

If Black men want to be part of the Euro-American structure in an 'intimate and non-superficial' way, they will have to give up the most important aspect of their being, their Blackness. And, in thought and actions, they will have to become white; a transformation that is ultimately impossible, but tempting enough to unconscious Black men that millions, in this century on a daily basis, unknowingly betray their people, themselves and the future of there children.[98]

This giving up of blackness presents additional problems for Black males, particularly those who seek to be role models. Those who want the world to see their success. As we move up the professional ladder toward the vice presidency, we find our mannerisms change. A point Nathan Hare makes, as he addresses the issue of the 'Mimic' "They chronically imitate white mannerisms in the quest for a feeling of similarity, or closeness, to their white ideal; as whites do, they do."[99]

In addition to this Hale-Benson states:

257

REACHING BLACK MALES THROUGH SPIRITUALITY

The Afro-American culture projects a hip walking, cool-talking model of masculinity. Dr. Ernie Smith of the University of California says that often Black Males reject models of Black professional men because their behaviors and mannerisms are considered effeminate; they do not project the raunchy macho of the ghetto. Dr. Smith also says that some boys feel they are flirting with homosexuality, if they give in to the pressure of the school to exhibit behaviors they consider feminine.[100]

It is rites-of-passage that takes one from boyhood to manhood. By no means do I suggest that black males display uncivilized behavior in higher education administration. How could I suggest this, when it was our fathers who civilized the world? I am suggesting that we take a close-look at the Anglo Male Cybernation (white male control). The truth is we KNOW we must take a passive role in order to progress in the system. We understand, we must not become a threat, we must appear 'safe'. In taking on this passive role, our mannerisms become effeminate, as we seek to mimic the educated power elite in the academy. In a culture such as this, being passive is associated with weakness and femininity, particularly among black males. We become so prim and proper, we lose the essence of who we are. While this is not true of many, it does hold true for most.

There is a need for the examination of maleness and manhood in higher education administration to be viewed from an afrocentric perspective. There is a need to view the rites-of-passage involved in bridging the gap, between the black culture and the white university (also, black colleges with white consciousnesses). This must be viewed with respect to the metamorphosis of the black male. Keeping in mind, there is always free cheese (promotion, tenure and etc.) in a mousetrap (denying culture, heritage, manhood), do we actually bridge the gap, or do we jump off the bridge?

ADDENDUM

Rites of Passage and the Black Male in Higher Education Administration

Dr. Molefi Kete Asante, the leading proponent in academia of the Afrocentric school of thought says, "Afrocentricity, means, literally, placing African ideals at the center of any analysis that involves African culture and behavior."[101]

Therefore, it is necessary to view the rites-of-passage of the black male in higher education administration from an African perspective. To speak of rites-of-passage is to suggest that one is conscious of the rhythm of life. That one has an understanding of the nature of man and his eventual destiny. However, to speak of rites of passage within the academy is also to suggest a consciousness of a rhythm. A rhythm that takes one at the symbolic state of childhood and evolves them through the portals of academic administration and deposits them in the seat of authority (i.e., Presidency. V.P., Dean or tenure). Verifying this rhythm and rites of passage, Hoskin (1978) writes:

> Similar to Black Administrators at predominantly Black institutions, white administrators at predominantly white institutions have traditionally risen from the ranks of the faculty, to dean and vice-president, and have often culminated their ascent with the presidency of an institution.[102]

Andrew J. Chishom of the University of South Carolina adds to this observation of Hoskins:

> Due to a rather rapid rise in Black student populations during the last five years, the majority of Black Administrators, at white institutions, are new to those systems and, to an extent, are limited in their professional ascension as compared to whites who, in similar positions, have followed an orderly progressive professional path.[103]

Thus, we see that the rites-of-passage for black administrators at white institutions does not entail the same rhythm as white administrators. Ra Un Nefer Amen, in his book, An Afrocentric Guide to A Spiritual Union, defines rites-of-passage as:

> Nothing more that a set of initiations aimed at leading individuals through the various evolutionary stages of life. For these initiations to succeed, they must be based on a full understanding of the spirit of man. Those who would conduct it must be in possession of such a knowledge.[104]

Here we have our first indication of serious conflict. When black males enter into the pipeline of higher education at white institutions, as students, faculty and administrators, do those who conduct the academic rites-of-passage have a full understanding of the spirit of man, black men in particular? As we witness white men's struggles with redefining of their manhood, in light of the rise of the women's movement and the climates of diversity and political correctness, we can only conclude that they do not have a full understanding of men, let alone black men. It would stand to reason, in light of these new threats to their manhood, white men would seek to hold on to the power they have, a fact that is validated by Dr. Joe R. Feagin in his book The Continuing Significance of Racism: U.S. Colleges and Universities, on page 11:

> Today, white men account for about 37 percent of the population, yet, after decades of affirmative action and anti-discrimination laws, they hold 90 – 100 percent of the top positions in most of the nation's major institutions.[105]

Furthermore, how can black men and females expect such an understanding of the spirit of man, when those in power have classified them as secondary? In fact according to Anthony T. Browder, in his

ADDENDUM

book, <u>Nile Valley Contributions To Civilization</u>, the myth that blacks
were inferior to whites got its origins in academia. He writes:

> The creation of this myth was fabricated in 1795 by Johann Fried-
> rich Blumenbach, a professor at Gottingen University in Germany.
> Blumenbach produced the first scholarly work on human racial clas-
> sification, and invented the term Caucasian. Martin Bernal, author
> of Black Athena, the Afroasiac Roots of Greece, discusses the im-
> pact of Blumenbach's research: Blumenbach was first to publicize
> the term 'Caucasian' which he used for the first time in the third
> edition of his great work (de Generis Humani Varictate Nativa) in
> 1765. According to him, the white or Caucasian, was the first and
> most beautiful and talented race, from which all the others had de-
> generated to become Chinese, Negroes, etc. Blumenbach justified
> the curious name 'Caucasian' on 'Scientific' and 'Racial' grounds.
> Blumenbach was conventional for his period in that he included
> 'Semites' and 'Egyptians' among his Caucasians.

> Between 1775 and 1800, Gottingen established the concept of the
> 'science of antiquity' upon which future universities would build.
> The slanted and distorted research which emerged for his institution
> established much of the intellectual framework within which later
> research and publication within the new professional disciplines
> was carried out, states Bernal.[106]

While history bears this claim false, one can see its effects on the
rites-of-passage of black males in higher education. On the notion of
Black inferiority, Browder provides comments of some of history's
most renowned, so-called, thinkers and scholars:

> Arnold Toynbee, historian:
> When, we classify mankind by color, the only one of the primary
> races... which has not made a creative contribution to any of our
> twenty-one civilizations is the black race.

David Hume, philosopher:
I am apt to suspect that Negroes... to be naturally inferior to the white. There never was a civilized nation of any other complexion that white, nor ever any individual eminent either in action or speculation, no ingenious manufacturers amongst them, no arts or sciences.

John Burgess, scholar:
A black skin means membership in a race of men, which have never created a civilization of any kind. There is something natural in the subordination of an inferior race even to the point of enslavement of the inferior race....

Richard Burton, explorer and writer:
The study of the Negro is the study of man's rudimentary mind. He would appear rather a degeneracy from the civilized man than a savage rising to the first step, were it not for his total incapacity for improvement ....

Benjamin Franklin, scientist:
Why increase the sons of Africa, by planting them in America, where we have so fair an opportunity, by excluding all blacks and tawnys, or increasing the lovely white and red?

Thomas Jefferson, president:
I advance it, therefore, as a suspicion only, that the blacks, whether originally a distinct race or made distinct by time or circumstances, are inferior to the whites in the endowments of both body and mind.

Abraham Lincoln, president:
Here is a physical difference between the white and black races which I believe will forever forbid the two races living together.... While they do remain together there must be the position of superior and inferior, and I as much as any man am in favor of having the superior position assigned to the white race.

ADDENDUM

Henru Berry, Virginia House of Representative:
We have, as far as possible, closed every avenue by which the light may enter the slave's mind. If we could extinguish the capacity to see the light, our work will be complete. They would then be on the level of the beast of the fields and we then should be safe.

Professor Peter Beyer of the University of Baltimore School of Law once said to me: "You can legislate change, but you cannot legislate the way people think."

While laws may have opened doors to the white universities, the position of the Black male within these institutions reflects the thoughts of the power elite. Black males occupy an inferior position within the administration of the academy. The reason being, the notion of black inferiority is very much alive and, even if black males learn to play the power game to its completion, they still do not and will not share in the power, equally.

Kwame Agyei Akoto in his book, Nation-building: Theory & Practice in Afrikan Centered Education says:

Education is the ritualized reaffirmation of the national identity. It is anchored in the real and idealized history of a people. The nation's education is shaped and given impetus by the cultural and ideological assumptions, dynamics, essential values, priorities and goals of the nation.[107]

Now, what was and is the national identity of America? What are the cultural and ideological assumptions that have shaped and continue to shape the American educational system? Melting-pot and multicultural society? The condition of Native Americans and the millions of disenfranchised Africans in America points out the fallacy of the melting-pot theory. The cultural and ideological assumptions on which the American educational system is shaped is white supremacy. As Dr. Everett Griffin writes in his book, The Politics of Education: The Deliberate Miseducation of Black Children:

> Education in America mirrors the larger society. The American society is foremost a class, ethnic, and color – conscious social order. On the social pyramid, ethnicity is higher than color. At the apex of the ethnic-color pyramid is the white Anglo-Saxon Protestant (WASP) and its descending class structure.[108]

It is the will of the WASP power elite that dominates the society. By virtue of skin color, other whites are given access to this inner circle. It is the black male who is kept out, and yet, he stands at the door of academia seeking rites of passage into a system, that was never designed for his inclusion. Of this, Griffin writes:

> America's white colleges and universities are citadels of racist ideology. They exemplify American racism in its purest form. Being socially isolated and insulated, they are closed environments where white racist theoreticians weave theories of social and moral justification for the racist activity that permeates a socially amoral society.

> The primary purpose for the American university existence is to preserve and perpetuate the intellectual heritage of a racist society, not to change it. They are quasi-intellectual 'museums' where the racist administrator and professor may be seen as curators of a racist ideology.[109]

A system of rites-of-passage, within this educational system, is to make one a curator of the cultural and ideological assumptions that shape the particular institution. This is all the more reason the black male administrator must be aware of the price he pays, as he progresses up the academic corporate ladder. As he seeks the cheese (power, promotion, tenure, position, etc.), he must be aware of the trap (loss of identity)! For it is only those black males who are willing to become the curators of the cultural and ideological assumptions of the institutions that are even considered to be able to put their feet on the first rung of the academic corporate ladder! He must be wiling to pay the ultimate price – his independent manhood!

In his book, African Religion and Philosophy, John Mbiti discusses the nature of rites-of-passage and its impact on the individual and community. He says:

> The rites of birth and childhood introduce the child to the corporate community, but this is only the introduction. The child is passive and has still a long way to go. He must grow out of childhood and into adulthood physically, socially, and religiously. This is also a change from passive to active membership in the community. Most African people have rites and ceremonies that mark this great change, but a few do not observe initiation and puberty rites. The initiation of the young is one of the key moments in the rhythm of individual life, which is also the rhythm of the corporate group of which the individual is a part.[110]

Thus, it becomes clear that rites-of-passage are to take one from a passive state of existence to an active state of adulthood. Rites-of-passage takes one from the passive state of childhood to that of adulthood, and from the passive non-married to that of married. With the Anglo male Cybernation, a few black males are taken from the symbolic state of childhood to the active state of responsibility, within higher education administration. However, this active state comes with limitations and compromise. Chishom writes:

> Roosevelt Johnson (1969) pointed out that Black Administrators are usually hired into important administrative positions, but they

lack power and authority to make administrative decisions in areas other than Black studies and minority affairs, primarily because no thought was given to the possibility of black administrators being on white campuses, prior to the mid 1960's. Therefore, concludes Johnson, until recently, Blacks have not had the chance to serve in meaningful administrative positions outside the predominantly Black institutions. Moore and Wagstaff (1974) support Johnson's contention by observing that "Black Administrators at white institutions are the administrative caricature in higher education. Even the worker in the kitchen, the attendant on the parking lot, and the custodian sweeping the floor know that most Black administrators are without power and authority.[111]

Regardless to how limited the authority, the Black administrator can be said to have experienced a rite-of-passage and been initiated to a limited aspect of the inner circle. On the subject of initiation, Mbiti writes that "Initiation rites have a great educational purpose. The occasion often marks the beginning of acquiring knowledge which is otherwise not accessible to those who have not been initiated."

Initiation involves, among other things, taking an oath, that one will uphold and be loyal to the goals and ideas of the organization. Furthermore, one's willingness to accept and uphold these goals will determine his future in the organization. This advancement is also predicated on the loss of a distinct consciousness of one's blackness. In a November 1992 Essence Magazine article, Why White Men Fear Black Men, Andrew Hacker, author of the best seller Two Nations; Black and White, Separate, Hostile, Unequal, says:

We don't give Black young men, starting at a certain age, a chance to develop impressive careers in this country. They have a certain number of career options- music, athletics –cliches, but the true reason is this is a white society. Now, we're suppose to deny this and say we're multicultural, but the fact remains that Time Warner,

ADDENDUM

Queens College, Cornell University, Redbook, PC magazine are all white organizations. What we mean by this simply is that you have to act and look white in order to be one of us. You have to have a demeanor. Now some people achieve this, hence our allusions to (General) Colin Powell, as often as we can. We say, "Hey, he can do it." But, what we really mean is- and Powell knows this better than we do – that he was able and willing to adapt to a white military organization. He put 99 percent of himself, or his Black self, on hold, on the back, because he was ambitious, wanted to get ahead, and did.[112]

We must ask ourselves, how much of our Blackness are we willing to put on hold? The Anglo Male Cybernation will not facilitate the initiation of Black men into the inner-circle of higher education administration, while it will accept unconscious black males. In the same article, Hacker says:

At this point, organizations are much more willing to promote Black women and Asians than Black men. That's because Black men are seen as having a chip on the shoulder - the rebel - not really willing to go along with the values of XYZ, Inc., or for that matter, Harvard University.[113]

It is for this reason Black men will never be initiated into the inner circle of higher administration. Dr. Walter Gill, in his book, Issues in African American Education, writes:

In Blacks on White Campuses: Problems and Perspectives, Edward Jackson contends that there is little contact between African American and White colleagues, they rarely socialize, and they seldom communicate about academic issues. Sheila J. Nickson, in status on Minority Professionals on Majority Campuses: Saviors, Victims or Survivors, points out that African American faculty have limited opportunity for attaining tenure and/or promotion to higher rank unless they 'fall into the academic identity of (their) departments', at the expense of their own African American identity.

William Banks (Networks, Linkages and the Socialization of Black Education) suggests that it is difficult to get white administrators and faculty to accept that race still influences the life and career chances of nonwhite and minority scholars. He states that the traditional old-boy network that facilitates the transition of young academicians is often less forthcoming to the most recent arrivals it they are African American, women, or Third World people.[114]

Rites-of-passage and initiation rituals are to facilitate development. While the rites-of-passage and initiation within higher education may take one from a lower level of administration to a higher one, they (rites-of-passage) also force one to make a conscious decision regarding his cultural and self-awareness, i.e. their Blackness. The conclusion is that while one advances towards the pinnacle of his academic career, he declines in consciousness and self-awareness. "What profits a man to gain the whole world and lose his soul," in the process? What makes matters worse is one knows this decline and he makes it anyway, under the guise of advancing the race. While this may have been true years ago, it is not true today, no, it is the advancement of self, we must be very clear on this! In fact, once we do make the necessary compromises to attain higher levels in administration, we turn around and become 'gatekeepers', always on the lookout for conscious Black men, insuring the gate is closed to them!

Just as all initiation processes require a symbolic death and re-birth, all too often, the initiation process in higher education is general and administration, in particular, requires the death of the budding Black manhood and the rebirth of the Negro or unconscious black male. Again, Andrew Chishom writes:

According to Moore and Wagstaff(1974), Blacks who are hired at the predominantly white colleges and universities are considered safe risks. In other words they will not 'rock the boat.' They view

Black administrators as hired interpreters. Their roles help the institution to better understand the students and provide better services to them.[115]

Why is the rebirth of the Negro so important for advancement in higher education administration? What does being a 'safe risk' and not 'rocking the boat' have to do with advancement in higher education administration? Besides not blowing the whistle on the many underhanded deals that go on in higher education, could there be another reason for being a safe risk? Drs. Nathan and Julia Hare write:

> In a white- dominated society (or situation within a sphere of white domination), it is the Black male who poses the primary threat to the white male patriarchy, who in the white male's mind can take his place in the male dominion.[116]

Could it be that, just as black males dominate in fields of athletics that same dominance can be transmuted to higher education? There is a resource wasting in this country that could change the face of the earth. This resource is the untapped, unlimited, creativity of Black men. While I have concentrated this work on Black men, by no means do I intend to discount Black women. Their impact and importance would require a separate work, for they, not only suffer the same racial discrimination, but sexism as well, the majority of which comes from their own black men.

It is time for men to address the issues of men! As Dr. Francis Cress Welsing once said, "Black men need to get together and admit their fear of the white man. In admitting that fear, they would seek ways to overcome it." This work is one such attempt.

II.
The Metamorphosis of the Black Male

Dr. Molefi Asante points out:

> To lose one's terms is to become a victim of the others attitudes, models, disciplines, and culture and the ultimate point of such massive loss is the destruction of self confidence, the distortion of history and psychological marginality.[117]

We have lost the meaning of manhood; as a result on the issue of manhood we accept the values, attitudes, models and cultural definition of someone else. We have so adopted these definitions until we (black males) in administration at white universities, have lost the sense of the black self, even though we try to cover it up with the wearing of Kente on our academic regalia! Our black colleges and universities are losing their distinct identities, while the physical manifestation is black; the administrative consciousness is an imitation of a white university! Haki Madhubuti echoes this point:

> Somehow, I think that in fighting our 'enemies' we've created new 'enemies'. For example, at many predominantly 'Black' or 'historically Black' universities, the 'New Negro' administrators run their institutions like 16th century plantations, as if the faculty are children and the students are babies. I worry about the current and next generation of African American students. For many of them to think for more than thirty seconds is a probable cause for brain damage. Yet, their examples (us) are often men and women (mainly men) who talk a good game and invent the 'right' words, but whose day-to-day actions – private and public- would, in a head-to-head competition, put soap operas out of business.[118]

While white administrators – presidents use the universities resources to fly their girl friends around the country, black administrators on

270

black campuses, are making bets to see who can get the new female administrator in bed first!

It is imperative that we begin to redefine manhood. We must approach this issue from an Afrocentric perspective, and define for ourselves who and what we are. Here is a need for black men to come to the healing circles of our Ancestors, that we might be taught by the Elders. However, for many of us, education has produced a pompous arrogance that has given rise to a rigid and limited range of thought. This limited range of thought will not allow us to see the benefits and superior understanding of our Ancestors. They understood well what it took to make men, how to produce men of character, respect and discipline. It matters not that you are the custodian, student, president or millionaire, it is time for the men to gather. We must reclaim our lost manhood. We must analyze our position and behavior in higher education administration with clear vision and begin to chart a new course.

REACHING BLACK MALES THROUGH SPIRITUALITY

ENDNOTES

1 Amen, Ra Un Nefer, *Metu Neter Vol. 2: The Kamitic Initation System*, Khamit Corp., Brooklyn, NY, 1994, p. 150-151

2 Ibid, p. 150-151

3 Ibid, p. 150-151

4 Ibid, p. 151

5 Amen, Ra Un Nefer, *Metu Neter Vol. 1: The Great Oracle of Tehuti and the Egyptian System of Spiritual Cultivation*, Khamit Corp., Brooklyn, NY, 1990, p. 46

6 Ibid, p. 65

7 Ibid, p. 65

8 Ram, *Siddha Yoga Meditation Teachings*, Siddha Yoga Foundation, Fallsburg, NY

9 Ibid

10 Rama, *Spirituality: Transformation Within and Without*, Himalayan Institute Press, Honesdale, PA, 1998, p. 129

11 Wallace, Keith, *The Physiology of Consciousness*, p. 4

12 Vanzant, Iyanla, *Tapping the Power Within*, p. 19

13 Ibid, p. 20

14 Some', Malidoma Patrice, *Ritual*, Swan/Raven & Co., Portland, Oregon, 1993, p. 28

15 Ibid, p. 30

16 Warfield-Coppock, Nsenga, *Afrocentric Theory and Applications Vol. 2: Advances in Adolescent Rites of Passage*, Baobab Associates, Washington, D.C., 1992

17 Bear, Sun, *Black Dawn Bright Day*

18 Boateng, Felix, *African Traditional Education: A tool for intergenerational Communication*, from the book 'African Culture'

19 Schwaller De Lubicz, R. A., *Symbol and the Symbolic: Ancient Egypt, Science, and the Evolution of Consciousness*, Inner Traditions International, New York, 1981, p. 55

20 Marciniak, Barbara, Family of Light: Pleiadian Tales and Lessons in Living, Bear & Co., Santa Fe, N.M., 1999

21 Colmant, Stephen A., & Rod J. Merta, *Using the Sweat Lodge Ceremony as Group Therapy for Navajo Youth*, Journal for Specialists in Group Work, Vol. 24, No. 1, March 1999

22 Mbiti, John S., *African Religions and Philosophy*, Heinemann, Oxford, Portsmouth, N.H., 1990, p.143

23 Welsing, Frances Cress, *The Isis Papers: The Keys to the Colors*, Third World Press, Chicago, 1991, p. 83

24 Ibid, p. 84

25 Ibid, p. 84

ENDNOTES

26 Wilson, Amos N., *Blueprint for Black Power: A Moral, Political, and Economic Imperative for the Twenty-first Century*, Afrikan World InfoSystems, New York, 1998, p. 311

27 Welsing, *The Isis Papers*, p. 85

28 Akbar, Na'im, *Visions for Black Men*, Winston-Derek Publishers, Nashville, TN, 1991, p. 33

29 Warfield-Coppock, Nsenga, *Afrocentric Theory and Applications Vol. 1: Adolescent Rites of Passage*, Baobab Associates, Washington, D.C., 1990

30 Mbiti, *African Religions and Philosophy*, p.158

31 Wilson, Amos N., *Black-on-Black Violence: The Psychodynamics of Black Self-Annihilation in Service of White Domination*, Afrikan World InfoSystems, New York, 1990, p. 83

32 Wilson, Amos N., *The Falsification of Afrikan Consciousness: Eurocentric History, Psychiatry, and the Politics of White Supremacy*, Afrikan World InfoSystems, New York, 1993, p. 28

33 Wilson, *Black-on-Black Violence*, p. 88

34 Bly, Robert, Iron John: A Book About Men, Addison-Wesley, Reading, Mass., 1990

35 Lynch, Willie

36 Lynch, Willie

37 Lynch, Willie

38 Hill, Paul Jr., Rites of Passage Institute, http://www.ritesofpassage.org/passage1.htm

39 Amen, *Metu Neter Vol. 2*, p. 149

40 Ibid, p. 149

41 Javane, Faith and Dusty Bunker, *Numerology and the Divine Triangle*, p.158

42 West, John Anthony, *Serpent in the Sky: The High Wisdom of Ancient Egypt*, Quest Books, Wheaton, Ill., p. 53

43 Mircea Eliade, *Rites and Symbols of Initiation*, Spring Publications, Originally Published

44 Ibid

45 Ibid

46 Ibid, XII

47 Amen, Ra Un Nefer, *An Afrocentric Guide to A Spiritual Union*, Khamit Corp., Bronx, NY, 1992, p.100

48 Karade, Baba Ifa, *The Handbook of Yoruba Concepts*, S. Weiser, York Beach, Me., 1994, p. 105

49 Amen, *An Afrocentric Guide to A Spiritual Union*, p.100

50 Some', Malidoma Patrice, *The Healing Wisdom of Africa*, Penguin Putnam Inc., New York, 1998, p. 277

ENDNOTES

51 Amen, *Metu Neter Vol. 2*, p. 149

52 Reid, Daniel, *The Complete Book of Chinese Health and Healing*, Barnes & Noble, Inc., New York, 1998, p. 277

53 Ashby, Muata, *Egyptian Yoga*, p. 23

54 Gawain, Shakti, *Living in the Light: A Guide to Personal and Planetary Transformation*, New World Library, Novato, CA, 1998, p. 39

55 Warfield-Coppock, *Afrocentric Theory and Applications Vol. 1*

56 Some', *The Healing Wisdom of Africa*

57 Amen, *Metu Neter Vol. 1*, p. 58

58 Some', *The Healing Wisdom of Africa*, p. 3

59 Karade, Baba Ifa, Address at the "5th Orisha World Congress", San Francisco, CA, 1997

60 Peek, Philip M., *African Divination Systems: Ways of Knowing*, Indiana University Press, Bloomington, 1991, p. 2

61 Some', *The Healing Wisdom of Africa*, p. 23

62 Karade, Akinkugbe, *Path to Priesthood: The Making of an African Priest in an American World*, Kanda Mukutu Books, Brooklyn, N.Y., 2001, p. 32

63 Andelin, Aubrey P., *Man of Steel and Velvet*, Pacific Press Santa Barbara, Santa Barbara, Calif., 1972, p. 13-14

64 Brownmiller, Susan, *Against Our Will: Men, Women, and Rape*, Fawcett Columbine, New York, 1993, p. 24-25, 27

65 Rama, *Spirituality*, p. 119, 122-123

66 Tiwari, Maya, *Ayurveda: A Life of Balance: The Complete Guide to Ayurvedic Nutrition and Body Types with Recipes*, Healing Arts Press, Rochester, VT, 1995, p. 11

67 Amen, *Metu Neter Vol. 1*, p. 39

68 Frawley, David and Subhash Ranade, *Ayurveda, Nature's Medicine*, Lotus, Twin Lakes, Wis., 2001, p. 9

69 Rajshekar Shetty, V. T., *Dalit: The Black Untouchables of India*, Clarity Press, Atlanta, 1987, p. 43

70 Ibid, p. 43

71 Ibid, p. 54

72 Feuerstein, Georg, Subhash Kak, and David Frawley, *In Search of the Cradle of Civilization: New Light on Ancient India*, Quest Books, Wheaton, IL, 1995, p. 140

73 Van Sertima, Ivan, and Runoko Rashidi, *African Presence in Early Asia*, Transaction Publishers, New Brunswick, U.S.A., 1988

74 Lad, Vasant, *The Complete Book of Ayurvedic Home Remedies*, Harmony Books, New York, 1998, p. 1

75 Frawley, *Ayurveda*, p. 9

ENDNOTES

76 Frawley, David, *Ayurveda and the Mind: The Healing of Consciousness*, Lotus Press, Twin Lakes, Wis., 1997, p. 110

77 Ashby, Egyptian Yoga, p. 124

78 Frawley, *Ayurveda*, p. 112

79 Ibid, p. 112

80 Reid, Daniel P., *The Tao of Health, Sex, and Longevity: A Modern Practical Guide to the Ancient Way*, Simon & Schuster, New York, 1989, p. 264

81 Ibid, p. 265

82 Ibid, p. 295

83 Afua, Queen, *Heal Thyself for Health and Longevity*, A&B, Brooklyn, N.Y., 1998, p. 127-128

84 West, *Serpent in the Sky*, p. 132-133

85 Ibid, p. 132-133

86 Warfield-Coppock, *Afrocentric Theory and Applications Vol. 1*

87 Akbar, *Visions for Black Men*

88 Ibid

89 Ibid

90 West, *Serpent in the Sky*

91 Amen, *An Afrocentric Guide to a Spiritual Union*, p. 8

92 Ibid, p. 7

93 Amen, *Metu Neter Vol. 1*, p. 281

94 Hoskins, Robert L., *Black Administrators in Higher Education*, Praege Publishers, N.Y., 1978

95 Sedlacek, William E., *Black Students in White Campuses: 20 Years of Research*, Journal of College Student Personnel, November 1987

96 Hale-Benson, Janice, *Black Children: Their Roots, Culture, and Learning Styles* (rev.ed.), The Johns Hopkins University (ED 226077) Baltimore, MD., 1986

97 Madhubit, Haki R., *Black Men, Obsolete, Single, Dangerours? The Afrikan American Family in Transition*, Third World Press, Chicago.

98 Ibid.

99 Hare, Nathan, *The Black Anglo-Saxons*, Third World Press

100 Hale-Benson, *Black Children*

101 Asante, Molefi A., *Africentricity and the African-American Student A Challenge*, The Black Collegian, March/April 1991

102 Hoskins, Ibid

ENDNOTES

103 Chishom, Andrew, *An Assessment of the Role of Black Administrators at Predominantly White Colleges and Universities*

104 Amen, *An Afrocentric Guide to a Spiritual Union*

105 Feagin, Joe. R., *The Continuing Significance of Racism: U.S. Colleges and Universities*, p. 11

106 Browder, Anthony T., *Nile Valley Contributions to Civilization: Exploding the Myths Vol. 1*, The Institute of Karmic Guidance, Washington, D.C., 1992

107 Akoto, Kwame Agyei, *Nationbuilding: Theory and Practice in Afrikan-centered Education*, Pan Afrikan World Institute, Washington, D.C., 1992

108 Griffin, Evertte, *The Politics of Education*, Adams Press, 1979

109 Ibid

110 Mbiti, *African Religions and Philosophy*

111 Chishom, Andrew, Ibid

112 Hacker, Andrew, *Two Nations: Black and White, Separate, Hostile, Unequal*, Scribner, New York, 2003

113 Ibid

114 Gill, Walter, Issues in African American Education, One Horn Press, Nashville, TN, 1991

115 Chishom, Andrew, Ibid

116 Hare, Nathan & Julia, *African-American Males on Campus*, The Black Collegian, March/April 1991

117 Asante, Molefi, Ibid

118 Madhubuti, Haki, Ibid

Index

INDEX

287

INDEX

ABOUT THE AUTHOR

Nashid Fakhrid-Deen, J.D. aka Koleoso Karade is well known and respected for his willingness to follow his spirit's direction and his soul's timeless wisdom. In his words he 'seeks to pierce the illusion of matter and become conscious of his divinity." He has traveled extensively studying and building unparalleled competence in well established spiritual traditions while remaining rooted in his African ancestry. His studies clearly indicate his commitment to learning those sacred philosophies and practices that help the seeker manifest the Creator, their Divine Self.

Nashid is a 'Pipe Carrier' in the Lakota tradition and conducts Sacred sweat lodge ceremonies around the country. He has participated in the Sacred Sun Dance and Vision Quest.

Like most, Nashid was raised in the Baptist Church yet his spiritual quest has lead him to being an active Minister in the Nation of Islam, and Imam of traditional Islam. He has been called 'shaman' and was also initiated by a Hindu Yogi, Rashun Nathji (may God be pleased with him). In 1998, Nashid was initiated priest of Shango in the Ifa-Yoruba tradition by Baba Ifa Karade. In 1999 he was initiated as a high priest, Babalawo of Ifa. His African name is "Koleoso Oduneye Karade." He is fondly referred to as "Baba", "Babaji" or "Baba Koleoso." Koleoso, which means "build the house of the seer," attests to his spiritual gift as a diviner. His book, "Tradition and Transformation: A Philosophical Treatise Based on the Ifa Religious System," attests to his ability to integrate his vast spiritual knowledge and bring that knowledge through African tradition.

With 25 years in higher education administration, he holds several degrees and is the recipient of numerous awards. However, after all is said and done, Nashid wants only that his bio reads,

"Nashid, one who is seeking to pierce the illusion of matter and become conscious of his divinity."

Please Visit us Online at

www.shekhempublishing.com

Printed in the United States
33045LVS00002B/499-522

9 780974 507019